"As the banking industry continues to disrupt at an ever-accelerating pace, this unputdownable book paints a future that is both exciting and inspiring. This is Brett, the King of futurism, at his compelling best! Speaking as a banker, you must read *Bank 4.0*."

— Suvo Sakar
Senior EVP and Group Head of Retail Banking
and Wealth Management, Emirates NBD

"Banking is being disrupted on a global basis and Brett's book helps to navigate through these rapid transformations. A must read in the new era of banking."

— Valentin Stalf
CEO and co-founder of N26

"Yet again, Brett King brings together some of the most knowledgeable and experienced figures in global FinTech for this authoritative guide to the very latest mega trends."

— Anne Boden
CEO and founder, Starling Bank

"'I don't think anyone else on the planet has Brett's ability to piece together what is happening around the globe and forecast the future of banking. A thoroughly researched, data-driven analysis from someone who has 'walked the walk'."

— Anthony Thompson
Founder and former chairman Atom Bank and Metro Bank,
co-author of *No Small Change*

"Two years ago on stage in Beirut, I called Brett King 'the King of Ban-King' and I stand by every word. This book continues his canon on the subject of where banking is going next. Everybody in a FinTech company should read it, everybody in traditional banking HAS to read it or they will be without a business in five years."

— Monty Munford
Founder of Mob76, SXSW emcee and Public Speaker,
writing for *The Economist*, BBC, *Forbes* and *Fast Company*

"The organizations we develop partnerships with know that our customers are in the driver's seat. We're innovating for them and that's non-negotiable. Brett King and Moven understood that from day one, and *Bank 4.0* is his manifesto."

— Rizwan Khalfan
EVP, Chief Digital and Payments Officer, TD Bank Group

BANK 4.0

BANK 4.0

Banking Everywhere, Never at a Bank

BRETT KING

WILEY

To Katie, with whom I am quantum entangled,
and my Dad, a role model, and whose energy allowed me
the freedom to go well beyond my limitations.

Contents

PART TWO: Banking reimagined for a real-time world

PART THREE: Why FinTech companies are proving banks aren't necessary

PART FOUR: Which banks survive, which don't

Preface

Bank 2.0 was written in 2009 when mobile had just started to become a significant part of retail banking, and just after the internet had surpassed all other banking channels for day-to-day access. Bitcoin had just launched. Betterment, Simple and Moven were yet to be announced, in fact, FinTech overall was not yet even a term for most of us. *Bank 2.0* was a simple exploration of the fact that customer behaviour was rapidly evolving as a result of technology, and this was creating an imperative for change within banking, which was undeniable.

By 2012 mobile was the next big thing. It was on track to surpass internet, and there was no longer an argument about whether or not banks should have a mobile application. The importance of day-to-day use of technology to access banking was clear, but most banks were still in the evolutionary mode, where mobile was considered simply a subset of internet banking and the technology team were still begging the executive floor for adequate funding. That was by no means an easy battle. *Bank 3.0* was the further realisation that you could be a bank based exclusively on emerging technology. As I wrote in *Bank 3.0*: "Banking is no longer somewhere you go, but something you do." Banking was moving out of the physical realm into the digital.

That was more than six years ago. That's a long time between drinks, as we say in Australia. The reason for the delay in me writing a *Bank 4.0* vision was simple—the future of where banking would go after the whole multi-channel realisation wasn't yet clear. It took some incredible changes in financial inclusion and technology adoption via unconventional, non-bank players for me to realise that there was a systemic shift in financial access that would undermine traditional bank models over the coming decade or two. The unexpected element of this was that the future of banking was, in fact, emerging out of developing economies, and not the established incumbent banking sphere.

Over the last 40 years we have moved from the branch as the only channel available for access to banking services, to multi-channel capability and then omni-channel, and finally to digital omni-channel for customers exclusively accessing banking via digital. The problem for most banks was that we were simply adding technology on top of the old, traditional banking model. We can tell this primarily because the products and processes were essentially identical, just retrofitted for digital. The application forms had just changed from the paper forms in the branch to electronic application forms online. We still shipped plastic cards, we still sent paper to customers in the mail, we still used signatures, we still maintained you needed a human for complex banking problems.

In markets like China, India, Kenya and elsewhere, however, non-conventional players were attacking payments, basic savings, micro-lending and other capabilities in ways that were nothing like how we banked through the branch traditionally. By building up new customer scenarios on mobile without an existing bank product as a reference point, we started to see new types of banking experiences that were influenced more by technology and behaviour than the processes or policies born from branch distribution. This evolution was led by technology players like m-Pesa, Ant Financial's AliPay, Tencent's WeChat, Paytm and many more. This combined with new FinTech operators in the established economies like Acorns, Digit, Robinhood and others who were creating behavioural models for savings and investing. There was a realisation that if you took the core utility and purpose of financial services, but optimised the design of that for the mobile world, then you'd get solutions that would scale better than retrofitting branch banking, and that would integrate into customer's lives more naturally.

If we observe the trend over the last 25-plus years since the commercial internet arrived, we can see that there's an overwhelming drift towards low-friction, low-latency engagement. Like every other service platform today, banking is being placed into a world that expects real-time, instant gratification. Banking, however, is not easily retrofitted into a real-time world if you're used to static processes that are based on a paper application form and hardwired compliance processes. Compared with many other industries, banking has been slower to adapt when it comes to the revenue aspects of e-commerce.

When technology-first players emerged in markets where there were large unbanked populations that had never visited a bank branch, there was no need to replicate branch-based thinking, there was just the need to facilitate access to the core utility of the bank. This, combined with the design possibilities afforded by technologies like mobile, allowed for some spectacular rethinking of how banking could be better embedded in our world. It turned out that these new approaches offered much better margin, better customer satisfaction, engendered trust that was just as good as the old-world incumbents, and businesses that held far more dynamic scaling potential.

This was when it became clear to me that the trajectory was shifting and that we were seeing an emerging template for the future of banking, one that wouldn't include most of the banks we know today. Why? Because if you're retrofitting the branch and human on to digital, you're going to miss the boat. Banking is being redesigned to fit in a world where technology is pervasive and ubiquitous; the only way you stay relevant in this world is by creating experiences purpose-built for that world. Iterating on the branch isn't going to be enough.

I hope you enjoy *Bank 4.0*.

Brett King
Founder of Moven
Host of Breaking Banks Radio

Acknowledgements

As with any book like this, it takes a tribe. This time around was much tougher to get the book done because Moven has been growing significantly and it required more focus. So the first people I'd like to thank are the team at Moven—specifically my executive team, including our new CEO Marek Forsyiak, Richard Radice, Kumar Ampani, Andrew Clark, Denny Brandt, Ryan Walter, and our teams dotted around the world in New York, Philly, Tokyo and Sydney. We work hard, but we have a mission we share and we have plenty of laughs along the way.

Secondly, the team at Marshall Cavendish, who remained extremely patient as I rolled past each consecutive deadline with constant apologies for the delays, including Melvin, Janine, Norjan, Mei and Mike and our partners for translation in markets like China, especially Daisy.

Thirdly, the team at Breaking Banks and Provoke Media that kept the pressure off by helping me get the radio show out each week, including JP Nicols, Jason Henrichs, Simon Spencer, Liesbeth Severiens and Rachel Morrissey.

The contributors for this book were also phenomenal. Anytime I get to collaborate with my FinTech Mafia pals Chris Skinner, Dave Birch, Jim Marous, Duena Blomstrom and others, you know it's going to be something special for readers. To the team at Ripple, Jo Ann Barefoot, Suvo at Emirates NBD, Brian Roemmele, Michael Jordan, Spiros Margaris, and John Chaplin—thank you.

I would be remiss not to thank the coffee shops that once again contributed to this tome.

Lastly, I couldn't have done this without the constant support of a small team who keep me sane daily. Jay Kemp and Tanja Markovic at

Provoke Management speaker bureau, and my social media team. To my dad, who despite daily challenges with his health remains my greatest fan, and my greatest mentor.

Most of all, my partner in life, Katie Schultz, who inspires me, drives me to new heights and puts up with my crazy schedule and global travels. Her, Charli, Matt, Hannah and Mr. T are a constant delight and make me one very happy author.

Part01

Bank 2050

1 Getting Back to First Principles

Everybody has a plan until they get punched in the mouth.
—Mike Tyson

Banking isn't rocket science, but as it turns out, rocket science is a great analogy for the future state of banking. Putting men on the moon is, to date, perhaps the greatest endeavour mankind has committed to. It inspired generations and, until we successfully put boots on the surface of Mars, will likely remain the single most significant technological and scientific achievement of the last 100 years. Getting men to the moon required massive expenditure, incredible advances in engineering, a fair bit of good old fashion luck and the "right stuff".

Before the US could get Neil Armstrong all the way up to the moon, they needed the right stuff in a different area—in figuring out the science.

At the end of World War II there was a very serious plan that would set the foundation for the entire Space Race and Cold War. It was the race for the best German scientists, engineers and technicians of the disintegrating Nazi regime. The predecessor to the CIA, the United States' OSS (Office of Strategic Services), were instrumental in bringing more than 1,500 German scientists and engineers back to America at the conclusion of World War II. The highly secretive operation responsible for this mass defection was codenamed "Overcast" (later to be renamed Operation "Paperclip"). The primary purpose of this operation was denying access to the best and brightest Nazi scientists to both the Russians and the British, who were both allies of the US at this time. "Paperclip" was based on a highly secretive document known within OSS circles as "The Black List", and there was one single name that was right at the top of that list: Wernher von Braun.

In the final stages of World War II, von Braun could see that the Germans were ultimately going to lose the war, and so in 1945 he assembled his key staff and asked them the question: who should they surrender to? The Russians, well known for their cruelty to German prisoners of war, were too much of a risk—they could just as easily kill von Braun's team as utilise them. Safely surrendering to the US became the focus for von Braun's own covert planning in the closing days of World War II. The question he faced was how to surrender without the remnants of the Nazi regime getting tipped off and putting an end to his scheme.

For this von Braun had to, twice, manipulate his superiors, forge paperwork, travel incognito and disguise himself as an SS officer to create a very small window of opportunity for surrender. Convincing his superior that he and his team needed to divert from Berlin to Austria, so that the V-2 rocket team was not at risk by invading Soviet forces, von Braun engineered an opportunity to surrender himself and his brother to the Americans. In the end, Magnus von Braun just walked up to an American private from the 44th Infantry Division on the streets of Austria and presented himself as the brother of the head of Germany's most elite secret weapons program[1].

> Suddenly a young German came to members of Anti-Tank Company, 324th Infantry and announced that the inventor of the deadly V-2 rocket bomb was a few hundred yards away—and wanted to come through the lines and surrender. The young German's name was Magnus von Braun, and he claimed that his brother Wernher was the inventor of the V-2 bomb. Pfc Fred Schneikert, Sheboygan, Wis., an interpreter, listened to the tale and said just what the rest of the infantrymen were thinking: "I think you're nuts," he told von Braun, "but we'll investigate."
>
> —The Battle History of the 44th Infantry Division: "Mission Accomplished"

Private First Class Fred Schneikert likely presided over the single greatest intelligence coup of World War II, save maybe for the capture of U-570 and its Enigma cipher machine.

To understand von Braun and his willingness to work on a WWII weapon of mass destruction like the V-2 rocket (which is estimated to have killed 2,754 civilians in London, with another 6,523 injured[2]), it needs to be understood that he simply saw the Nazi ballistic missile program as a means to an end. In von Braun's mind, the V2 was simply a prototype of rockets that would one day carry men into space—that was his end game.

The images and engineering principles of spacecraft we have from the 1950s we owe largely to von Braun's designs. The three-stage design of modern rockets, the chosen propellants and fuel, the recovery ship system for returning capsules, the initial NASA designs for space stations and Mars programs, all came from von Braun's early musings and engineering drawings. Sixteen years after von Braun's surrender to Allied forces, President John F. Kennedy Jr announced that by the end of the decade the US would put a man on the moon. It would be in a rocket built by Wernher von Braun.

The Saturn V was an astounding piece of engineering. Today, it remains the largest and most complex vehicle ever built. A total of 13 Saturn Vs were launched between 1967 and 1973 carrying the Apollo and Skylab missions. The Saturn V first stage carried 203,400 gallons (770,000 litres) of kerosene fuel and 318,000 gallons (1.2 million litres) of liquid oxygen needed for combustion. At lift-off, the stage's five F-1 rocket engines produced an incredible 7.5 million pounds of thrust, or about 25 times that of an Airbus A380's four engines at take-off. In today's money, each Apollo launch and flight cost around $1.2 billion.

However, despite the incredible advances of von Braun's program in the 1950s and 1960s, manned spaceflight hasn't progressed significantly since. In fact, one could argue that the US' capabilities in this area have been declining ever since Apollo. On 20 July 1969, the Americans landed Neil Armstrong and Buzz Aldrin on the lunar surface, but after December 1972 no further manned missions were launched. In the 1980s the US had the Space Shuttle and could get to low-earth orbit, but today they are renting seats on Russian Soyuz vehicles to get NASA astronauts to the International Space Station.

First principles design thinking

While the cost of launching commercial payloads into space has decreased by some 50–60 percent since the Apollo days, the core technology behind the space industry has simply gone through multiple derivative iterations of von Braun's initial V-2 work. The rocket design, production process, and mechanics all are essentially based on the work of NASA in the Apollo era, which itself was based on the V-2 design. This process of iterative design, or engineering, is known to engineers as "design by analogy"[3].

Design by analogy works on the philosophy that as engineering capabilities and knowledge improve, engineers find better ways to iterate on a base design, perhaps finding technical solutions to previous limitations. But design by analogy creates limitations in engineering thinking, because you're starting with a template—the work is derivative. To create something truly revolutionary you have to be prepared to start from scratch.

Enter Elon Musk. Like von Braun, Musk has an unyielding vision for space travel. Musk isn't interested in just returning to the Moon though, he has his sights set on Mars. For Musk, this is about nothing short of the survival of humanity. In discussing his obsession with Mars, Musk refers to the fact that on at least five occasions the Earth has faced an extinction level event, and that we're due for another one at any moment. We've had dinosaur-killer scale asteroids sail past Earth on near collision courses on multiple occasions in recent years, too. Thus, Musk argues, we must build the "insurance policy" of off-world colonies.

After his successful exit from PayPal, Musk created three major new businesses: Tesla, SpaceX and Solar City[4]. Instrumental in Musk's approach to each of these businesses was his belief in the engineering and design concept called *first principles*. Unlike design-by-analogy or derivative design, first principles take problems back to the constituent components, right back to the physics of the design—what the design was intended to do. A great example of first principles design is the motor vehicle. At the time that Carl Benz invented the first two-seater lightweight gasoline car in 1885, everyone else was trying to optimise carriage design for use with horses. Benz took the fundamentals of transport and applied the capabilities of the combustion engine to create something new.

> I think it's important to reason from first principles rather than by analogy. The normal way we conduct our lives is we reason by analogy. [With analogy] we are doing this because it's like something else that was done, or it is like what other people are doing. [With first principles] you boil things down to the most fundamental truths…and then reason up from there.
>
> —Elon Musk, YouTube video, First Principles[5]

To get to Mars, Musk has reckoned that we need to reduce the cost to orbit by a factor of 10. A tall order for NASA, a seemingly impossible task for a software engineer who had never built a rocket before. As noted in Musk's recent biography (Vance, 2015), Musk has the unique ability to learn new skills to an extremely high level of proficiency in very short time frames. Thus, when it came to rocket design, he simply taught himself— not just the engineering of pressure vessels, rocket engine chambers and avionics, but the physics behind every aspect of rocketry—and even the chemistry involved. Musk reasoned, if he was to start from scratch based upon the computing capability, engineering techniques, materials sciences and improved physics understanding we have today, would we build rockets the same way we had for the last 50 years? The answer was clearly no.

In 2010 NASA was paying roughly $380 million per launch. SpaceX currently advertises a $65 million launch cost for the Falcon 9, and $90 million for the Falcon Heavy. SpaceX's current cost per kilogram of cargo to low-earth orbit of $1,100 is well below the $14,000–39,000 per kilogram launch cost of United Launch Alliance, the lowest priced direct competitor for SpaceX in the United States.

The last major manned space program of the US, the Space Shuttle program, averaged a cost per kilo to orbit of $18,000. Now that SpaceX has figured out how to land their first stage vehicles back on land and on their oceangoing drones[6], such as JUST READ THE INSTRUCTIONS and VANDENBERG OF COURSE I STILL LOVE YOU[7], the reusability factor will reduce their cost per kilo to orbit of their Falcon Heavy launch vehicle down to around $400 over the next few years. This means that SpaceX will have reduced the cost to orbit by more than 90 percent in the 14 short years of their commercial operations. NASA's nearest competitor to the Falcon Heavy will be the Space Launch System, with a payload capacity of 70 metric tons, and an expected launch cost of $1 billion per launch. The Falcon Heavy at 64 metric tons and $90 million per launch represents one-tenth of the cost, before reusability.

Figure 1: Part of the secret to lower cost is advancements SpaceX has made in integrated manufacturing.

A greater than 90 percent cost to orbit reduction, reusability with rockets that land themselves, and a fuel source that is easily manufactured and stored on Mars.

Welcome to the revolutionary benefits of first principles design thinking.

The first principles iPhone

Musk isn't the only one to believe in the philosophy of first principles design. Steve Jobs was a believer in getting back to basics for redesigning well-worn concepts. Instead of iterating on the famous Motorola flip phone, the Blackberry, or the Nokia "Banana" phone, Jobs started from scratch in reimagining a phone, browser and iPod combined into a personal "smart" device.

> There's the great story about how Steve carried a block of wood around the office while the team was creating the iPhone. He wanted to remind everyone around him that things should be simple. Jobs understood that technology is only as powerful as the ability for real people to use it. And it's simple, usable functionality—not ridiculous over engineering—that makes for technological power.
>
> —Bill Wise, MediaBank, quoted in *Business Insider*,
> 12 October 2011

Now in fairness, Jobs may have got the "block of wood" prototyping idea from Jeff Hawkins, the lead inventor of the PalmPilot. The story goes that when he first imagined the PalmPilot, he carried blocks of wood the approximate size of the device he would later build around with him everyday. Whenever Hawkins saw a need for the device in his daily routine, he would tap on it, scribbling on the block of wood, or in his notebook, simulating or prototyping how the device might be used to solve that problem, whether it was a calendar entry, jotting down some notes or swapping contact details with a colleague.

Figure 2: The iPhone is a great example of first principles product design.

Jobs and Jony Ive, Apple's chief design officer, didn't try to iterate on an existing device design and improve on it; they started from scratch. It's why the iPhone ended up with a revolutionary touch screen design, aluminium housing, no keyboard and an app ecosystem. Do you remember the debate when the iPhone launched over the value of the Blackberry RIM keyboard versus Apple's lower accuracy touch screen keyboard? Many commentators were sure the Blackberry keyboard would win out. But it didn't.

Why am I focusing on this? Ask yourself a couple of simple questions. If you were starting from scratch today, building a banking, monetary and financial system for the world, a banking system for a single country or geography or just designing a bank account from scratch, would you build it the same way it has evolved today? Would you start with physical bank branches, insist on physical currency on paper or polymers, "wet" signatures on application forms, passbooks, plastic cards, cheque books, and the need to rock up with 17 different pieces of paper and three forms of ID for a mortgage application?

No, I'm sorry—that's just plain crazy talk. If you were starting from scratch with all the technologies and capabilities we have today, you would design something very, very different in respect to how banking would fit into people's lives. Let us then apply first principles to banking and see if there are any examples of this type of thinking emerging today. Are we seeing systems emerge that are fundamentally different?

Applying first principles to banking

The banking system we have today is a direct descendent of banking from the Middle Ages. The Medici family in Florence, Italy, arguably created the formal structure of the bank that we still retain today, after many developments. The paper currency we have today is an iteration on coins used before the first century. Today's payments networks are iterations on the 12th century European network of the Knights Templar, who used to securely move money around for banks, royalty and wealthy aristocrats of the period. The debit cards we have today are iterations on the bank passbook that you might have owned if you had had a bank account in the year 1850. Apple Pay is itself an iteration on the debit card—effectively a tokenised version of the plastic artifact reproduced inside an iPhone. And bank branches? Well, they haven't materially changed since the oldest bank in the world, Monte Dei Paschi de Sienna, opened their doors to the public 750 years ago.

When web and mobile came along, we simply took products and concepts from the branch-based system of distribution and iterated them to fit on to those new channels. Instead of asking the question whether we need an application form in the online process at all, we just built web pages to duplicate the process we had in the branch[8]. For many banks and regulators today, they are still so married to this process of a signature on a piece of paper and of mitigating risk to the bank through a legal physical paper record, that in many parts of the world you still can't open a bank account online or on your phone—and that's a quarter of a century after the commercial internet was launched.

Think about the absurdity of that situation for a moment. We're tied to using a first century artifact, namely a "wet signature" to uniquely and securely identify an individual for the purpose of opening a bank account. But signatures aren't secure, they aren't regularly verified, they aren't really unique, they are easily compromised, easily copied, and in the case of an identity thief using stolen or fabricated identity documents, a signature provided might not bear any resemblance to the authentic account owner's actual signature—as long as it is the first signature that particular bank gets, then they have to presume the signature matches the owner of the account.

Don't even get me started on branches[9].

Hence the big question. If you started from scratch today, designing a new banking system, would any of the structures we are used to seeing survive? If not, like Elon Musk's approach to SpaceX rockets or Steve Jobs' approach to smartphones, the only way we're going to get exponential progress and real efficiencies is through a first principles rethink of the banking system.

So, what would a "first principles" bank or bank account look like today?

In first principles, utility is king

Let's strip it down to the constituent physics, as Musk suggested. What does a bank do that no other organisation can do, or at least do consistently well? Or what do we rely on banks to provide that would remain in a re-imagined, first principles version of banking?

I would suggest banks have traditionally provided three core pieces of utility:

1. **A value store**—The ability to store money safely (investments fall into this category)
2. **Money movement**—The ability to move your money safely
3. **Access to credit**—The ability to loan money when you need it

If you describe the essence of what you want from your bank as a customer (and it doesn't matter whether that is as a retail consumer or as a business owner), ultimately you don't start off with saying I need "product A" or "product B". Ultimately, you come up with stuff like:

- "I need to keep my money safe."
- "I need to send money fast."
- "I need to save money for [insert need/dream/wish here]."
- "I need my employer to be able to pay me."
- "I can't afford to buy this thing and I need some short-term credit."
- "I need to be able to pay my staff."
- "I want to buy a home."
- "I need to pay this bill."
- "How am I going to pay when I'm in another country?"
- "How do I make more money to pay my bills?"

Whenever we talk about what a bank does for us, or what we need from our bank, we generally don't describe channels, bank departments or products—we describe utility and functionality. Banks have tried very, very hard to train us to think in terms of products, and to some extent they have been successful.

Since the emergence of banking during the 14th century, as banks we've taken that core utility and we've added structure. Initially this structure was about network—*where* you could bank. Banks then added structure around the business of banking, trust and identity—*who* could bank, what was a bank and how you had to bank. Today you could argue that these structures have been reducing risk to both banks and consumers, rather than reducing risk or complexity around utility. Today, as users of banking, we must fight through more friction than ever before just to get to that underlying utility.

Technology now affords us the ability to radically eliminate that friction and create banking *embedded* in the world around us, delivering banking when and where we need it the most. My good friend Chris Skinner calls this "Semantic Banking".

> The semantic web today is all around us. It is immersive, ubiquitous, informed and contextual. The semantic bank will have these features, too. It will prompt us with the things we need, and warn us against doing things that will damage our financial health. It will be personalized, proactive, predictive, cognitive and contextual. We will never need to call the bank, as the semantic bank is always with us, non-stop and in real-time. As a result, nearly every bank function we think about today—paying, checking, reconciling, searching—go away as the semantic bank and web do all of this for us. We just live our lives, with our embedded financial advisor and the core utility of banking as an extension to our digital lives.
>
> —Chris Skinner, author of *ValueWeb*

In a world where banking can be delivered in real time, based on predictive algorithms and surfaced using voice-user interfaces like Alexa and Siri, in a mixed-reality head-up display like Magic Leap or HoloLens, in an autonomous car or home, or just in increasingly smarter watches and phones that you carry everywhere, banking simply becomes both embedded and ubiquitous. But let's be clear—it is not the bank products of today that will ultimately become embedded in this smart world. Only the purest form of banking utility.

When it comes to this new augmented world, banks are significantly disadvantaged over the real owners of utility, and they must constantly jostle for a seat at the new table. The utility today isn't via a branch or an ATM, but the smartphone, the IP layer, data, interfaces and AI.

In this emerging world of instant payment utility, for example, the artifacts and products we associate with payments today—hard currency, cheque books[10], debit and credit cards, wire transfers, etc—will simply disappear. Ultimately, they represent only structural *friction* in enabling payment utility. A good illustration of this is the capability we see emerging in the likes of Amazon Echo[11] or Google Home, where you can now conduct simple commerce and transactions by using your voice. As smart assistants like this get smarter, we're going to delegate more and more of our day-to-day transactional and commerce behaviour to an AI-based agent[12]:

"Alexa, pay my telephone bill."

"Siri, transfer $100 to my daughter's allowance account."

"Cortana, can I afford to go out for dinner tonight?"

"Alexa, reorder me a pair of Bresciani socks."[13]

In this AI and agency-imbued world, utility is the core—products become invisible as they are transformed into everyday, technology-embedded experiences.

In a world where you delegate Amazon Alexa to make a payment on your behalf, triggered by your voice, does the airline miles program you have linked to your credit card make any difference which payment method you choose? I'd argue, absolutely not. Once you have configured Alexa with your preferred payment method, the improved utility will simply demand more and more transactions go through that account—you won't stop a voice transaction to get your physical card out and read 16 digits to Alexa. The promise of rewards simply won't be enough to disrupt that core payment utility.

Amazon, Apple, Facebook, Alibaba and others own those layers of technology that deliver experiences and utility today. Banks are already being forced to submit to app store rules just to be a part of their ecosystem. If you're a bank that does a deal with Uber or Amazon to provide some sort of bank utility to an Uber driver or an Amazon small business, you have the advantage of access and scale, but you no longer "own the customer". It's no longer about having a building on the High Street or a piece of paper you can sign, it's about the most efficient delivery of banking to the customer in real time.

We've been hearing about the threat of the "Facebook of banking", the "Uber of banking", or the "Amazon of banking" for many years now, but if you step back from the hype, we've already seen the emergence of new *first principles* competitors.

A bank that is always with you

In a host of countries around the world you can instantly sign up for a bank or mobile money account on your phone in minutes. In countries like China, Kenya, Canada, US, UK, Australia, Thailand, Singapore, Hong Kong and throughout Europe you can pay by simply tapping your phone or scanning a bar code. You can send money to friends via the internet instantly in more than 190 countries today[14]. You can pay bills in real time and increasingly just let your phone or bank account look after those payments for you. Real *first principles* thinking in banking isn't happening in established, developed economies. The real action is in emerging markets or developing countries where legacy is poor.

In 2005 if you lived in Kenya there was a 70 percent chance you didn't have a bank account, nor could you store money safely and it's unlikely you were saving, unless it was under your mattress. Today, if you're an adult living in Kenya there's a near 100 percent likelihood that you have used a mobile money account (stored in your phone SIM), and that you can transfer money instantly to any other adult in Kenya. Today, data shows that Kenyans trust their phone more than they trust cash in terms of safety and utility, with people sewing sim cards into their clothes or hiding them in their shoes so they can more safely carry their money with them. This is all possible because of a mobile money service called M-Pesa, created by the telecommunications operator Safaricom. Today at least 40 percent of Kenya's GDP runs across the rails of their mobile money service called M-Pesa[15].

> We're currently sitting at about 22 million customers out of a total mobile customer base of about 26 million. Now, if you take the population of Kenya as being 45 million, half of whom are adults, you can see we're capturing pretty much every adult in the country. We are transmitting the equivalent of 40 percent of the country's GDP through the system and at peak we're doing about 600 transactions per second, which is faster and more voluminous than any other banking system.
>
> —Bob Collymore, CEO of Safaricom/M-Pesa[16]

The road to 100 percent financial inclusion via mobile wasn't without its challenges. In December of 2008, it was reported in Kenya's *The Star*[17] that a probe instigated by the finance ministry was actually as a result of pressure coming from the major banks in Kenya. By this stage it was already too late for the banks. By 2008, M-Pesa was already in the pockets of more Kenyans than those that already had a conventional bank account. The impact M-Pesa was already having on financial inclusion in Kenya meant the regulator simply wasn't going to shut it down to curry favour with the incumbent banks. Financial inclusion was a bolder ideal than incumbent protection.

Figure 3: M-Pesa is a first principles approach to financial inclusion.

Today there are more than 200,000 M-Pesa agents or distributors spread across Kenya. More than every bank branch, ATM, currency exchange provider or other financial providers. Those M-Pesa agents are at the heart of the ability to get cash in and out of the network, but being a part of that network allows them to accept mobile payments for goods and services also. It is not unusual to find M-Pesa agents who have trebled their business since taking on M-Pesa, or those that see 60–70 percent of in-store payments being made via a phone. On average, the central bank estimates that the average Kenyan saves 20 percent more today than the days prior to mobile money.

Kenya isn't the only one to have found the mobile to be transformational for financial access. Today there are more than 20 countries[18] in the world where more people have a value store or account on their mobile phone than via a traditional bank. In sub-Saharan Africa, a population of close to 1 billion people is amongst the least banked population in the world, with fewer than 25 percent of them having a traditional bank account. However, today more than 30 percent of them already have a mobile money account, and that is growing year on year by double digits. If you wanted to bank these individuals in the traditional way, you'd need to get them to a bank branch and they'd need a traditional form of identity. Research by Standard Bank in 2015 showed that 70 percent of these so-called "unbanked" people would have to spend more than an entire month's salary just on transportation to physically get to a branch. Branch-based banking was actually guaranteeing financial exclusion for these individuals.

The introduction of mobile money accounts has also had a profound effect on the banking system. The big banks that once plotted to kill M-Pesa have found incredible opportunities for expanding their horizons.

> When I took this job two years ago my vision was that we were not delivering the experience the customers were asking us to, we were stuck in the traditional mode of asking customers to come to the branch. I wanted an account where you can use your mobile device to get our services. So when we started [working with M-Pesa]

we had a target to reach 2.5 million customers in one year, but then in just one year we had already reached 7.5 million customers. We had kind of broken all the goals that we set up for ourselves...our credit products have already done $180 million so far.

—Joshua Oigara, CEO of Kenya Commercial Bank[19]

Kenya Commercial Bank quadrupled their customer base from just over 2 million customers to more than 8 million customers in just two years by deploying a basic savings and credit function on top of the M-Pesa rails. A 124-year-old bank that took 122 years to reach its first 2 million customers, and just two years to reach the next six million. That's all thanks to mobile. Another Kenyan bank, CBA, had equally as impressive results, going from just tens of thousands of customers to more than 12 million today, thanks to their M-Shwari savings product that they launched on top of the M-Pesa rails. Pre M-Pesa just 27 percent of the Kenyan population was banked; today almost every adult in Kenya has a mobile money account. That is a revolutionary transformation.

While M-Pesa's effect on financial inclusion has been nothing short of phenomenal, the really big numbers aren't happening in Africa, they're happening in China. The transaction volume of Chinese mobile payments reached 10 trillion[20] Chinese yuan (US$1.45 trillion) in 2015[21], and they reached 112 trillion yuan (US$17 trillion) in 2017. In comparison, the equivalent figure for mobile payments in the United States stood at a meagre US$8.71 billion in 2015[22] and US$120 billion in 2017, less than 0.1 percent of China's traction. Even though the US is expected to approach $300 billion on mobile payments in 2021, they're still not even within shouting distance of China in terms of per capita volume, transaction volume or mobile payments adoption rates. In 2018, China's mobile payments activity will overtake global plastic payments—that's the scale we're talking about. That meteoric growth is down to several factors, but most notably because China is today dominated by non-bank payments capability on mobile that has massive, massive scale due to non-bank ecosystems.

By the end of 2015 more than 350 million Chinese were regularly using their mobile phones to purchase goods and services that exceeded

750 million in 2017. Alipay is handling a huge portion of that traffic, making it the world's largest payments network by a wide margin, but WeChat Pay exceeded both Mastercard and Visa in transaction volume in 2017 as well. To help you understand how much larger Alipay is than conventional payments networks, in 2015 Visa reportedly peaked at 9,000 transactions per second across their network, while Alipay delivered 87,000 transactions per second at peak—almost 10 times that of Visa. Alipay is now available in 89 countries across the globe, and Jack Ma is expanding that rapidly. On 11 November 2017 alone, Alipay settled RMB 159.9 billion (US$25.3 billion) of gross merchandise volume (GMV) through its network—84 percent of that via mobile handsets.

Given that PayPal, Apple Pay, Android Pay and Samsung Pay hit US$9 billion in mobile payments volume for the same year, the US is significantly behind China. Visa's market cap today is $260 billion. In comparison Ant Financial (Alipay's parent company) looks like a huge buy opportunity right now, with a valuation at their last investment round of approximately $150 billion[23]. The mobile payments market in China is growing at 40–60 percent year on year and Ant Financial (Alipay) and Tencent (WeChat/WePay) claim more than 92 percent of that volume today[24]. Yes, you read that correctly, 92 percent of mobile payments in China are handled by two tech players—not by UnionPay, Mastercard, Visa, Swift or the Chinese banks. By tech companies. In Q1 of 2017, mobile payments accounted for 18.8 trillion yuan (US$2.8 trillion) in China, and they finished out the year with a staggering US$17 trillion in volume.

Ant Financial has demonstrated better than any other company in the world, with the possible exceptions of Starbucks[25] and WeChat, the ability to leverage mobile for deposit-taking and payments. In 2017, Alipay, through their Yu'e Bao wealth management platform, managed $226 billion in AuM (and growing)—all via mobile and online channels. Alipay has no physical branches for taking deposits. It is the largest money market fund in the world today[26] beating out JPMC's US treasury bond market fund. Yu'e Bao has proved that the most successful channel in the world for deposit-taking is not a branch, it's your mobile phone. Something that is only viable using first principles thinking.

This has spurred a mobile deposit and payments war in the Middle Kingdom with Apple, Tencent, UnionPay and Baidu launching their own competing initiatives. WeChat's online savings fund raked in US$130 million just on its first day of operation. The downside for Chinese banks is that now that a quarter of all deposits have shifted to technology platforms, the cost of liabilities and the risk to deposits has increased by 40 percent[27]. Competitors building new branch networks aren't the threat, the utility of mobile and messaging platforms are.

With the largest mobile deposit product in the world, access to more than 80 countries, investments in US-based Moneygram, Korea's Kakao Pay, Philippines GCash (Globe Telecom), Paytm in India and others, Ant Financial is no longer just an internet-based payments network in China. Today, Ant Financial is on track to become the largest single financial institution in the world. Seriously.

Within 10 years, based on current growth, Ant Financial will be valued at more than US$500 billion, and by 2030 it will likely be approaching $1 trillion in market cap value. This would make it four times bigger than the largest bank in the world today, ICBC of China. Today, Ant Financial is worth roughly the same as UBS and Goldman Sachs, two of the most well-respected banking players in the world. Ant Financial has a first mover advantage as a true first principles financial institution built upon the utility of mobile. Ant Financial is not a bank, it is a FinTech, or more accurately a *TechFin* company—a technology company focused on financial services.

Ant Financial is clearly the 800-pound Unicorn in the bunch, but when you look for first principles in financial services, you see an overwhelming representation by FinTechs, startups, tech companies and pure-plays. I guess that's the nature of it—for an incumbent to go back to first principles they'd have to burn it all down and start again. Even when you look at the more innovative incumbent banks in the world, banks like mBank, BBVA, CapitalOne and DBS, you still rarely see evidence of even an iPhone-type "first principles" product design—it is still vastly skewed towards reducing friction for derivative products; design by analogy again. Products that were essentially created for distribution through physical branches are simply being retrofitted on to digital channels. For example, DBS' Digibank in

India and Atom Bank of the UK are just digital treatments of traditional bank products and services fitted onto a mobile phone—they're derivative. Yes, they are mobile or digital optimised, but the product features and names all remain essentially the same as those you would have received from branches in the past.

For example, we haven't seen incumbent banks come up with a savings capability that isn't APR[28] based, or where interest isn't received in anything but a very traditional manner—with one possible exception. Dubai-based Emirates NBD launched a savings product in 2016 that allowed customers to be rewarded based on physical activity measured via a wearable device that counted steps. Well played, Emirates NBD.

Other examples of first principles approaches to savings have all come from FinTechs. Digit and Acorns are two examples of behaviourally-based approaches to savings—apps that modify people's day-to-day behaviour to save more, not just simply offering a higher interest rate for holding your deposit longer. Fidor was the first bank in the world to launch an interest rate based on social media interactions[29].

We haven't seen the incumbent industry come up with credit products that aren't based on the same models we've seen for hundreds of years. PayPal Mafioso Max Levchin launched Affirm in 2014, which provides credit based on buying patterns, geolocation and behaviour. We've seen Grameen in Bangladesh pioneer micro-credit and Zopa in the UK pioneer P2P lending, but the banks that followed were largely derivative of these pioneers. You don't see banks reinventing credit based on behavioural models.

We have very rarely seen incumbent players abandon their reliance on application form-based credit scoring or reference checks to determine someone's suitability for a loan or credit card. Yet we see startups like Sesame Credit (Ant Financial), Lenddo and Vouch experiment with social-based scoring, and LendUp creating loans that boost credit scores for consumers instead of simply rejecting them.

When it comes to money itself, you can't effectively argue that Bitcoin isn't a first principles approach to the problems of currency, identity and the challenges of cross-border digital transfers. When you look at the money transfers themselves, you don't see players like SWIFT, Western Union or others using first principles or adapting blockchain (yet) to solve the problem, but you do see M-Pesa, Abra, Ripple and others solving money movement issues with great aplomb.

Distributed ledger technology like the blockchain clearly has the potential to be a first principles platform for a range of things, the most illustrative example being the creation of the DAO or decentralized autonomous organisation. It was the first AI-based company that allowed participants to invest Ether cryptocurrency into Ethereum/Blockchain startups managed purely on a code and consensus basis. Technically the DAO was a stateless, cryptocurrency based, investor-directed venture capital fund, with no risk or compliance officers, no management, and no traditional company structure. You can't argue that this isn't a first principles approach to VC investment.

When you look for first principles approaches to banking you can find plenty of examples, just not amongst incumbent banks. That is the threat.

Is it too late for the banks?

Elon Musk's SpaceX isn't the only company in the world to make rockets today, but it does have the cheapest kilogram-to-orbit platform. Tesla isn't the only electric vehicle in the world, but it is the most widely known and sold, and has reframed the motor vehicle industry with the likes of Volvo and others responding in kind because of Tesla's success. Apple's iPhone isn't the only smartphone on the planet, but it did completely redefine what we considered a phone and personal computing device. Daimler and Benz aren't the only automobile manufacturers in the world, but you don't see horses on our streets today because of their first principles approach to transportation.

Ant Financial, Tencent, Safaricom and thousands of FinTech startups are redefining what it means to bank today. Redefining how people use a bank account, or more accurately a value store that is embedded in their phone.

Bank 4.0, however, will be about more than new value stores, payment and credit utility. Bank 4.0 is going to be embedded in cars that can pay in a drive-through without the need for plastic, or autonomous vehicles that generate their own income and pay their own road tolls. Bank 4.0 is going to be embedded in voice-based smart assistants like Alexa and Siri, available at your command to pay, book, transact, enquire, save or invest. It is going to be embedded in mixed-reality smart glasses that can tell you, just by looking at something—like a new television or a new car—whether you can afford it. Bank 4.0 is about the ability to access the utility of banking wherever and whenever you need a money solution, in real time, tailored to your unique behaviours.

The emergence of Bank 4.0 means that either your bank is embedded in the world of your customers, or it isn't. It means that your bank adapts to this connected world, removing friction and enabling utility, or it becomes a victim of that change. The bankers of tomorrow are not bankers at all—the bankers of tomorrow are technologists who enable banking experiences your customers will use across the digital landscape. The bankers of today, the bank artifacts of today, the bank products of today, are all on borrowed time.

Is it too late for the banks? In one sense, yes. This transformation into the semantic, augmented world is happening because of a whole range of technology changes outside of banking, and the constant demand by consumers for the next big thing. The only way banks could hope for first principles NOT to undermine their businesses is if they could successfully stop all adoption of new technologies like smartphones and voice-based AI. That is patently impossible. Markets that are successful in slowing down the adoption of things like mobile payments become outliers and simply look out of date in a transformed world.

Case in point. Two-thirds of the world's cheques today are written in the United States, along with the highest card fraud volume in the world, and as you read earlier the volume of mobile payments in the US is fractional compared with the likes of China. This outlying behaviour is permitted by a system suffused with legacy, payments regulation ruled by consensus, point-of-sale architecture that is a decade behind the rest of the world, and reluctance by incumbents to remove this embedded friction because it will weaken their oligopolies. However, the fact remains: when it comes to mobile payments, Kenya is a far more advanced economy than the United States. When it comes to financial inclusion, Kenya has done more to improve the lot of its populace in the last 10 years than the US has in the last 50 years through legislation like the Community Reinvestment Act. Indeed, Kenya today has higher financial inclusion than the United States—a mind-blowing and clearly inconvenient statistic.

The US banking system is a macro example of design by analogy versus design by first principles, whereas China and Kenya are becoming the opposite. The more legacy behaviour and regulation your economy has supporting the friction of the old system, the harder it will be for your bank to be 4.0 ready because it forces slow adaptation to new technology. It is why London and Singapore are pushing so hard for regulatory reform in financial services—they know that is how the future centres of finance will be defined in 2030 and beyond.

Ultimately, this fight will occur across the global stage, and the new metric for developed economies won't be things like GDP and economic growth, but the ability to leverage new technologies to become smart economies, the ability to enable automation, investments in smart infrastructure and the ability to capitalise transformation. Banking is a key part of the infrastructure of the global economy, but if your banking system is built on dumb rails, you will find more and more competition coming from offshore, and more and more blockchain and AI-based attempts at rendering you completely irrelevant.

If you're a bank steeped in tradition, run by lots of bankers, with an old core, in a market with tons of regulation, reliant on branch traffic for revenue then, yes, it is very likely too late. A complete transformation of a bank to being a provider of embedded banking utility, driven by behaviour, location, sensors, machine learning and AI, needs more than an innovation department, an incubator, a mobile app and a Google Glass demonstrator video.

Bank 4.0 is about that radical transformation and how the best banks in the world are responding to these shifts, and how first principles competitors are forcing us to think about banking in different ways. Bank 4.0 is about regulators that are rethinking friction, licensing and regulations themselves. Bank 4.0 is about new capabilities, new jobs and skills that underwrite competencies banks have never needed until now. Bank 4.0 is about the ability of FinTech startups to create transformative experiences faster and cheaper than any incumbent bank could ever do.

If you want to be Bank 4.0 ready, you need to strip your bank back to first principles and rebuild. If not, it's largely just a matter of time before your business is no longer economically viable, especially if you're a bank with under $1 billion in assets. If this prospect scares you, I've successfully whet your appetite for what comes next.

If you're looking for a book that describes how you take your bank from where it is today into the world of tomorrow, then keep reading. This may be your last chance to make the necessary changes to survive through the next decade. Otherwise, feel free to continue the slow decline into obsolescence.

Endnotes

1   2 May 1945.

2   Source: British Ministry of Home Security Statistics from 1939–1945—
    http://myweb.tiscali.co.uk/homefront/arp/arp4a.html.

3   As we'll find out later in the chapter, this is the sole mechanism we've used to progress the banking system over the last 100 years.

4   I'm not counting Hyperloop and his LAX-based tunnelling machine, purely because they are not yet separate businesses run by Musk.

5   Elon Musk explains "first principles"—https://youtu.be/NV3sBlRgzTI (Source: Innomind.org).

6   ASDS—Automated Spaceport Drone Ship.

7   SpaceX names their ocean drones and landing platforms after ships in Iain Bank's science fiction stories from the world of the "culture".

8   In *Bank 2.0* I was able to find an example of a bank that had done this so judiciously that their online credit card application form asked you to staple proof of income to the form—an electronic form on a screen requiring a "stapled" proof of income.

9   We'll get to branches later—I assure you.

10 As only the US uses the spelling "checks", we'll use the globally accepted anglicised version in this book—cheques.

11 More generally known also as "Alexa".

12 For a more detailed analysis of this trend, please see my *Augmented: Life in the Smart Lane.*

13 Much of this is possible now, or close to possible. Check out the Alexa ad featuring Alec Baldwin, where he orders Bresciani socks.

14 This is just for PayPal coverage alone. AliPay is already in 80 countries and growing, too.

15 Source: *The Economist*—A new East Africa campaign, 9 July 2015.

16 Breaking Banks Radio interview—aired 9 February 2017.

17 Source: *The Star*—Big Banks in Plot to Kill M-Pesa, 23 December 2008.

18 Source: WorldBank—those countries include China, Kenya, Tanzania and Nigeria.

19 Breaking Banks Radio interview—aired 9 February 2017.

20 With a capital "T".

21 Source: iResearch—http://www.iresearchchina.com/content/details7_21238.html.

22 Source: CIO Magazine, "7 reasons mobile payments still aren't mainstream", James A Martin, 7 June 2016.

23 As of their $4bn capital raise April 2016. To be fair, it could be argued that they are worth well in excess of $100 billion today, based on their current revenues and activity.

24 Source: ChinaDaily.com, 3 August 2017; "Alipay, WeChat Pay vie for customers"—http://www.chinadaily.com.cn/bizchina/tech/2017-08/03/content_30337784.htm.

25 In 2016 Starbucks saw approximately $8 billion loaded onto their mobile-based "cards" (Source: Starbucks Investor call).

26 "Chinese money market fund becomes the world's biggest", *Financial Times*, 26 April 2017—https://www.ft.com/content/28d4e100-2a6d-11e7-bc4b-5528796fe35c.

27 Source: Asian Banking Journal.

28 Annual Percentage Rate.

29 Incidentally, this would technically be illegal in jurisdictions like the US today due to disclosure requirements around savings accounts that require APR rates to be published according to a strict schedule.

When Alipay was created, we hoped to create
an equal environment in China so that everyone
can have equal access to financial support. We hoped
to see that every honest person, every good person,
even though penniless, can create sufficient wealth
and value for one's honesty and virtues.
—Jack Ma, Chairman of Alibaba and Ant Financial

For 20 years, I have been watching developments in financial services in China closely. My first exposure to the Chinese system was in 1997, just before the Asian financial crisis. The Bank of China proudly showed off their Beijing head office, staffed by 300,000 people, with most of it being to drive money from citizens towards government-initiated projects. There were high levels of savings and little credit availability. Customer service was of zero interest and the major focus was supporting State-Owned Enterprises (SOEs). Back then, bank tellers had to take a proficiency test in using an abacus before they were given a job.

A decade later, China had opened up to world trade and had seen a phenomenal expansion of growth in the economy. I had been caught out by the emerging social network called QQ, which had achieved 300 million users, and was amazed at how quickly the market was changing. Visiting Shanghai, you could see the change. The riverside financial district had literally emerged from the ground up in the previous decade, and was now vying to be a global financial centre. It had a long way to go, but was getting there. Hu Jintao noted in 2006:

"From 1978 to 2003, China's GDP increased from US$147.3 billion to over US$1.4 trillion, with an average annual increase rate of 9.4 percent; its total foreign trade volume grew from US$20.6 billion to US$851.2 billion, with an average annual growth rate of 16.1 percent; and the poverty-stricken population in the rural areas dropped from 250 million to about 29 million."

I wrote extensively about the changes in China in 2006[1] and, back then, was predicting that the biggest banks in the world within a decade would all be Chinese. Today, they are:

Rank (prev)	Bank	Country	Tier 1 capital ($m)
1 (1)	ICBC	China	281,262
2 (2)	China Construction Bank	China	255,838
3 (3)	JPMorgan	US	208,112
4 (4)	Bank of China	China	199,189
5 (6)	Bank of America	US	190,315
6 (5)	Agricultural Bank of China	China	188,624
7 (7)	Citigroup	US	178,387
8 (8)	Wells Fargo	US	171,364
9 (9)	HSBC	UK	138,022
10 (10)	Mitsubishi UFJ Financial Group	Japan	135,944

Table 1: Top 10 world banks 2017. Source: *The Banker* magazine, July 2017.

Today, China's phenomenal growth has started to slow, government policies to support such growth are being questioned and concerns over the whole shadow financial system are raising global systemic worries. No matter. The country is still seeing progress and QQ is now WeChat, part of the Tencent group. The group operates alongside several other massive

Chinese internet giants, including Alibaba (the Amazon of China), Baidu (the Google of China) and more, to challenge the thinking of all.

In so doing, the country has leapfrogged their legacy competitors. America struggles with the conversion of mag stripe points of sale to migrate to chip & PIN, while Europe tries to work out how to hold together their union in light of Brexit. China, by contrast, has transformed—and specifically transformed their financial markets. Ant Financial are expected to IPO some time in the next couple of years.

However, Ant Financial go way back, beyond 2014. In fact, their humble roots began in 2003, when Alibaba came head to head with a big American giant who wanted to take root in China. That giant was eBay. Here begins a story that should fascinate everyone, especially as Ant Financial are realising the dream widely discussed in this book: the creation of a financial system for the fourth age of humanity[2].

Through a series of meetings in July 2017, I spent time in Hangzhou, China and London talking with Ant Financial and Alipay executives about their views of the past, present and future of the company. I also spent time touring China, and talking with real people about their views of the company. The following represents the summary of those experiences.

The Alibaba stories

In order to understand how Ant Financial made its mark, we first need a brief history of its origins within Alibaba. There are many ways in which you can catch up with the Alibaba story, with Porter Erisman's book, *Alibaba's World*, quite an easy read. I saw Porter present this story, from when he was involved in the early days of Alibaba, having lived in China since 1994.

The origins of Alibaba actually date back to 1980 when an Australian Communist sympathiser, Ken Morley, travelled around China on a summer vacation. When visiting Hangzhou, Ken and his family went down to the main tourist area, the West Lake. There they met a young Jack Ma who, back then, went by the name Ma Yun. Ma Yun was 16 years old, learning English, and liked to hang around the West Lake most days he could, in order to improve his English by talking with tourists. Ken's son David was also 16 years old, and the two boys struck up an unlikely long-term relationship.

Figure 1: Ma Yun and David Morley in 1980.

From the chance encounter with the Morleys, Ma Yun started a pen pal relationship with David. They would exchange letters with Ma Yun, leaving every other line free for David's father, Ken, to make corrections to Ma's English spelling. Ken decided to see if he could help his son's young pen pal by inviting him to visit Australia in 1985 when Ma Yun, now Jack Ma, was just 21 years old.

This was when the doors of China were still firmly closed and an individual could not get a travel visa. However, Jack Ma was determined and travelled to Beijing to see if he could get permission. Seven times he was told no. At that time, visas were only issued for service, family or studying purposes, not for general visits or tourism. So, Jack Ma almost lost all hope after his visa was rejected seven times in a row. Ken Morley was also worried about this, and even sent a telegram to the Australian embassy in China, hoping they could issue a visa for Jack Ma.

Jack Ma stayed in Beijing for a week, diligently applying for the visa every single day, as the trip to the capital cost all the money he had. The last time he stepped into the embassy, he ran towards the first visa officer he met and said: "I have been here for a week so this might be my last chance. I want my visa, and I want to talk to you seriously."

"What do you want to talk about?" said the clerk.

"I have been rejected for a visa seven times during the past week. I have no money anymore so I have to go back home. But I need to know the reason for my rejections."

Impressed by Jack Ma's persistence, the visa officer listened carefully to the story of his relationship with the Morley family and, afterwards, Jack Ma finally got his Australia visa. This changed his life and, many years later, Jack recalls: "I am very thankful for Australia for that 29 days in Newcastle [a suburb of Sydney]...when I arrived in Australia I was so shocked and amazed by the wonderful things, the people, the culture, the landscapes, the products...I was...educated in China that China was the best and richest country in the world...when I arrived in Australia I saw the world was so different."

After this, everything changed in Jack Ma's thinking, although he could not realise his dreams at that point. Instead, he returned to Hangzhou to teach English. However, his Australian trip stayed with him and, combining this with a visit to America in 1995, his life's path was clear.

Jack visited the United States in early 1995, as the first roots of search engines and trade were emerging, and this was when Jack discovered the internet. He was inspired and it changed the path of his life, creating his first business, a "Yellow Pages" for China, upon his return. The business failed but Jack was undeterred and, in 1999, Alibaba was formed. Alibaba is based upon Amazon, but it is different because it is Chinese. For example,

Amazon emerged from a Western economy that had moved from mom-and-pop stores to large malls, grocery stores and urban shopping centres. As a result, the retail model replicated the offers of these centralised centres and replaced them on margin over time.

China didn't have that structure. China in the 1990s just had the mom-and-pop stores, and no large shopping centres and malls. So, Alibaba's original idea was to create a global marketplace, connecting small Chinese businesses with the world's buyers. It was described as being an online tradeshow for Chinese businesses to demonstrate what they could do for the rest of the world, and Jack Ma sold it to Chinese firms that way. Alibaba in 1999 was building a massive Expo for Chinese business to engage with the world's manufacturers. That was the original idea, and it went well. So well that Jack Ma and his team saw an opportunity to provide a service connecting people, called Taobao. Taobao was launched in 2003, and aimed to emulate the eBay success in America, but in a different way. After all, Chinese consumers didn't buy collectables at that time, as there really wasn't anything worth collecting, or so they thought. The only thing Chinese people had that was collectable in the early 2000s was Chairman Mao's Red Book, and most people were trying to get rid of those.

This is why Taobao, which means "digging for treasure", focused upon connecting small Chinese businesses and sole traders—the mom-and-pop stores, as there weren't many big firms—to Chinese citizens. It worked, but not before being exposed and made potentially vulnerable to the entry of eBay into the Chinese markets.

---

ebay is a shark in the ocean.
We are a crocodile in the Yangtze River.

If we fight in the ocean, we will lose.
But if we fight in the river, we will win.

—Jack Ma, CEO, Alibaba Group

---

eBay entered China by buying heavily into its Chinese equivalent, EachNet. Jack Ma knew that eBay could eradicate Alibaba, and determined that the US auction service was not right for China. But Alibaba at the time was tiny compared to the mighty eBay, which had millions of dollars to invest in the Chinese market. However, eBay was not Chinese and did not understand Chinese markets like Jack Ma and his team at Alibaba. For example, eBay cut back on features that Chinese consumers liked, such as emoticons and animations.

Taobao ramped up these features to be a far more social commerce model, as well as adding the sprinkler of being free. eBay did not offer a free version to compete and made other mistakes, eventually pulling out of China completely, having lost millions of dollars.

At this point Alibaba had won and began to diversify into other areas. For example, Alipay was launched in 2004 as an escrow account service to allow consumers to hold funds until they were happy with the goods they received. This was key to Taobao's growth, as China had very poor consumer protection laws. In 2008, they launched Tmall, a B2C site for the sale of key branded goods and services as an offshoot of Taobao.

In 2013, Alibaba's money fund Yu'e Bao ("leftover treasure") was launched and marketed to users of Alipay. They then expanded into banking in 2015, launching MyBank during the summer and, in an audacious move, opened their bank capabilities to other Chinese banks through an open marketplace of apps and APIs.

All of these financial activities—Alipay, MyBank, Yu'e Bao, open banking—are consolidated into the brand Ant Financial. Ants are a good metaphor for the business, as ants are weak individually but together are strong. That's the message Ant Financial wanted to send to Chinese citizens and it seems to be working as Ant Financial was worth $45 billion in 2015, $60 billion in 2016 and looks likely to top $100 billion by the time of its IPO in early 2019.

Just to put this in context: what Alibaba with Taobao, Tmall, Alipay, Yu'e Bao and more of its affiliates have put in place is like an Amazon,

Facebook, Netflix, PayPal and more all in one ecosystem. For example, a vision for Alibaba is that:

- you can advertise movie concepts and ask customers to crowdfund the movie ideas they like, all channelled through Alibaba Pictures;
- once a movie is funded and gets made, you can buy tickets to see the movie through Taobao;
- when you see the movie, you might want to watch the digital release at home on Youku, Alibaba's version of Netflix;
- if you like the movie that much, you can buy branded memorabilia on Tmall;
- all of it is paid for and funded through your Ant Financial accounts.

In other words, it offers a digital marketplace that manages the complete process of digital creation from start to finish. The banking stuff is simply embedded in this ecosystem. This concept is nicely summarised by Jack in his presentation to the Taobao annual partners meeting, nicknamed "Netrepeneurs: Made in Internet", in 2017. I attended this meeting in Hangzhou, and it was an immersive experience. A mixture of online teenage celebrities streaming their ideas to entrepreneurial Taobao businesses talking about their business models and dreams, it was all very Chinese.

The meeting concluded with an interview with Jack, and here are my main notes and takeaways from what he said:

- "It is impossible to do business today offline as everything has to have something online, which is why we need more netrepreneurs. The whole supply chain will be impacted by the internet. I talk about these challenges at many conferences and people don't believe me, but I'm used to this. It's like climbing a mountain. What you see at the foot of the hill is very different to what you see when you're halfway up. What's at the top of the mountain are those who change their mindsets and, in the next three decades, the world will change more than you can ever imagine."

- "In the next 10 years all industries will change due to AI, big data and cloud. Industries will be turned on their head. This means that, in the future, there will be no "made in", as in "Made in China" or "Made in India". You will just have designed, ideated, printed and made it in the internet. Equally, everything can now be customised. It's expensive to customise today but, if you can't do it tomorrow, your company will fail."
- "Alibaba doesn't do e-commerce. We only provide the platform. So, the more success our partners have, the more successful are we."
- "Three years ago, we bet that cloud and big data would be key. Most critical are data and computing. We put all of our resources into data, computing and data services. But still what we do is just a fraction of the total. Soon we will have IoT and all these devices will create data, and this is why we are panicked. There will be a huge amount of data to deal with."
- "In the age of data, we can no longer have this idea of controlling everything. A monopoly is an idea of the industrial era. We just want to help people, not be a monopoly. We want to connect everyone."
- "We provide payments and logistics and shipping. We can deliver anywhere in China within 24 hours. That's too slow for Beijing and Shanghai but, for the villages, we want to build that infrastructure across all China. We will never be a logistics company, however. We partner with others for this. So, we focus on the things that others cannot do or are not willing to do. We focus on things SMEs cannot do. We only want to compete with companies that won't share or partner with others."
- "If you are having a difficult time as a startup, we were like that, but we had a dream and now we have got there. Now we are a huge company, but if we stay there and don't share those riches, then everyone will hate us. So, we have to make everyone richer. If you are the only rich person in a village of paupers, the paupers will kill you."

- "Alibaba is a tool for everyone that should benefit everyone, especially young people. Remember I was a teacher—and any company will diminish ultimately. I want people to say Alibaba is great, not because we sell a lot of product, but because we helped young people and our society."

- "Management. The word is there for regular companies. At Alibaba, we treat it more like governing an economy, as we have to manage so many companies dependent upon us as partners. Any SME with an idea now has a way to realise that idea. Alibaba marketplace can find you buyers and sellers; we can provide you with computing through cloud; we can distribute and deliver your products. By 2036 we will have built an economy that can support 100 million businesses for billions of users. We won't own that economy. We will just govern it."

- "Having great, smart experiences will be the keywords for our next decade."

- "FinTech is there to empower the financial sector. I want to do that for consumers so they have equal access to finance. I don't want people to be waiting for money or for pity. I want to empower them through access and inclusion, and get things to people a lot faster and easier."

- "This year is very different to five years ago. This year we focus upon 'Made in Internet'. Your business model is to redefine your consumers, supply chain and financing methods for the Made in Internet age. I tell all retailers and manufacturers and banks to do this urgently as I've been saying it for over a decade. You don't have so much time left."

Figure 2: Jack Ma at the M@de in Internet Alibaba event in China.

Finally, here are the top 10 messages that Jack gives people for business:

1. On chasing dreams: dream big, really big
2. Remember: the bigger the problem, the greater the opportunity
3. Today is tough, but the day after tomorrow is beautiful
4. Focus on the customer and the rest will follow
5. Learn from competitors, but never copy them
6. It's more important to be best than first
7. Find opportunity in crisis
8. Use your competitors' strength against them
9. Don't dwell on mistakes
10. The team should work for the goal, not for the boss

Driving Alipay's innovation?

When it began, as an escrow system, the exchange of information was based upon fax messaging. Fax messages to and from the bank and seller via Alibaba allowed Taobao orders to be fulfilled. Roll on five years, and that had changed.

In the summer of 2011, China's Alipay developed a QR-code payment system to support payments, and this was the revolution that turbo-charged a payments transformation in China. This is because China had few credit and debit cards in the hands of the population, but everyone had a mobile phone. At the time using the phone for payments wasn't easy. Then the roll-out of the QR-code system changed all that. Similar to the Starbucks app that had made Starbucks become a payments phenomenon in America, Alipay did the same thing, generating a unique QR-code at checkout that merchants can scan with a barcode reader or their own smartphone camera. The system draws funds from a user's credit card or a prepaid Alipay account.

This move also led to some problems though, as Jack Ma made the controversial decision to spin out Alipay as a separate company, without approval from Yahoo or Softbank, who owned 40 percent and 30 percent of Alibaba at the time. The move needed to be made because the firm could not continue to act as a payments processor without a third-party payments license from the government. This license would not be issued unless Alipay was set up as a dedicated payments processor. The controversy was settled by agreeing that a certain percentage of Alipay's revenues would flow back through Alibaba, but it did cause a bad taste in the investor's mouths.

Singles' Day is just one of several events created to promote the use of mobile payments in China, finding its source in the battle between Alipay and WeChat Pay over the red envelope day to celebrate Chinese New Year.

The idea began in 2014 when Tencent promoted its 400 million WeChat users to send each other virtual red envelopes, which would be deposited into their mobile payment accounts. The gimmick became a big hit with 40 million virtual envelopes being exchanged, worth a record 400 million yuan ($64 million). Jack Ma called it a "Pearl Harbor moment" for his company, and ramped up the game in 2015 by announcing it would give away more than 600 million yuan ($96 million) to its 190 million users as "lucky money" gifts if they used its red envelope messaging system. Tencent responded within hours by saying it would also gift 800 million yuan ($125 million) to users of its virtual red envelopes service, and blocked Alipay users from their WeChat friends. Tencent's WeChat won that battle, with over one billion virtual red envelopes sent on 18 February, compared

with 240 million sent through the Alipay Wallet—and, as can be seen, the
rivalry between the two firms is intense.

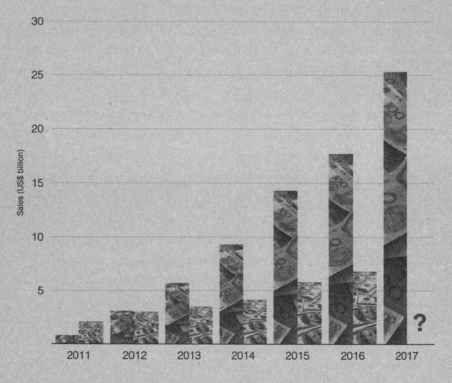

Figure 3: Alipay's Singles' Day is the world's largest single day of commerce. Visa averages 1,750 tps and scales to 24,000 tps; during Singles' Day Alipay beats that handsomely, with transaction volumes exceeding 300,000 tps.

Meanwhile, Alipay extended its tentacles into other areas, such as
creating a savings fund for customers to store their balances when not using
Alipay. Called Yu'e Bao ("leftover treasure", as mentioned earlier), it acts as
a method of moving prepaid funds from a balance on Alipay to an amount
that can gain interest on Yu'e Bao. Western media call it a "money market
fund", but Ant Financial take exception to this, as they see it as just a way
of gaining interest on unused funds—a behavioural savings feature.

Another move occurred in 2014, when China's regulators offered
private companies the opportunity to apply for banking licenses, resulting

in Ant Financial launching a bank in 2015 called MyBank. Ant Financial hold a 30 percent stake in MyBank alongside other main shareholders, including Fosun Industrial, Wanxiang Sannong, and Ningbo Jinrun—three Chinese conglomerates with investments in agriculture, insurance, machinery, and other industries. The founders' initial investment is four billion yuan (about $644 million). MyBank's most important partner is Alibaba, however, as the main offering of loans is based upon user's transaction history in Taobao and Tmall.

MyBank focuses upon supporting small businesses on Taobao, which supports over five million merchants. At its launch Eric Jing, MyBank's executive chairman, said that their mission is "answering to the needs of those who have limited access to financial services in China" and "is here to give affordable loans for small and micro enterprises".

A good example of such a service is a Taobao-subscribed shop owner who sells beef jerky. Each time they receive an order, they can immediately turn that order into cash through a short-term MyBank microloan. This particular store owner has had 3,795 such loans in the last five years, an average of two loans a day, with the amounts varying from three yuan (half a dollar) to 56,000 yuan (US$8,000).

The learning Alibaba gained through MyBank enabled the company to open its services to other Chinese banks to use when, in 2013, Alibaba verticalised their cloud with the announcement of Ali Cloud for Financial Services, or the Ali Finance Cloud for short.

The development of the Ali Finance Cloud was part of a perfect storm for Ant Financial. They had applied for their MyBank license and obviously needed to have a future-proofed, core-banking system. Rather than look to an external provider, they decided to develop it internally.

A bank developing its core banking system internally is not unique in China, but Ant Financial went one step further by deciding to sell the cloud-based solution to other banks in China. The breadth of the solution is extensive, including risk management, lending, deposits, mobile apps, infrastructure-as-a-service (IaaS), platform-as-a-service (PaaS), know-your-customer (KYC) and more.

It is difficult to overstate the potential impact of Ali Finance Cloud on the Chinese banking industry, or the potential implications globally. Adoption and usage of the Ali Finance Cloud in China has been swift, with around 40 organisations using the service, including banks, payment providers and even peer-to-peer (P2P) platforms.

Ant Financial: Building a better China

One of the big things about Ant Financial is its principles and mission, which is all about using technology to improve society and the economy. Here is the opening statement from their 2016 Sustainability Report.[3]

The evolutionary and civilized history of the human being, in the simplest way, can be seen as a progressive history where a marginal species climbed rapidly to the top of the ecological chain by developing cognition, agriculture, industry, science and technology. At present, human beings are in a golden age of the so-called third industrial revolution.

As a tech company, what we want to do and are currently doing is to use technology to bring society back to the origin of human beings: simple, equal and free. For example, our daily errands, can we handle them easily without queuing, begging people or even going out? This is the simple principle. Can a grandmother and a bank president enjoy the same quality and equally convenient financial services? This is the equal principle. Can we say goodbye to complicated passwords, cash or even ID cards and passports, paying bills easily with a face and the credit data behind it?

Technology is at the heart of this vision and, more importantly, it is at the heart of this business. For example, the company states openly that creditworthiness is the passport to a better society. Creditworthiness has been difficult historically, as you need some form of credit history to evaluate people; without data, that is hard.

This is all changed today, thanks to the development of cloud computing, machine learning and big data. Creditworthiness, which used to be regarded as a moral evaluation, is now becoming direct and quantitative and can be analysed as well as utilised in real time. Ant Financial therefore created a brand new credit evaluation system called

Zhima Credit, which enables more people to enjoy convenience in finance, life and other sectors.

The Zhima Credit score is based on your financial behaviours and trustworthiness with money, and a key part of this is ensuring people pay back. Zhima Credit scoring works with the support of intelligent decision-making, and this is a core part of Ant Financial's operations based upon a well-established creditworthiness evaluation and risk forecasting system that operates in real time. As a result, farmers without bank statements can obtain loans to buy fertiliser and seeds through MyBank.

Ant Financial illustrates this through the stories of their partners.

A key backdrop to the Zhima Credit score, creditworthiness, microloans and inclusiveness is Ant Financial's continual real-time analytics and risk management. This enables the company to deliver its "3, 1, 0 strategy": it takes *three minutes* to apply for a loan; *one second* to transfer the funds to the applicant's account; and there is *zero manual intervention* in the whole process.

MyBank has helped many blue-collar workers, undergraduate students and migrant workers to embark on a new life. By the end of April 2017, 6.5 million people had borrowed over 800 billion yuan (US$125 billion) in just two years.

This is bringing a convergence between creditworthiness and wealth to help people from all walks of life to realise their dreams. Creditworthiness is linked not only to wealth, but also to the operation and governance of society. It is closely related to everyone's daily life. This is why the usage of technology to extend credit to everyone creates a more inclusive economy and a more equal society.

Ant Financial believe that, in the near future, it is likely that cameras in restaurants, subways and airports will automatically identify your credit status. People will be able to go out without a mobile phone, cash or even an identity card. They can go anywhere using only their face as their authentication system. From your face the cloud, and the big data of creditworthiness behind it, will become everyone's passport in society. The trustworthy will be welcomed everywhere, while the untrustworthy will be rebuffed at every step.

That is why creditworthiness is a critical factor driving Ant Financial, Chinese society and the economy forward, with the company regularly acting as a mediator between those who can be trusted and those who cannot. It is why Ant Financial's Zhima Credit system is working with China's Supreme People's Court to punish dishonest credit behaviours. By January 2017, Zhima Credit had assisted the Supreme People's Court to punish over 730,000 dishonest debtors, almost 50,000 of whom have paid off their debt. This is another key tenet of Ant Financial's vision, in using creditworthiness to improve social governance and make integrity a highly valued attribute of society.

People born in the 1990s have grown up in an environment where the concepts and applications of creditworthiness are being popularised. For example, one in four Chinese people born since 1990 use Ant Credit Pay for consumption. Therefore, they have a clearer understanding of creditworthiness, and value it more than the older generations. Statistics on Ant Credit Pay show that the proportion of people born in the 1990s who repay their debt on time is 99 percent. A society that values and upholds integrity is taking shape.

When I attended the Alibaba partners conference in July 2017, they hosted many of their most successful Taobao businesses in Hangzhou, China. Many of these are young people who are now entrepreneurs. Intriguingly some of these businesses are based in rural villages—because they can be. This is a massive change in society in China and, from a digital age platform, the world. The fact is that anyone, anywhere—even in the most remote villages—can become an entrepreneur if they have an internet connection and, increasingly, everyone has this through their mobile smartphone.

But it's not just commerce and society that Ant Financial focuses upon. Equally, it is worth underlining that Ant Financial is not first and foremost a financial firm. They are a technology firm, focused upon leverage technologies to improve society and the economy. This is illustrated well by their services to government.

A final element worth mentioning in Ant Financial's strategy is building a greener planet. This is achieved through their program of gamification, called "Ant Forest".

The idea of Ant Forest originates from the carbon emissions account of Alipay, which is by far the largest platform for personal carbon accounts in the world. In the Alipay carbon account, users are educated in using some of the common global practices in energy conservation and emission reduction. It is the first carbon account using a bottom-up approach to reduce carbon emissions. Specifically, Ant Forest encourages users to choose greener lifestyles by taking public transport, paying utility bills digitally and booking tickets online. It is also the first in the world that encourages hundreds of millions of people to lead a low-carbon life voluntarily, rather than forcing this approach top-down.

Embedded banking: understanding not selling

Ant Financial is the only company worldwide today focused upon building a global financial inclusion platform. A platform that can support and connect potentially seven-and-a-half billion people in real time. At the very least, a platform that will include all those who are currently excluded from the financial network, by offering them a connection via the mobile network and simple technologies that are interoperable between operators in all countries.

Their strategy is based upon finding companies in other countries who offer an e-wallet payments service, and then to invest in those firms and share their technologies with them. Eventually, it is likely that Alipay and Ant Financial's base technologies would be powering the core infrastructure of e-wallets globally—a sort of globally aggregated wallet service.

First, they invest in equivalent products and services in similar markets, such as India and Thailand. That is why Ant Financial's leadership team talks about inclusiveness, as that's a great strategy with a mobile wallet. Hence, they invested $680 million in India's Paytm in September 2015, just before demonetisation stimulated Indians to open 200 million wallets on Paytm. In November 2016, Ant partnered with Thailand's Ascend Money, which also runs a digital wallet service. Under the agreement, Ant Financial will assist Ascend Money to grow its online and offline payments and financial services ecosystem. It is notable that Ascend may be based in Thailand, but also operates in Indonesia, the Philippines, Vietnam, Myanmar and Cambodia.

In February 2017, they announced a $3 billion debt financing deal to expand their investment portfolio and, interestingly, moved into the US market with a bid to acquire MoneyGram for $880 million. This was followed by a strategic investment in the Korean messaging service Kakao, which offers Kakao Pay; also, in March 2017, they increased their stake in Paytm, so that Ant Financial is now the majority owner of the service.

Meantime, apart from heading for inclusiveness, Ant Financial has also expanded into the USA and Europe. At the end of 2015, the company signed a deal with Wirecard to give them access to Europe for merchant checkout using their wallet for Chinese tourists. This was followed with a partnership with Ingenico to further enhance their European presence and then a deal with First Data to give them a similar coverage of North America.

The media positions the Wirecard, Ingenico and First Data moves as being a pure provision of service for Chinese tourists, but it is not as simple as this. This is a fast-moving company that is expanding non-stop in its mission to be the dominant global mobile wallet.

That is the mission and was articulated by Ant Financial CEO Eric Jing at Davos in January 2017, where he stated: "We have an ambition to be a global company. My vision [is] that we want to serve two billion people in the next 10 years by using technology, by working together with partners...to serve those underserved."

How Ant Financial thinks is radically different to US and European FinTech firms, because it is automating a market that had nothing before. When Alipay began, there was no e-commerce in China. Alibaba and Alipay created it.

That's a radical difference from the American internet giants like Amazon and eBay, who had major bricks-and-mortar competitors also competing online, and began without any payments integration. Equally, the US giants were serving a developed market, where consumers had sophisticated online needs; Alibaba and Alipay were serving markets that were changing dynamically as Chinese citizens moved from rural, agricultural work to the rapidly expanding cities, where manufacturing offered a rapid uplift from poverty to riches. In fact, Amazon runs a 14-year-old ACH payments system today, showing one of the core differences between Alibaba and the US commerce giant.

In creating this revolution of commerce in China, both manufacturing and online, Ant has emerged as the leader, and they talk about empowering digital FinLife globally. This is important, since it's not a payments app or a mobile wallet, but a complete social, commercial and financial systems in one. Imagine Facebook, Amazon and PayPal all integrated into one app. That's what Ant has got.

And their business model is fundamentally based upon deep user understanding, not cross-selling.

This is an abbreviated version of a detailed case study of Ant Financial in Chris Skinner's new book, Digital Human. *The full version includes five interviews covering the past, present and future of Ant Financial, from the person who wrote the first code to the head of strategy building the company's future.*

Endnotes

1   See https://www.finextra.com/resources/feature.aspx?featureid=845.

2   Read more in Chris' latest book *Digital Human.*

3   Many of the facts and statements made in this section draw on Ant Financial's 2016 Sustainability Report—https://os.alipayobjects.com/rmsportal/omkAQCxPyHDDqtqBDnlh.pdf.

2 The Regulator's Dilemma
By Brett King and Jo Ann Barefoot

One can see an emerging requirement for a body
that will carry out the functions of a kind of "central world
bank" that regulates the flow and system of monetary
exchanges, as do the national central banks.
—Vatican's Pontifical Council for Justice and Peace, paper 2011

If there's one area that is going to need a total, first principles rethink, it is regulation. Presently, we are in the vernacular of the software industry, madly adding "patches" to the system, trying to retrofit decades-old regulations and core systems for all these new channels, behaviours and technologies that are emerging. But the more we try to add fixes into the system, the more we get a sort of conflated banking spaghetti code—a system that threatens to lose its coherence at any time, with legacy system and platform limitations that are already decades out of date. Developed countries, in particular, have elaborate and rigid regulatory systems built in an analog era where everything was paper-based, when data was scarce and computing power was also scarce and extremely expensive. Now, both data and computing are ubiquitous and cheap, and paper is increasingly viewed as hard-to-remove friction. We need to create a whole new model for the digital age, in order both to regulate digital markets and to deploy new technology in the regulatory process.

What's needed is digitally-native regulation. It should be designed from scratch, planted beside the old system and replacing it gradually. It needs to incorporate small-scale testing. And, as discussed below, it should build on a breakthrough experiment conducted in late 2017 by the UK Financial Conduct Authority on "machine-executable regulation"—rules issued not as words, but as computer code, self-implementing.

Change won't be easy. Regulators face a diabolical version of the Innovators' Dilemma made famous by Harvard University's Clayton Christensen. In his landmark 1997 book[1], Christensen argued that successful companies become captive to legacy products and practices that are working too well to abandon, and so are vulnerable to displacement by superior disruptive technologies. Regulators face this risk too, holding to traditions built on long histories of painfully-learned lessons. The regulators' challenge is compounded by the risky and constrained frameworks in which they operate. Even more so than banks, regulators are simply not built for rapid change.

One can debate how well regulatory systems have worked in the past, but they have been intentionally designed to have features that make them ill-suited to today's challenges. Financial regulatory frameworks are, and are supposed to be, risk-averse, deliberate (read slow) and clear (read rigid). While some agencies have mandates to promote goals like competition and financial inclusion, most regulators have as their primary mission to detect and address risk to the financial system and its customers. They are not meant to spearhead or promote particular kinds of market changes. They are not meant to spot hot new products and services that deserve a regulatory boost or regulatory relief—a process that could eventually put regulators, not innovators, in the lead in designing financial products by making some safer than others to offer.

Ironically, the very traits that have made regulators effective have suddenly become top contributors to new risks, as a gulf widens between the velocity of market and regulatory change. Regulators must rapidly address new technologies they don't understand and which are rapidly exposing current regulatory moulds. Regulators are left walking a knife-edge between neither blocking emerging benefits nor allowing new risks to proliferate. The chance of this all going smoothly with minimal failures is, honestly, zero. In fact, the most likely thing to go wrong in the Bank 4.0 model is that we will regulate it badly, or that we fail to future proof the sector so our institutions remain globally competitive.

The obstacles to regulatory innovation are numerous, massive and intertwined. They include structures and domains (many are built on foundations dating from the 19th century and even earlier), organisational cultures, incentive systems, external and internal politics, skill sets, legal frameworks, cumbersome procedures, slow pace, constraints on communication and collaboration, pre-digital age leaders, regulatory "capture" by incumbent industries threatened by change, and of course existing laws and regulations themselves.

These last are not only difficult to alter but are also notoriously complex and intertwined. Reforming any part of them is like trying to remove one strand of a spider's web without moving anything else. There is a reason why the US Dodd-Frank Act weighed in at 2,300 pages and spawned tens of thousands more pages of rules (a count that is still rising, 10 years later). Regulatory change is extremely complicated. It is also hideously expensive, which means that even companies that wish for reform often oppose actual efforts to undertake it because of the cost. They know that, once started, reform efforts can go awry, making things worse rather than better or yielding only marginal improvements that are not worth the massive costs of implementing them.

The financial crisis and the iPhone both arrived in 2007. Ever since, policymakers have been consumed with rearview mirror mandates arising from the crisis, even as the whole world has been changing around them.

The risk of regulation that inhibits innovation

The current nature of innovation is very much policy and process-based. Government sets policy, which is implemented into law, or with the creation of new regulatory bodies and modes of conduct. Rules and standards are published, and examiners are mobilised to ensure compliance with those rules. Breaches of the rules are documented and dealt with and where policies or rules are found to be unworkable or fall out of favour, feedback to the policymakers results in slow changes as Acts of Parliament or Congress are drafted and executed, before the cycle starts again.

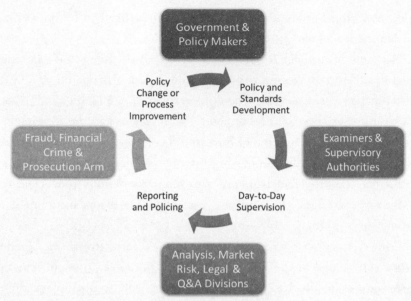

Figure 1: Typical regulatory structure at a market level.

Changes in regulation require both an identification of a system change or emerging market risk, and often changes in law or operational structure to implement. Such changes take years, in typical terms, to be effected. Policy is often the purview of the current government administration, and can change when there is a change at the government level. These ebbs and flows work counter to the way the market we see is innovating today. With few exceptions, regulators are not innovators, and respond to innovation as a risk to the market—a virus that must be killed off by the regulatory immune response.

Here are some examples of rapidly emerging technologies that could be seen as undermining our current regulatory environment, and that illustrate well the risks of restricting regulatory innovation:

Bitcoin—Alt-currency, Ponzi scheme bubble or monetary evolution?

From a purely regulatory perspective how do we classify Bitcoin? Is it a currency? Is it a marketplace, an exchange? Is it a payments network? Is it a new asset class? Is it a tool for money laundering? Is it a tool to circumvent taxation or cross-border currency controls? Is it a threat to central banks and the concept of fiat currency?

Depending on which regulatory body is looking at Bitcoin, at a specific point in time or via specific actors, it could exhibit any one of, or all of, these different characteristics. The decentralised nature of Bitcoin, a lack of a clear internal oversight (as opposed to consensus) and the appearance of anonymity make regulation of Bitcoin difficult. There are countries that over time have issued decrees making Bitcoin technically illegal, and there are further countries that have put significant restrictions and licensing on Bitcoin exchanges, the platforms that allow for the exchange of fiat currency into the digital cryptocurrency.

However, even if exchanging US dollars for Bitcoin was made permanently illegal in the US, for illustrative purposes, it would remain almost impossible for the US government to actually stop people trading in or mining new Bitcoins. In fact, the US government would have to shut down the internet to make Bitcoin completely inaccessible, and even then people could still meet up and trade Bitcoin in person. It's how it was done before Bitcoin was legal in the first place.

Any regulator that thinks they can successfully regulate Bitcoin almost certainly doesn't understand the phenomenon. You can't stop Bitcoin any more than you can stop the internet from working today[2]. As such, Bitcoin presents a significant problem for governments and central banks, which tend towards control. While Bitcoin is extremely unlikely to bring down the banking system (as some of the purists contend or maybe hope for), if Bitcoin achieves a high enough level of utility and becomes a stable form of value exchange, it could actually be more effective for cross-border commerce than even the most popular forms of fiat currency. As the world moves towards globalised online commerce, there's really no advantage in a geographical-based currency on the IP-layer, and as such a popular digital cryptocurrency could easily start to compete with traditional fiat currencies based purely on utility. It's easy to see why central banks might want to attempt to ban, or at a minimum inhibit, Bitcoin.

The reality is that Bitcoin has a design problem that prevents it from being the first truly digital, global currency—and that is the current trend of hoarding Bitcoin[3] and speculating around its possible future value. A ton of Bitcoin holders persist in the belief that Bitcoin's scarcity is one day going to drive the price of a single Bitcoin up to $100,000 or even $1 million, and so they hold on to it like gold or Apple Computer Inc. stock, waiting for the right day to cash out. This behaviour significantly undermines the likely viability of Bitcoin as a pure currency for now, because no one wants to spend it. As a result Bitcoin has very low utility compared with fiat currencies like US dollars. This could be perceived as a design flaw, but primarily this has emerged as an issue through user behaviour.

Unless Bitcoin crashes in value, finds some stable level of value that means it behaves more like paper money, and then people start spending it again, Bitcoin will likely act as a learning foundation for a future digital currency somewhere down the line that will be even more disruptive and ubiquitous.

At the time of writing there are roughly 4,500 cryptocurrencies and altcoins to choose from. If regulators attempt outright to stop BTC, ETH, XRP and others, then their markets become unattractive for investors and entrepreneurs alike.

The development of autonomous networks, smart contracts and smart assets and infrastructure is likely to involve the creation of new methods of value exchange optimised around platforms. For example, the Sun Exchange, a solar startup on the African continent, not only allows you to buy solar panels for local villages using Bitcoin, but the return that is generated off each kilowatt of energy produced is captured in a "solar coin". This is a template for the sort of optimised value exchange systems we're likely to see in the smart world. Artificial intelligence, the blockchain and the need for smart contracts will lead to IP-optimised value exchange systems that circumvent currency controls by necessity.

If a regulator inhibits cryptocurrency models or blockchain deployment, by necessity their economies will start to slow.

The Decentralised Autonomous Organisation (DAO) and ICOs
The DAO is a computer code-based venture capital investment fund or organisation sitting on the Ethereum blockchain. With no typical corporate governance structure, it used a cryptocurrency called Ether for

its underlying asset architecture. Technically the DAO was an AI-based, or automated smart contract between the community members participating in the experiment, but from a regulatory perspective it was, well, an absolute nightmare. It represents a template for future business operations that will be commonplace in 10–15 years, and yet current regulation would prohibit these types of entities in most global jurisdictions.

The DAO doesn't have a management board, a charter or business license. As a proxy for a modern corporation, AI-based or not, it is technically illegal. There are no officers of the "corporation" to hold ultimately responsible for decisions executed within the DAO's operating structure, which is entirely built in code. There are no by-laws, no management structure, no employees and no governance, there's just code that executes instructions. There was no CFO or CEO who took fiduciary duty on the financial governance of the company. No one who could be sued for breach of tax laws. In fact, the DAO operated without any conventional revenue sources or income, so technically would not have paid tax either.

From an investment perspective, while the DAO creators or programmers did explain that investments of Ether coins (the underlying altcoin behind the DAO) carried risk, this investment approach breached securities rules in most developed markets. Investors that invested in the DAO didn't do so through a registered investment fund, they didn't receive advice from an investment advisor, and there was no securities commission oversight in respect to the investment process. No risk profile questionnaires were done, no signatures accepting risk were received. That didn't stop $150 million worth of Ether being deployed within the DAO's engine in the first weeks of operation, and given the increase in price of Ether, we're now talking well over $1 billion of investment in today's terms. A very significant investment pool indeed.

This investment in a blockchain startup using cryptocurrencies was not the first such unregulated, crowdfunded coin offering—that honour goes to Mastercoin in 2013. Unless you are living under a Wi-Fi barred rock today, you've heard the buzz on ICOs or initial coin offerings. Essentially Mastercoin, the DAO, Ethereum, Blockchain Capital[4] and a plethora of others have all raised billions through cryptocurrency-based, over-the-counter trades or issues of ICOs.

Technically considered by law to be a securities issuance (at least in SEC terms[5]) as of the first half of 2017 we've been seeing about 30–40 new ICO offerings per month. Will the SEC, FSA, MAS, HKMA, ASIC and others permanently outlaw ICOs? Will ICO creators be fined for being in breach of securities law?

If regulators want to encourage capital flows and investment in entrepreneurial endeavours, shutting down ICOs wouldn't encourage the free movement of capital, it would restrict it for some of the most innovative startups in their space—risks to consumers aside. The bigger problem is that ICOs could essentially be issued without jurisdiction, making enforcement a sticky problem. A startup that is incorporated in one country, operated in another, with a coin offering taking investment from investors in cryptocurrencies all over the world, could simply move their cryptocoins to another jurisdiction without any operational impact. The only issue would be cashing out their coins. However, if staff, contractors and suppliers are willing to accept altcoins instead of cash, this would be virtually unstoppable.

This doesn't mean regulators won't try to stamp out ICOs (the SEC are making it very tough to legally issue tokens). It does mean that doing so might present significant challenges at law, and may make the markets where cryptocurrency-based offerings are illegal far less competitive and attractive for startups. A regulator that want's to encourage rapid innovation and investment in the emerging FinTech ecosystem would be much more likely to take a light touch on ICOs from a regulatory perspective so that both funding and innovation keep flowing. A regulator that outlaws ICOs would be heavily limiting its options at the market level for participation in the future of financial services, as the best innovations that get the most ICO-based funding would simply flee their jurisdiction. More on this in Chapter 5.

The underlying legal problem with the DAO as an AI-based company is that it wasn't a business subject to human laws in the traditional sense; it was a construct operated via instructions in its code base. While law is how we get our codes or ethics as humans and as corporations, the DAO essentially used its code as law for the internal operation of the business.

For machines, code is law, for us humans, law is our code. When we mix up these concepts, we wind up with situations like the DAO, which doesn't fit any of our current definitions of investment, companies and risk.

Ultimately a flaw in the DAO smart contract allowed certain programmers to siphon off one-third of the DAO's value held (roughly $50 million). Thus, it has been framed as a failure by many, an experiment that came to nothing. However, we've learned from the DAO experience—and it's very likely not the last AI-based company.

Regulators might want to stop future instances of AI-based corporations or smart contracts like the DAO, or force the programmers who write the code to be held to securities law and provisions for regulation of investment businesses, but that would be a mistake. It's clear that in the future we're going to have more and more AI-based execution of smart contracts, particularly as trading floors disappear and are replaced with code. In that instance, any regulator who bans AI-based platforms like this might find their market woefully uncompetitive in a world where AI execution is becoming increasingly normal.

Will AIs trading in the future have to pass a FINRA Series 7, OFQUAL or SFC licensing exam? When code is executing investment decisions en mass, will we still be insisting financial advisors are licensed and leaving code to run amok? Giving preference to humans because they've sat some licensing exam isn't the answer either. As we'll learn later, robo-advisors are already performing at a similar level to human advisors and will likely exceed them for general portfolio management in the next few years.

A flawed approach to financial crime and KYC

Almost 30 years ago[6] the Financial Action Task Force, a body attached to the OECD and sponsored by the G7 member governments and central banks from 37 countries, put in place 40 recommendations on combating money laundering (and nine on terrorist financing). These recommendations are now enshrined in law in major financial centres around the world. Amongst these changes were the requirements for banks to report *suspicious transactions* that could indicate money laundering. The definitions of these suspicious transactions were in themselves a little problematic.

If a financial institution suspects or has reasonable grounds to suspect that funds are the proceeds of a criminal activity, or are related to terrorist financing, it should be required, by law, to report promptly its suspicions to the financial intelligence unit (FIU).
—Recommendation 20, The FATF Recommendations (2012)

Banks find themselves today being the unwitting police force for a global anti-money laundering machine that is amazingly ineffectual.

The AML (anti-money laundering) laws contain three elements. First, banks must authenticate the identities of people opening accounts under complex "Know Your Customer" or KYC rules. Then they must monitor customers' transactions to understand normal patterns, including cash handling, and detect anomalies. Third, they must investigate anomalies and if necessary report them by filing Suspicious Activity Reports, or SARs.

Despite partial automation, these efforts are still configured largely as they were from the beginning, in an era when the best way to find and report suspected money laundering was to have a bank teller or analyst fill out a form. Not surprisingly, they are failing.

The United Nations reports that financial crime today amounts to two to five percent of global GDP—as much as US$2 trillion annually—and that current AML efforts catch less than one percent of current illicit financial flows[7]. Unfortunately, that miserably ineffective result comes with an enormous price tag for banks. In the United States alone, banks spend an estimated $50 billion collectively each year on AML compliance alone[8]. This means that to catch all the financial crime that happens today would require spending the annual equivalent of the GDP of the United Kingdom just on AML policing. The current model is not scalable, nor is it effective.

AML compliance costs are compounded by massive risks for banks—fines have exceeded a billion dollars for a single institution[9]. Fear of aggressive enforcement encourages over-reporting of suspicious activity, which in turn mires law enforcement in low-value data and impedes detection of serious crime. In the United States, major cities have inter-agency task forces that print out reams of SAR reports each month and gather around tables laden with stacks of paper and yellow highlighters, searching for meaningful information. This is probably why the reporting is so ineffective. The hard end of enforcement comes down to yellow highlighters!

Another unintended consequence of this low-tech system is it can block whole sectors of the economy from financial access due to regulatory mandates for "de-risking". Customers whose industries, locations, and circumstances are potentially high risk are screened out simply because, under the current KYC procedures, banks find it simply too difficult, too costly, and too risky to accurately sort the law-abiding people from the bad. This is a major concern of policymakers in the developing world[10]. In the US it has been called the "new redlining".

One side effect of this simple process today has meant that some laws have rendered entire populations of customers unsustainable. The US FACTA (Fair and Accurate Credit Transactions Act of 2003) policing provisions require banks, wherever they are in the world, to report to the IRS when they onboard a US citizen as a customer. This has simply led numerous banks around the world to reject any US citizen even applying for a bank account[11].

AML challenges will continue to mount.

Evolution of the payments space means regulators will have to deal with increasingly diverse types of value stores and payments vehicles, many of them that fall outside of regulation. For example, consider Bitcoin, Ether or XRP coins, Starbucks or Xbox credits—if someone transfers more than US$10,000 using these, they currently wouldn't be reported in an STR[12]. In China today, 90 percent of mobile payments run across Alipay and Tencent's WeChat network, and the trillions of annual payments flying across those networks today are virtually impossible to monitor from the reference point of a traditional banking system.

The process of reporting a US$10,000 transaction that falls outside of predicted patterns is woefully ineffective at finding money launderers today. What we really need is a system that monitors flows of funds, looking for patterns where those funds converge. This requires an AI-based monitoring capability at a minimum on a country-wide basis, but probably on a global basis with coordination between different authorities. Such a transaction flow monitoring system would, on an aggregated basis, be much more effective at finding where money laundering is taking place and the identity of the players involved than the current reporting system.

New technology throws into doubt even the core logic of AML regulation. The system is designed to keep criminals and terrorists out of the financial system, but at a time when arguably technology should be deployed inside regulators for sophisticated data analysis that could be applied to detecting, monitoring and catching them, we are policing using paper-based reporting and human eyeballs. According to a recent University of Chicago report, in their "generous" assessment they estimated that only *0.2% of money that is laundered is successfully seized.* That means for every dollar caught by AML regulation today, $499 is still successfully laundered. We're spending globally $50–100 billion each year for a 0.2% success rate in AML. That's appallingly ineffectual. Massive regulation, billions of man hours and efforts expended, customers disrupted and accused, regulatory enforcement action taken, and it simply doesn't work.

The technology already exists to make AML efforts effective and efficient. The system needs updated reporting designs and norms, greater sharing of secure data, greater information security, faster and more accurate pattern analysis, and tools that remove manual work and free bank specialists and law enforcement. Some countries, such as Singapore, are exploring creating a shared data utility between government and industry for KYC. More regulators will need to engage.

Current KYC laws are a path to exclusion

But let's think about KYC moving forward for a moment. While Uber has been making some big losses the last few years, things seem to be on the up[13]. In Q2 of 2017, Uber's bookings were up 17 percent, and they were up 10 percent in the quarter before that, with almost $9 billion in revenue. For the first 20 years of Amazon's life it made a loss, so it appears Uber's investors are willing to trade off losses for growth for now. But as Uber grows it is definitely changing driving habits for millennials in particular. My daughter, Hannah, is 17 now and when living in New York it became clear she really had no intention of getting her driver's license; in fact, when

I talked about getting her a car she said, "Don't bother Dad, just give me an Uber allowance."

As autonomous vehicles kick in and as services like Uber abound, the expectation is clearly that our sons and daughters will be driving less than we did. A report from the Frontier Group in the United States in 2016 showed the six-decade-long driving boom seen in the United States is already over[14]; based on other factors, Uber will just accelerate this decline.

> The Driving Boom of the second half of the 20th century coincided with rapid economic, cultural and demographic changes in the United States. Those changes largely pointed in the same direction: toward a more automobile-oriented society. Many of those trends, however, have either reached their natural limits or have reversed direction...those trends point to the conclusion that the trajectory toward increased per capita driving that prevailed during the Driving Boom has likely reached its end.
>
> —Frontier Group assessment on the Future of Driving in the United States

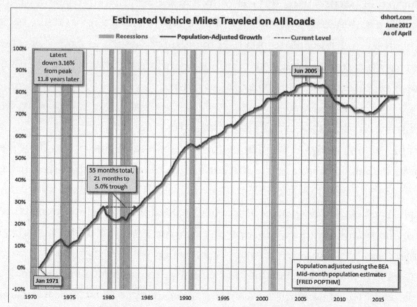

Figure 2: Fewer miles, fewer drivers, fewer driver's licenses for KYC.

Thus, when we combine lower incentives or tendency to drive, the increasingly ubiquitous nature of shared transportation services like Uber, and the medium-term impact of autonomous or self-driving cars, one thing is abundantly clear: fewer drivers means fewer driving licenses, means fewer identity qualifications, and this means greater financial exclusion based on current KYC rules in markets like the United States[15].

In developing economies like sub-Saharan Africa, branching as a mechanism for financial inclusion has stalled. Research from Accenture and Standard Bank showed that 70 percent of the currently unbanked on the African continent would be required to spend more than an entire month's salary just to physically get to an available bank branch[16]. Something similar was found in India. Initially the Reserve Bank required banks based in India to deploy a minimum of 25 percent of new branches in rural areas to focus on unbanked customers; however, this measure didn't affect inclusion significantly enough because of the inability of the unbanked there to meet account opening identity requirements. This is why India's initiative to deploy the Aadhaar card has been such a boon for financial inclusion—it changed the game. As of 15 August 2017, more than 1.171 billion have been enrolled in the Aadhaar card program. That's 88 percent of the Indian population.

The effect of identity reform in India is that the number of those included in the financial system has skyrocketed. The segment of the population most excluded in the old banking system—lower income households and women—have seen 100 percent year-on-year growth every year since the Aadhaar card initiative was launched. As of 2015 more than 358 million Indian women (61 percent) now have bank accounts, up from 281 million (48 percent) in 2014. This is the biggest single jump for "banked" women among eight South Asian and African countries[17]. You can either lower identity requirements or create new identity structures to support inclusion, but you can't create IDV requirements that need driver's licenses and passports for a population that doesn't drive and doesn't travel and expects financial inclusion through branches. That model is a recipe for financial exclusion as the 25 percent of US households that are underbanked already know.

From a regulation perspective, however, the question should be asked, who has the best IDV capability today? Who is well placed to support financial inclusion and access over the next couple of decades? Frankly, it isn't the banks.

The largest holders of broad identity data sets today are Facebook, Apple, Tencent, Amazon, Alibaba/Alipay, Uber, Snapchat and other platforms with massive scale. Those platforms not only have basic identity data, but they often have quite sophisticated behavioural data sets along with biometric data like facial recognition, etc. It is likely that Facebook[18] today has better identity information than the majority of retail banks in the world. Oh, and they are all on the cloud.

As real-time delivery capability becomes essential for competitiveness, the need to present at a branch to provide an identity document that large swathes of the population no longer use is simply a structural impediment to inclusion. Regulators that insist that face-to-face verification is required using a driver's license or passport, along with a physical signature, are not securing banking for consumers, they are part of the problem. It is a problem that is only going to get worse. Face-to-face verification backed by a wet signature will guarantee disruption from frictionless FinTech's providing alternate value stores on top of ubiquitous platforms like those mentioned above.

The only way for regulators to guarantee incumbents stay competitive is to remove both the face-to-face and cloud platform constraints. By 2025, we could see most banks outsourcing identity to identity brokers like Facebook or the Aadhaar card. It simply doesn't make sense for banks to be collectors and holders of identity data in the future. It's far more likely banks will interface with identity services and just pass enough information across to verify the identity of the new customer is accurate. Not to mention that technology like software-based facial recognition is 15–20 times more accurate at identifying a customer than a typical face-to-face interaction[19]. A fact that would indicate face-to-face account opening is no longer safe—it's probably statistically the single riskiest thing a bank could do in this day and age.

But read later the chapter on blockchain, where I will argue that regulators and banks won't have to worry about identity collection and KYC regulations for much longer.

Heads in the cloud?

Another key challenge is that regulators must join the global technology migration to cloud computing. Until recently, examiners in the US routinely required banks to produce things like physical e-card keys for accessing server rooms and written fire suppression plans for protecting servers—these have been mandatory elements in IT risk management. FinTechs, in contrast, don't have server rooms. The data is in the cloud. When Moven first migrated our technology to Canada, the Canadian regulator wanted Amazon Web Services (AWS) to tell us where the physical servers that stored anonymised, tokenised customer data were housed. Needless to say AWS didn't comply with the request.

Regulators have generally frowned on cloud-based systems due to security concerns. Done right, however, cloud systems like Amazon Web Services are actually far more secure, not less. This is mainly because they are much easier to defend. Traditional bank IT systems have numerous weak links, because every point of access is a potential vulnerability. In banks, points of access are everywhere—in multiple server rooms in many locations; in systems that typically run numerous kinds of software, often in versions that are not fully up to date; and in the leaky pipes between these systems, which are full of cracks in security where data can be lost or stolen. The stealing can be done by hackers, and also by the many bank employees who must have access simply to maintain it all.

More critically though, cloud-based providers like AWS or Microsoft Azure have grown up in a combative security environment where they are constantly being probed by hackers, and their cyber security teams are the best in the world. Over time this acts like an immune system, enabling the big cloud providers to build military grade security[20] of their platforms—platforms that routinely outperform bank-owned IT systems on both security and performance criteria.

In a cloud system the data is all online, which means it's protected from physical disasters like fire, and it can be secured efficiently. Regulators should focus on security outcomes, not forms. If the bank and regulators properly run penetration testing to assure that the environment is secure, it shouldn't matter how the security is being achieved, as long as customer data remains secure.

Regulators are increasingly open to this, but they need to make a full conversion to permitting and even encouraging cloud-based systems. Both the banks and their consumers will be better off for it. So will the regulators themselves, who will be increasingly able to monitor banks' compliance performance through RegTech strategies that analyse easily-gathered data.

The trend of regulators to require on-premises solutions is effectively building stand-alone "islands" in the technology architecture of future financial systems. These islands prevent banks from working seamlessly with other providers.

We have to assume that in the future more cloud-based financial service providers will emerge than not. In fact, it's likely that the majority of experience-based capabilities will have a cloud element. By restricting the use of cloud as a platform for regulated entities, regulators are actually ensuring that their banks won't be able to sustain competitive platforms against emerging FinTechs and technology leaders. In turn, cloud prohibitions will make a financial services marketplace less effective and less competitive over all. Restricting the cloud today will increase the gap between the most progressive financial markets and your own.

Improvements in credit access

Another widening gulf between old regulation and new technology is in credit risk assessment, and therefore financial inclusion. Today, lenders can use new kinds of data and machine learning to fine tune risk evaluation models that were developed in an era when, again, data and computing power were both scarce. Combined with the mobile phone, which is bringing financial access to billions of people never served by brick and mortar branches, this data revolution is the most democratising force in the history of finance. Unfortunately, public policy and bias towards incumbent lending institutions threaten to block much of this potential, especially in countries like the United States where credit agencies are very well established.

While US regulators permit many kinds of data modelling for risk analysis, policymakers have created a special risk zone around using new kinds of data for consumer lending. The laws that prohibit credit discrimination include the concept of illegal "disparate impact", meaning non-intentional discrimination in the form of statistical disparity in lending outcomes for "protected classes" such as women and minorities. Lending that shows such statistical patterns may be challenged as illegal unless the provider can prove a business need and can demonstrate that this need cannot be met with a less discriminatory approach.

All lending produces different outcomes for different groups of borrowers, and these disparities are often adverse for racial and ethnic minority populations that have lower income, wealth, job security and other attributes that can impact creditworthiness. Long ago, regulators blessed the use of certain models, despite such impacts, viewing them as statistically sound and predictive. These approved models generally rely heavily on use of credit scores, and so work well for consumers who have good scores. However, they can inadvertently exclude or penalise people with "thin" credit files, no credit history, or complex histories that are hard to evaluate efficiently through available data (such as a past financial setback due to a health problem). With such customers, reliance on credit scores can exclude people who are actually creditworthy and could prove it, if the lender could evaluate more information about them.

Technology makes that possible. Lenders today can readily learn much more about people beyond their credit histories and scores—in fact, they routinely do so in areas like detecting fraud and complying with the anti-money laundering KYC rules. In credit, most lenders are afraid to use alternative data, because regulators have not clarified how such practices will be evaluated for discriminatory disparate impact.

In the United States, an estimated 80–130 million Americans live at the fringes of the financial system, relying on high-cost services[21]. Millions could be brought into accessing well-priced mainstream credit, on terms they can afford, if the regulation can catch up with the technology[22].

The future form and function of regulation

Returning to first principles, we need to ask why we created regulation in the first place. At bottom, it's a function, not a form. In modern finance, though, the function has become encased in old and rigid structures that are increasingly mismatched to the task.

The oldest remaining central bank, and technically the first government regulator of money, was Riksbank[23] in Sweden, which began operations in 1668. Government involvement in control of money is not a new phenomenon, however. The earliest examples of state controls over currencies go back to Egypt around 2750 BC, where the state-issued shat[24] unit of currency was pegged to gold. The Bank of England was established soon after Riksbank in 1694, but as a mechanism to raise money for war with Louis XIV of France.

Central banks originally were the private banks of the government or royal families. As such, their role in regulating the financial system effectively evolved over the 18th and 19th centuries. Until 1844, commercial banks in Britain were able to issue their own notes. After this date, issuance of new bank notes was restricted to the central bank, and backed by gold (generally referred to as "seigniorage"). Over time central banks came to manage the banking market as a whole, including licensing of banks for commercial operations. Later, economic policy also became the purview of central bankers and monetary authorities as a means to regulate growth. It is fairly clear today that after the Global Financial Crisis of 2007–2008, central banks can no longer effectively boost economic growth with monetary policy alone.

Regulation of banks came with central bank controls on issuance of notes—only a licensed bank could issue notes or take deposits. This all changed in the 1930s with the Great Depression, as regulation was introduced to protect consumers more broadly from failing banks and stock markets.

Thus, regulation of institutions that take deposits or issue currency is the historical role of central banks, but in a world where cryptocurrencies can be issued by a collective group of programmers, or a technology company like Ant Financial, Microsoft (with XBox credits), or Starbucks can hold more deposits (read funds) on behalf of their customers than a modern bank—the control and structural elements start to break down.

There is a very real question of what value a banking license itself will hold in the near future, as value stores become more fungible and as utility is increasingly owned by non-bank actors. Should Microsoft be forced to issue an FDIC deposit guarantee on the funds it holds for you? Should Ant Financial, Facebook or Amazon be forced to get a banking or payments license to be able to move money around the economy?

However, what if Alipay (for example) is issued a payments license in China, but half of its users are outside of China? Should Alipay be required to get a payments license in every country it operates? This is what current regulation would assume. But what about deposits or value held in its wallet—should Ant Financial be required to get a banking license in every country where they hold deposits? I think only regulators would assume this is a reasonable ask—shareholders in Ant Financial would argue it is not reasonable. Operationally, you could very well have laws in China that restrict a company like Ant Financial from operating in the United States, or you could have regulations that are in conflict. A non-bank entity in the UK that has an e-money license or a challenger bank charter is still prohibited from taking deposits from a customer in the US. What if they allowed a US resident to deposit cross-border using Bitcoin and then issued a UK debit card to the US resident? This would be in breach of US regulations, but would be very difficult to police and prevent.

The reality is that as our economy becomes increasingly global, and as money movement becomes less and less defined by geography, the role of central banks to authorise a technology actor to act as an extension to the traditional banking system assumes that the traditional banking system works efficiently. However, in pure economic terms, the way we license banks and the way we limit the ownership of bank accounts will fail to cater for the plethora of new types of value stores and value exchange systems we see emerging in the future world of finance.

Take, for example, the ability of AI agents or smart assistants like Siri and Alexa to act as agents conducting commerce on your behalf in a few years' time: "Alexa, book me a restaurant in Chinatown Friday night for five people. Make sure they serve dim sum for dinner and it's rated 4-stars or better."

In this scenario, if the restaurant in question also has an AI agent handling bookings, it's fairly certain that before long payments will be fully automated by these agents. These two AI agents will negotiate between each other to facilitate the payment, but the underlying value store won't matter—an AI probably won't stop because you don't have a MasterCard linked to your Alexa account. If you're a Chinese tourist visiting Chinatown in New York City, your AI will likely be powered by a WeChat or Alipay style value store enabled in the cloud and built into your phone; so by the time that you've finished your meal the restaurant AI would poll the tourists' agent requesting payment, and some clearing house would facilitate a payment from Alipay to the restaurant's Citibank bank account held in New York.

To extend the analogy: what if the restaurant receives delivery of foodstuffs via a delivery robot and has to pay the robot a delivery charge? The robot will have a value store to accept payment; but which bank is going to enable robots to open traditional bank accounts so they can be issued a 16-digit card number from their social security number? It's far more likely that this value store will be more like a stored value GPR prepaid card or a so-called e-wallet (PayPal, Venmo, Alipay, WeChat, etc) construct than a traditional bank account. When a sizeable chunk of commerce shifts to non-bank value stores, do we license every variety of value store and insist on a deposit guarantee? Or do we simply monitor that activity to protect consumers?

What could go wrong?

A parade of horribles will arise out of the coming regulatory failures in overlapping categories.

First, over-regulation will inevitably throttle desirable and helpful innovation. This will happen because regulators do not understand the upside potential but are built to see the downside risks. Innovation, especially by small startups, inherently involves business and technology risk. Some innovators will fail, leaving customers stranded, including people who were storing value in uninsured instruments, and will lose their money. Innovators will also experience security breaches. Such breaches are, of course, common in today's highly-regulated banks as well, but there will be public and regulatory backlash against newer kinds of entities. In other cases, policymakers will frequently seek to block innovation due to political pressure from incumbents seeking regulatory protection from more agile competition.

Second, under-regulation and gaps in legacy regulatory domains will allow new risks to emerge and grow. These will include loss of consumer privacy and cyber security, rising money laundering, bias and inaccuracy in algorithmic decision-making, and instability in the financial system. The fact is, innovative methods of financial service are evolving at a rate faster than regulators can adapt. So expect these gaps to grow.

A third type of failure will be regulatory inconsistency producing market distortions and also systemic uncertainty that chills the entry of new capital into promising fields. In most countries, multiple regulators have overlapping mandates and jurisdictions with, generally, only weak (and very slow) mechanisms for collaboration and coordination. The United States has a uniquely intense version of this problem, with five national agencies directly supervising financial institutions, another two dozen involved in financial regulatory matters, and 50 states also overseeing banks and non-bank financial companies. Despite some coordinating bodies, this splintered structure causes extensive inconsistency, which breeds regulatory uncertainty and risk and again deters innovation.

Finally, regulations will simply become increasingly ineffective in achieving their goals. Regulators built on analogy technology will increasingly lag behind industry (as well as criminals and terrorists) using advanced digital and computational approaches grounded in massive data and AI.

These kinds of failures will certainly threaten the soundness of the financial system. Banks are far more regulated and supervised than non-banks, a pattern likely to intensify as market change accelerates. Banks will probably continue to be forced to carry higher regulatory costs and risks than competitors and to maintain old systems, such as to keep branches open, especially in lower-income areas. One result will be loss of market share. Another will be likely failures of banks that don't adapt. All these problems will tend to spiral, as regulatory strictures and costs continue to drive innovation out of the banking sector and into less-scrutinised space. There, risks will rise, undetected, sometimes leading to crises that produce reactive policies that may make matters worse long term (as happened in the subprime mortgage crisis, sparking popularisation of the term "shadow banking.") These trends could bring systemic crises in system liquidity, capital and public trust.

Don't expect this to negatively impact non-bank players necessarily. While many banks point to "trust in banks" as a core of their ability to service the market, the reality is players like M-Pesa, Alipay and WeChat Pay have established strong trust through their utility, which is in turn amplified by network effect.

Private companies that don't adapt rapidly to new technology will be replaced by ones that do, ones with better utility. In the regulatory realm, however, institutions are created by sovereign governments. Despite some likely restructuring, most are here to stay. To avert the regulatory disasters described above, these organisations will have to change. The journey to a 21st century financial regulatory system will be long and hard.

Elements of reform

Success will require strategies grounded in first principles of assuring financial system stability, customer fairness, and curtailing money laundering (and in some countries, fostering economic growth by promoting competition and financial inclusion for consumers and small businesses). Below are the critical elements:

RegTech and SupTech: principles-based, data-driven supervision: Policymakers will have to de-emphasize rules-based regulation and rely increasingly on principles-based supervision married to data-intensive monitoring against quantified metrics. Rules-based regulation can work in some realms, but prescriptive, procedural requirements will increasingly lag behind tech-driven change in products and practices. (In advanced economies, it can take several years to create a new regulation, making many likely to be obsolete at issuance.)

Instead, regulators must move to data-intensive, AI-driven monitoring of transactions, business conduct, and market patterns, using "RegTech" for regulators, or supervision technology, often called "SuperTech" or "SupTech". This will require setting quantified, measurable standards for satisfying the principles embodied in the goals of each regulation, ranging from adequacy of risk-adjusted capital and preventing insider trading to non-discriminatory treatment of consumers.

Digitally-native regulation: Reform should create new systems that are digitally-native, not mere enhancements of old analog processes. They should determine what data and analysis are needed to achieve the goal and then digitise the regulatory design to make it better, faster and cheaper all at once, as happens with all things that are digitised. In many areas, these new approaches should be established in parallel with the analog model and industry should be allowed to choose between the two, as a means of easing transition.

Machine-executable regulation: In November 2017, the UK Financial Conduct Authority (FCA) conducted an experiment in machine-executable regulation. Convening a collaborative hackathon with industry, they coded a change in a regulatory reporting mandate, applied it to a set of dummy data, and successfully produced a report reflecting the revised rule, machine to machine. The reporting change, which might have taken months or years to execute through traditional means, was implemented in about 10 seconds. The FCA has issued a report on the test, requested public input on next steps, and reached out to engage regulators from other countries. Machine-executable regulation would not work for some purposes but where it can, it could save vast amounts of time and money for both government and industry. It should be central to regulatory reform.

AML network monitoring: As discussed earlier. For example, the future won't be based on a reporting mechanism that requires banks to act as a virtual police force for tracking down suspicious transactions and suspicious account owners. Instead, AIs will track transactions en masse, looking for suspicious flows and identifying the centres of AML activity that need policing response. Bad actors could be flagged in much the same way fake phishing websites are identified today, and banks would automatically know not to transact with those entities.

Test beds, sandboxes and Reg-Labs: Regulators will need new strategies that can enable them to formulate and test technology-driven change before adopting it system-wide. Similarly, industry will need a carefully designed safe space within which to test promising innovation that does not fit squarely within current regulatory requirements. For both, regulators should create and permit test beds, Reg-Labs, or regulatory "sandboxes" under clear, thoughtful limits and at a very small scale.

These are already spreading worldwide. Inspired by the one created by the UK's Financial Conduct Authority, more than 20 countries have created or are exploring establishment of Reg-Labs[25].

Changes in missions, cultures, skills and protocols: Most current regulatory bodies will need rethinking regarding missions, scope and protocols. They will need to change training and to recruit new skills, especially in data science. They may need to reorganise around tech-centred issues and create new leadership roles like chief innovation officer or chief data officer. They will also have to alter cultures that are conservative and focused heavily on risk avoidance, rather than open to the upside of innovation. Changes may be needed to enhance their freedom to collaborate with industry and other interested parties and in some cases to "co-create" regulations and shared databases. Other changes will be required in regulatory procedure protocols that require lengthy formal periods for public comment—although constant input will be more important than ever.

Structural modernisation will have to include updating which companies can access central payments systems and how, and how this should be regulated. This will also mean thinking through the challenges of regulating cryptocurrencies, and the nature of banking itself.

Regulatory agility, open platforms, and code: Regulators will have to speed up their cycles for creating and updating regulations. Some might be structured to function like GitHub or an app store, operating on an open platform that would prescribe standards and then permit innovation in how to meet them. Eventually, regulators may promulgate some regulations in the form of computer code that simply plugs into industry systems and creates self-executing compliance. The ability to deploy cloud-based systems in their markets will be essential for new players, incumbents and the regulators themselves.

Practical implementation roadmap: If we were starting today from scratch, few if any people would design the regulatory systems we now have, with their pre-digital assumptions, missions, technologies and structures. However, we are not starting from scratch. While change can come to the private sector through competition, the regulatory world can only change through the will of policymakers. The regulators' dilemma will most likely work against that happening—like an immune system attacking the virus of change.

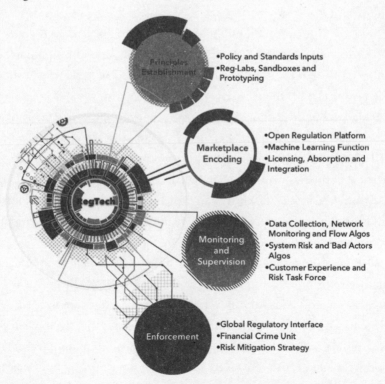

Figure 3: Regulation is largely about absorbing tech, monitoring algos and risk mitigation in real time.

It is crucial, therefore, to create not only a vision of possibilities, but also a practical pathway that can get us there from here. No such pathway exists using traditional methods for changing the government—new laws, new regulations, regulatory reorganisation, and the like.

Where do regulators start?

Instead, regulators need to do three concrete things and start small, but fast.

First, regulators must use the test-beds described above as small-scale learning laboratories where they can develop empirical proof that key changes will produce benefit and little risk or harm (the testing can determine what harm-mitigation steps should be built in). The empirical proof can help build support for needed reforms by convincing sceptics of their merits, while the testing process provides the needed insight on how to go forward.

Second, regulators must build these Reg-Lab learnings into an experimental, alternative regulatory channel that works through data and AI. Again, this channel should start small. Furthermore, crucially, it should be made optional for the industry.

Regulated entities should be given a choice: they can remain in the traditional regulatory process they hate but know, or they can elect a new data-driven RegTech channel, submit to intensive, real-time scrutiny, and be relieved of process-oriented compliance requirements. The government's stance would be that if the entity can prove through data that it is meeting desired outcomes, measured using transparent and empirical standards, then regulators need not care how they got there.

Making this new channel optional would avoid the biggest obstacle to regulatory reform, namely the need to force change on the entire system at once. Regulators today don't even know what changes are needed—this needs to be learned through testing and other means—but even when they do, the system will exert massive political resistance to major change, due to both fear of the risks involved in opening up set rules and fear that the reform's benefits won't outweigh the transition costs of adopting them. Removing that fear makes it possible to spread new regulatory norms gradually through the financial system, learning and refining at small scale before scaling up.

Lastly, regulators must retool—the most critical change is one of leadership focused on technology-based or *digitally-native* supervision, rather than policy and process-based regulation. The skill set required by the regulator of 2030 is not one of policymaking and examiner-based compliance; it is almost entirely technology supervision based and the ability to respond and correct the market in a very dynamic, real-time capability. This evolution will happen quickly in regulatory terms over just 10–15 years.

These changes will require strong leadership and courage by policymakers. Fortunately, many leaders are already stepping up.

Endnotes

1 *The Innovator's Dilemma*, by Clayton Christensen. See https://www.google.com/url?sa=t&rct=j&q=&esrc=s&source=web&cd=3&cad=rja&uact=8&ved=0ahUKEwj9rOKe_uDVAhUMmoMKHb1-CBkQFgg0MAI&url=http percent3A percent2F percent2Fwww.claytonchristensen.com per cent2Fbooks percent2Fthe-innovators-dilemma percent2F&usg=AFQjCNHyfrCGTv2MBU9wUzlWnNrj8n2SrA.

2 Even in countries like China where the "Great Firewall" restricts access, the proliferation of VPN (virtual private networks) has allowed circumventing these restrictions for years.

3 Bitcoiners even have a slang term for this mantra of retention, which is HODL or "Hold On for Dear Life!"

4 "Are cryptocurrencies about to go mainstream?", *The Observer*, 1 July 2017—https://www.theguardian.com/technology/2017/jul/01/cryptocurrencies-mainstream-finance-bitcoin-ethereum.

5 SEC Investor Bulletin: Initial Coin Offerings —https://www.sec.gov/oiea/investor-alerts-and-bulletins/ib_coinofferings.

6 Founded in 1989 at the G7 Summit in Paris, also known by its French name, *Groupe d'action financière* (GAFI).

7 Source: FATF/United Nations Office on Drugs and Crime (UNODC).

8 https://www.unodc.org/unodc/en/money-laundering/globalization.html.

9 HSBC were fined $1.9 billion—https://www.google.com/url?sa=t&rct=j&q=&esrc=s&source=web&cd=2&cad=rja&uact=8&ved=0ahUKEwi7qbb4hOHVAhXBfyYKHa5-DcAQFggtMAE&url=https percent3A percent2F percent2Fdealbook.nytimes.com percent2F2012 percent2F12 percent2F10 percent2Fhsbc-said-to-near-1-9-billion-settlement-over-money-laundering percent2F percent3Fmcubz pe rcent3D1&usg=AFQjCNGaAgOEpYZrn0Pp0WaupEedz3rwIw.

10 Alliance for Financial Inclusion report on pillars for financial inclusion—http://www.afi-global.org/publications/2458/The-2016-Global-Policy-Forum-GPF-Report-Building-the-Pillars-of-Sustainable-Inclusion.

11 "Overseas Americans can't open foreign bank accounts because of FACTA? Court says tough luck!", AngloInfo.com, 29 April 2016 by Virgina La Torre Jeker.

12 Suspicious Transaction Report.

13 "Uber second-quarter bookings increase, loss narrows", Reuters Technology News, 24 August 2017.

14 "A New Direction: Our Changing Relationship with Driving and the Implications for America's Future".

15 Fewer voting rights, too.

16 Source: Standard Bank/Accenture Research (2015).

17 Source: Intermedia.

18 Fake profiles aside.

19 Research shows that Australian Customs and Border Patrol Officers doing face-to-face verification missed one in seven fake IDs—http://theconversation.com/passport-staff-miss-one-in-seven-fake-id-checks-30606.

20 Amazon literally provides cloud services for the U.S. Department of Defense (see https://aws.amazon.com/compliance/dod/).

21 *Report on the Economic Wellbeing of U.S. Households in 2015*, Federal Reserve Board of Governors, May 2016—https://www.federalreserve.gov/2015-report-economic-well-being-us-households-201605.pdf.

22 At this writing the US Consumer Financial Protection Bureau is evaluating this issue and may undertake rulemaking or other guidance to address it.

23 Effectively translates as "Bank of the Estates of the Realm".

24 I swear—I'm serious.

25 Aspen Institute Report—https://www.google.com/url?sa=t&rct=j&q=&esrc=s&source=web&cd=1&cad=rja&uact=8&ved=0ahUKEwjj1unioOHVAhVk6YMKHeOtANEQFggmMAA&url=https percent3A percent2F percent2Fassets.aspeninstitute.org percent2Fcontent percent2Fuploads percent2F2017 percent2F07 percent2FModernizing-Reglabs.pdf&usg=AFQjCNEZSooEnB6NYEFmWRbZVvyiOyNMKA.

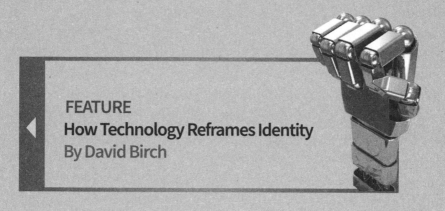

There is no doubt at all that the future of banking is entangled with the future of identity. Digital identity is a key resource in the new economy and banks, just like other organisations, will need to develop digital identity strategies. But what should these be? And, we might speculate, what happens if banks do not develop these strategies?

We have all read countless articles and sat through countless conference presentations and seen countless blog posts and noted countless tweets that all highlight the key role of digital identity in the new economy. The authors may not all be entirely clear on what a digital identity actually is, but they do share the common suspicion that unless we have some form of digital identity infrastructure in place then the potential growth and attendant benefits of the transition to a new online economy cannot be fully realised. I more than share this suspicion. In fact, I think it's an absolute certainty that unless an appropriate infrastructure can be put into place, then we have no chance of moving forwards.

Digital identity is, not to put too fine a point on it, critical infrastructure for the future. But how will it work? Who will be in charge of it? When it comes to thinking about this sort of thing, I admit to having some form. I've been working in the space for many years and indeed have something of a reputation for my modest intellectual contributions to the evolution of the subject. Along with my colleagues at Consult Hyperion, I developed a pretty good model of digital identity that has been tried and tested and found useful in a number of different areas. This model, the "three domain identity" (3DID), as shown in Figure 1, frames digital identity as the bridge between the mundane and virtual worlds and sets out a clear framework for thinking about the dynamics of the bindings with either of them. At a high level, it's sufficient to know only that these bindings are highly asymmetric: it is time-consuming, complicated and expensive to bind a digital identity to something in the real world but it is inexpensive and quick to bind the digital identity to something in the virtual world. It's all about encryption and keys and how you manage them (see "A Model for Digital Identity" in *Digital Identity Management*, edited by yours truly back in 2007).

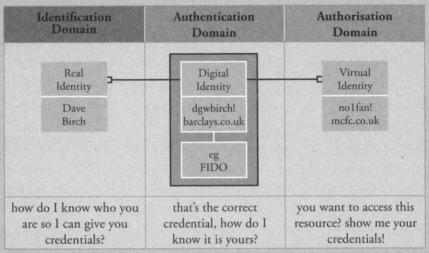

Figure 1: The "three domain identity" model.

There are a number of reasons for thinking that while there are a wide variety of organisations that could instantiate these bindings, and indeed a number of different institutional arrangements that could come into existence around these bindings, it is a plausible hypothesis that it should include banks who could be vanguard providers of digital identity. A few years ago, I wrote a book about this (*Identity is the New Money*, LPP: 2014) to explore some of the issues around identity infrastructure, making some positive suggestions about how we might construct a better identity infrastructure more suited to the modern world and explaining why it was that banks might be the right organisations to create and manage these bindings.

On the whole, I think that my arguments still hold true. I was reminded of them recently when a friend of mine had some problems with his Facebook account being taken over by fraudsters. He was extremely frustrated by his efforts to contact Facebook and have something done about it. As I pointed out to him, I could not see any reason why he should have expected anything different. Facebook has no statutory obligation to remedy such problems[1]. Banks, on the other hand, are regulated financial institutions—were they to provide identity services—and would be obligated via regulation to ensure your identity was protected. If your bank account was taken over by thieves, then you might reasonably expect the bank to do something about it and have some procedures to establish who the rightful owner of the bank account was, restore control of the account to that person and provide appropriate compensation if the bank had behaved negligently in some way.

I like this vision of the future. Let's imagine a non-financial use case to see what I mean. Internet dating sites provide a rich and practical environment for exploring different notions of identity, so let's use them as our example. Let's imagine I go to the dating site and create an account. As part of this process the dating site asked me to log in via my bank account. At this point it bounces me to my bank, where I carry out the appropriate two-factor authentication to establish my identity to the bank's satisfaction. The bank then returns an appropriate cryptographic token to the internet dating site, which tells them that I am over 18, resident on Jersey and that I have funds available for them to bill against. In this example my real identity is safely locked up in the bank vault, but it has been bound to a virtual identity that I can use for online interactions. So my internet dating persona contains no Personally Identifiable Information (PII), but if I use that persona to get up to no good then the dating sites can provide the token to the police, the police can see that the token comes from Barclays and Barclays will tell them that it belongs to Dave Birch[2]. This seems to me a very appropriate distribution of responsibilities. When the internet dating site gets hacked, as they inevitably do, all the criminals will obtain is a meaningless token: they have no idea who it belongs to, and Barclays won't tell them.

One of the key attractions of this architecture—and I'm sure that I am not the only person who thinks this—is that it gives an expectation of redress in the event of inevitable failure. Things always go wrong. What's important is what the structures, mechanisms and processes for dealing with those failures are. If some fraudsters take over my bank account and use my identity to create a fake profile on a dating site, then I'd expect the bank to have mechanisms in place to revoke the tokens and inform both the dating site and me that such revocation has taken place, without disclosing any of my personal identifiable information. This is important, because PII is in essence a kind of toxic waste that no companies really want to deal with unless they absolutely have to. Under the new provisions of the General Data Protection Regulation (GDPR), the potential fines for disclosing PII without the consent of the data subject are astronomical. Hence the complete cycle needs to be thought through, because it will be crazy to have an infrastructure that protects my personal data when the system is operating normally but gives it up when the system fails, or when we attempt recovery from failure.

To see how banks are beginning to take advantage of the new opportunities in this space, let's have a quick world tour to examine what Barclays are doing in the UK, what itsme is doing in Belgium, what Toronto Dominion are doing in Canada and what the Commonwealth Bank of Australia (CBA) is up to down under.

Barclays are one of the "identity providers" for the British government's identity service. In order to use this service to access a variety of government services online, you have to first create an online identity. To do this, you can choose one of a number of private sector organisations to validate your personal details and bind them to the online identity. Barclays is one of these organisations. To date, this scheme has met with limited success, since there are few places to use the government identity, but Sarah Munro (Director of Information Propositions at Barclays) says that it is a model that will develop.

In Belgium, the itsme service[3] launched in 2017 shows a very different approach. It's a very interesting collaboration between the Belgian banks and Belgian mobile operators: Belfius, BNP Paribas, KBC/CBC and ING working with Orange, Proximus and Telenet. To use this, you download the itsme app and verify your identity (which is easy in Belgium, since everyone already has an eID card), then use it to log in to participating websites. To begin with these sites are (as usual!) tax filings, but insurance companies and retailers are joining the program. Soon, users will be able to sign official documents using their mobile phones and have secure remote access to a wide variety of systems. The combination of the identity, the SIM and the app delivers a very secure and reliable environment. To be completely honest, I don't understand why banks and mobile operators were not co-operating in this way a decade ago!

The leading Canadian banks (including BMO, CIBC, RBC, National Bank, Scotiabank and Toronto Dominion) are part of a nationwide consortium[4] developing a sophisticated digital identity infrastructure to bring security and convenience to their marketplace. As in the case of itsme, customers will use the service via an app, but in the Canadian scheme the trusted credentials are stored on a shared ledger built using IBM's blockchain service (implementing Hyperledger Fabric). The scheme uses a "triple blinding" implementation so that the people relying on the trusted credentials and the people providing these credentials never see each other's identity.

CBA have begun a pilot service with Airtasker to provide verification services. In the growing "gig economy" it is a significant step, because providing identity infrastructure to these marketplaces is a way for banks to be involved in the transactions. Airtasker is an Australian online community, similar to Task Rabbit in the US, where people and businesses can outsource tasks (eg build my IKEA furniture for me!). If you have an Airtasker profile you can go through the CBA verification process and the system will add a badge to your profile. The badge tells people that CBA know who you are. It does not give away any personal information, it merely tells prospective users of your skills and time. This simple expression of reputation gives comfort to these prospective users and illustrates a central point about the coming collaborative economy, which is that reputation is much more important than identity (and it is much harder to counterfeit). Banks ought to obtain significant advantage as infrastructure providers here, because the collaborative economy stakeholders do not want to have to create their own identification, authentication and authorisation infrastructures. This not a purely technological perspective. As the *Financial Times* reported way back in 2014, British banks believe that they have a future role as repositories of digital identities (Davies, S.: "Banks want to keep your digital ID in their vaults", *Financial Times*, 2 September 2014).

I hope these examples illustrate the potential market for bank services in the digital identity field, but it isn't all about profits. One of the reasons why we should want regulated financial institutions to provide the digital infrastructure is because that infrastructure will form an essential element of a sound strategy for the financial sector as a whole. Right now, we don't want criminals and terrorists obtaining bank accounts, we don't want drug dealers and corrupt politicians to be able to shuffle money around the system, and we don't want our institutions to be subverted by dirty money. Therefore, we let the banks have certain privileges, but in return we ask them to shoulder the burden of knowing your customer (KYC), anti-money laundering (AML), counterterrorist financing (CTF) and the exclusion of politically exposed persons (PEPs).

Incidentally, a major problem for banks is that the costs of the current approach are absolutely unsustainable and with new AML regulations on the way, they are going to get worse. Perhaps it is time for some thought experiments around alternatives, exploring where RegTech might create new mechanisms for monitoring money flows. Hence, we might reflect on an apparently radical alternative: rather than try to keep people out of the system, we could do everything possible to get everybody into the system. Why? Well, because when people are excluded from the system you have absolutely no idea what they're doing. This is very evident in the case of the "de-risking" of money transfer services in key remittance corridors. A good example is the UK–Somalia corridor, which was the subject of detailed study and comment in the British Parliament. As part of the de-risking the banks withdrew services. The result was not, of course, that money stopped flowing to Somalia with some of it ending up in questionable destinations. Instead of the money flowing through electronic channels where we could at least monitor what was going on and have some potential to discover what the bad guys might be up to, the cash moves in suitcases out of Stansted Airport—and nobody has any idea what is happening, with no opportunity to track or monitor criminal behaviour.

But. And this is a big but…There is no inevitability about this bank-centric vision. On the contrary, it is entirely possible to construct an alternative view that is based not on banks and bindings and regulated financial institutions, but on big data, artificial intelligence and a more inclusive view of the world.

Let's go back to that internet dating example, because it's useful to explore. I go to the internet dating site and create an identity. During this process, the internet dating site asks me to validate my identity. I go to Microsoft, Amazon, Facebook, Apple or Google and log in, and get bounced back to the dating site with a cryptographic token that says that (for example) Amazon knows I am over 18 and resident in the UK and, crucially, that Amazon will accept liability to a maximum amount if either of these credentials turns out to be incorrect. Amazon can be pretty sure about these facts because, apart from anything else, Amazon has access to my bank account because of open banking initiatives. Amazon also knows everything I buy, where I am and when my salary gets paid into the account. They can give the dating site a pretty accurate picture of me, without disclosing any PII. And they can allow the dating site to bill against the token if necessary.

There is, as the World Economic Forum made clear, a role for regulated financial institutions here ("A Blueprint for Digital Identity—the Role of Financial Institutions in Building Digital Identity", World Economic Forum: Geneva, 2016). However, digital identity does not offer the right to banks to exploit it. If banks do not offer digital identity services that are relevant to the post-industrial revolution, they won't simply miss out on the opportunity to offset some of their costs with some revenue generating (and generally useful) new services. Instead, they will cut themselves off from the sources of data that they need to feed their artificial intelligence engines of the future. They will not be able to do risk analysis or information management of any value, and access the vast quantities of information, relationship and reputation data that are needed to feed the voracious appetites of the machine-learning behemoths that will be at the heart of the next generation of banks. Digital identity should be central to bank and regulatory strategy moving forward. Without it, you're not just a number, you are nobody in the digital world.

Endnotes

1 Although recent Facebook problems may lead towards increasing regulation over data usage.

2 Why the police are worried about my dating website is a whole other story.

3 See https://www.itsme.be/en.

4 Called Secure Key—https://securekey.com/.

Part 02

Banking reimagined for a real-time world

3 Embedded Banking

There are better, faster, more convenient, less costly payment
methodologies in place, but with those comes the technology-
adoption hurdle that a lot of companies just can't get over…
[The United States] have probably the most antiquated
payment system in the whole world. It would be much
harder to get a mandate to eliminate checks from a cultural
standpoint, but also from a central bank standpoint.
—Tom Hunt, Director of Treasury Services,
Association for Financial Professionals

For many of the approximately 700 million users of WeChat Pay in China, they don't have a debit card they use regularly—their primary value store or payment vehicle is either cash or their phone. Increasingly in urban China it is only their phone, and even if people do have a bank account, they're not using it other than for transfers, top-ups and withdrawing cash. The primary challenge for banks is that once money goes into the WeChat or Alipay ecosystem, it rarely leaves—and banks have zero visibility of it once that happens. The battle for mobile payments appears over in China. Soon the battle for deposits will be also.

This is not just about a chat app that has been adapted for payments. We can see through first principles that the two-and-a-half billion great "unbanked" will more than likely not need so-called "real" bank accounts in the future. In fact, by 2030, the bank account itself is likely to be just a value store on the phone for the vast majority of consumers who have come into the banking system in the 21st century. The fact that you'll have a wallet or value store on your phone, and the money might be stored in a bank account somewhere, is almost incidental.

In 2000, financial inclusion in Bangladesh was just 14 percent; today almost 40 percent of the adult population is on bKash and doing their day-to-day payments via mobile[1], and increasingly people are simply getting paid to their mobile phone. When the central bank put restrictions on mobile financial service (MFS) providers, then people in Bangladesh just got more SIM cards so they could continue to store cash on their phones.

In 2000, financial inclusion in Kenya was 27 percent and today almost 100 percent of the adult population is using M-Pesa mobile money regularly, saving 20 percent more than they did prior to M-Pesa. In 2011, India had 557 million unbanked, and by 2015 that had halved to 233 million due to mobile access[2] and the new Aadhaar identity card scheme. Paytm, India's leading mobile wallet, now has 280 million users[3], is aiming for 500 million within three years, and has teamed up with both Softbank from Japan and Alipay from China.

More interestingly, consider the way Uber, Alibaba and Amazon are innovating around banking. Uber launched its own debit card, not to become a bank, but so that they could onboard drivers faster to grow their business[4]. However, by embedding banking in the driver onboarding process they circumvented the friction of having to have an unbanked driver visit a bank branch to get a piece of plastic. Today, Uber can pay their drivers up to three times per day using their new "instant pay" capability, which is only possible through the Uber driver debit card. By issuing their own debit card, Uber instantly became one of the largest acquirers of new SME bank accounts in the USA, but that wasn't their goal—they just wanted to accelerate the growth of their business, which banks were slowing down.

Alibaba and Amazon have increasingly started to offer business banking services to entrepreneurs on their platform. Whether that is a store front through their platform, small business loans, foreign exchange, capital management, taxation and other operational elements, increasingly these platforms will enable business users to do more of their banking and finance integrated into their platforms. They want businesses running all of their operations on their platform and not needing to go to a bank branch for functions they can provide.

The 21st century bank account is not a physical artifact that consumers or small businesses will need to get from a branch, it's just a piece of utility that will be engineered into their world through technology. The physical card, books and statements of the 19th century banking system will be relics of a time long past when it comes to banking for our children and their children. The developing world will get there first, as already emphasized by Chris Skinner's coverage of Ant Financial, because these newly "banked" consumers don't have legacy behaviour built around traditional banking and commerce. The fact that some people still write cheques in the United States is not evidence that bank accounts will survive in their current form[5], and this is evidenced by the fact that cheque use has declined almost 70 percent in the US since 2000 alone.

Behaviour is switching to mobile and digital payments globally, and will be almost exclusively digital by 2030. Voice-based commerce and mixed reality technologies will speed up the shift away from physical artifacts.

The nature of the bank account will have to change significantly in this environment to stay relevant. In the 19th and 20th centuries the value of a bank account was primarily that it "kept your money safe", that you could save money securely, and you could pay for stuff based on the authority of the bank—when you wrote a cheque people would trust it as a mechanism of value exchange because a bank was behind it. The value in a 21st century bank account will be in how it provides utility in context, how it adapts to your financial life and your behaviour. The bank account is transitioning to a smart money artifact—bank utility embedded in our world enhanced by artificial intelligence that responds to your financial needs as and when they present themselves.

Let's examine the principles behind a 21st century embedded, smart bank account and how it will change the way you live with your money.

Friction isn't valuable in the new world

If you examine challenger and FinTech banks around the world, you'll see a consistent theme. See if you can guess what the message is…

Simple was started out of frustration with banks. We're positive, passionate people who are serious about creating an experience for our customers that's unlike any personal finance product you've ever used.

—Simple

Get Moven with Smart Banking and take control of your finances. Whether you're buying groceries, dining out, or saving for something on your wish-list, Moven automatically analyzes your spending and gives you instant receipts and insights so you can spend, save & live smarter.

—Moven

Life doesn't have boundaries, so why should your banking? We're making banking easier, intuitive and there whenever you need it, all on your mobile.

—Atom Bank

Monzo is a bank that makes life easier, not harder. We are building a smart bank on your smartphone.

—Monzo

For incumbent banks, the message consistently promoted when you visit a bank is essentially "our bank has the best product".

Figure 1: Sample homepages of banks around the world (emphasis on product).

At the core of the difference between challenger/FinTech banks and incumbents is their mission: challenger/FinTechs want to radically simplify the banking experience, but incumbents seem much more intent on wanting you to choose their bank products over their competitors.

Friction is the antithesis of the design premise for FinTech banks. Every FinTech is trying to take friction out of the experience, making it faster, easier and sexier[6].

Incumbents are admittedly iterating on the friction, but have to butt up against compliance, legal and risk departments constantly trying to retain as much of the friction as possible. It takes a really strong CEO and executive team to reform that systemic thinking.

Writing this may shock many of you, but the reality is that FinTech's can't realistically go far enough to beat the banks entirely. They can't do this because the real winners of the bank account battle will be those that own the technology layers you'll use everyday—voice, AR, AI agents and smart assistants, the day-to-day commerce and messaging platforms, because that is where banking will reside. As written in Chapter 1, banks will never own this layer either. Thus, when it comes to the future of banking, both challenger banks and conventional banks may miss out—namely because the bank account of tomorrow is primarily an activated, cloud-based value store that reacts through technology where you are using your money. It's not an app, a website or a branch. Having said that, a frictionless value store that is already digitally enabled will be able to transition to this new state significantly faster than one restricted to sale in a physical building requiring a signature on a paper form.

The key problem with designing better banking really begins with how incredibly difficult bankers find it to think outside of the branch.

New experiences don't start in the branch

When banks launched the first automated teller machines[7] in the 1960s and 70s they were an attempt at just that, automating the function of the in-branch teller that could help you with a cash withdrawal. When the internet came along, unlike most retail businesses, banking didn't start with building e-commerce applications; it started with transactional functions straight out of the branch. When banks did introduce e-commerce, they simply took application forms from the branch and put them online.

When banks built early versions of "internet banking" they just tried to do simple transactions—stuff they would normally ask the tellers at the branch to do. When Wells Fargo launched "on-line" banking in 1995, all you could do was get an account balance[8]. After that banks just put virtual bank statements online. Later banks added transfers between accounts. Every step of the way banks added more and more of the stuff a teller did and simply put it online. In fact, for most banks you had to visit the branch even to "register" for online banking.

Figure 2: Early bank homepages (Credit: Wells Fargo, Bank of America).

When mobile came along, banks simply took what they had built for internet banking and tried to shrink it down to fit on a smaller screen.

Figure 3: When Citi launched mobile in April 2007, you could view 150 transactions in app and could search for branch and ATM locations (Credit: Citibank).

There's virtually no innovative thinking here. From a design perspective, banks did have to learn new tools like interaction design and usability testing, but they weren't designing new systems on top of mobile or the web, they were iterating on the old. Whether web or mobile, the thinking was still very much based on the branch and this is perhaps the hardest thing to displace from a design perspective.

Figure 4: The CEO of Bank of New Zealand claimed in February of 2017 that the biggest BNZ branch was the website.

> Our busiest branch in 2014 is the 7:01 from Reading to Paddington— over 167,000 of our customers use our Mobile Banking app between 7am and 8am on their commute to work every day. Over 2.1 million customers use our mobile app every week.
>
> —Ross McEwan, CEO of RBS 2014

Design by analogy is hard-coded into most banks' DNA. When the Apple rumour mill started to suggest Apple might launch an NFC-enabled iPhone, rather than try to build completely new thinking around payments, the main payment rail providers, Mastercard and Visa, forced Apple to simply add mock plastic cards inside the phone. While tokenisation was added for additional security, it was more iteration on the old system, no first principles thinking in sight.

There are a number of reasons for this. Firstly, *legacy* systems have evolved to encode branch operations on mainframe systems, and when you have to adapt legacy systems to the new digital layer, it is easier to just enable a digital version of the branch product and process rather than start from scratch with something new. Secondly, *regulation* inhibits innovation, often by enforcing branch-based product structures and processes. Indeed, the greatest challenge many face around mobile today is getting permission from the regulator to allow someone to sign up for a new product or service *without a signature*. When at Moven we tried to innovate around savings APR[9] in the US, we were hemmed in by regulations that required our savings rate to be published in the customer disclosures and be consistent from one customer to the next, rather than a savings rate that could be dynamic based on our credscore™ algorithm.

Lastly, legacy systems, rails and regulation mean *legacy customer behaviour*, and the ability to change that behaviour, such as the use of cheques in the United States, is often just as difficult. It is why markets like Africa and China are getting much faster rates of mobile payments adoption than the US—they generally don't have to move people off legacy behaviour.

As discussed in Chapter 1, while first principles thinking is evident in technology and FinTech, it's rarely evident in incumbents because of this branch-first mindset. The real innovation of embedded banking, however, will not be limited to channels or products, but be focused on advice.

Advice, when and where you need it

For a long time, bankers have held the belief that advice from a human is what would continue to differentiate the branch experience from technologies like web and mobile, especially in the areas of investment or what bankers like to call "complex products". That core belief is being tested today as more and more robo-advisor and chat-bot style advisory capabilities become embedded in day-to-day banking experiences. The reality is, however, the advice you're likely to get from your bank through technologies like voice and AI in the future will be very different from the advice you get today.

Figure 5: The typical positioning of "advice" within a bank today.

Today if you visit a bank to get advice on buying a home, it inevitably is really about positioning which mortgage is right for you. If you visit a bank to get investing advice or talk about retirement planning, the inevitable advice is which asset class or investment product you should be investing in. If you go into a bank to get advice on just everyday banking, you'll walk out with a bank account, not advice on using your money more effectively. The advice we get today is rarely just "advice"; it's typically product selling or position couched as advice.

This sort of advice is not very sticky—it doesn't engender long-term loyalty, it is more about short-term selling for the bank. In regards to whether or not that advice is better off coming from a human in a bank versus an AI, I'm honestly doubtful that humans will remain competitive in this space for much longer. Let me illustrate.

Information asymmetry and AI

Advisors in investing, private banking, mortgage-lending and other disciplines in financial services have traditionally justified themselves by asserting that you need an advisor because they know more about the subject than you do.

> Asymmetric information, sometimes referred to as information failure, is present whenever one party to an economic transaction

possesses greater material knowledge than the other party. This normally manifests itself when the seller of a good or service has greater knowledge than the buyer, although the opposite is possible. Almost all economic transactions involve information asymmetries.

—Asymmetric Information, Investopedia definition

Let's use an emerging AI technology as an example of information asymmetry in machines.

Emerging technology in self-driving cars includes sensors such as cameras, lidar (light detection and ranging), point mapping, sonar, radar, lasers and so forth. A human eye can see about 250 feet (76 metres) at night assisted by headlights, but a robocar's radar can see about 820 feet (250 metres) today, and across 360 degrees. Machines can react to a potential obstacle on a dry road in about 0.5 seconds, compared with the typical human who takes on average 1.6 seconds. Some autonomous vehicles today are capturing around 1,000 times more information than your visual cortex is capable of processing. All this suggests that in 10–20 years, when this technology is truly mature, no human driver will be as safe as an AI-driven automobile. Why? Information asymmetry.

Figure 6: Autonomous vehicles will soon beat humans at driving because of information asymmetry—more data through a suite of technologies that lead to better decision-making.

A self-driving car can process more data much faster than a human brain. Once mature, no human will match an autonomous vehicle for safety[10] alone because of this ability. Is it really that hard to imagine an algorithm in banking that might be able to recommend a mortgage product or an investment strategy better, faster and based on more data than a human advisor? Self-driving cars could eliminate 3,000 deaths per day, more than 95 percent of which occur due to human error. This will eventually lead to human drivers being considered too lethal for many environments—like city centres[11].

AIs that are better at budgeting than your accountant

But the advice our AI smart assistant built into our home, car and smart devices won't be like the advice we get from a banker today. The real benefit of a smart bank account of the future is that once we've established a basic set of parameters, we'll get personalised advice that will be like having a money coach in your back pocket full-time. This won't be product advice like "buy this mortgage versus that mortgage". It will be simple stuff like "Hey, Siri, can I afford to go out for dinner tonight?"

Figure 7: Financial advice in the age of AIs will be much more personalised (Credit: Moven Siri implementation).

Budgeting emerged in the early 18th century as a mechanism for improving the financial stability, not of consumers, but of governments. The origins of the word "budget" lie in the French term "bougette"—a leather wallet in which documents or money could be kept. The bursting of the South Sea Bubble in 1720 wrecked the British economy's balance sheet and led to the imprisonment of the Chancellor in the Tower of London. Toward the end of the same century, in 1799, Pitt the Younger introduced income tax as a way of helping fund war. These became the drivers for a commonsense annual process for managing inflows and outflows from the British treasury.

In the early 1900s personal budgeting was all the rage, with ready-made budget ledger pages being available for households and newspapers like *The Evening World of New York* running a thrift campaign in 1916, encouraging using envelopes for budgeting.

There's only one problem today: with 70 percent of US households[12] and 65 percent of British households[13] being unable to absorb a small financial shock of one sort or another, clearly budgeting has failed the vast majority of our society.

This is where AI is likely to make a massive change in the way we think about our connection with money: a bank account will shift from being a value store with payments utility to being something we're much more reliant on.

Budgeting today requires the right tools, but more importantly, like making a New Year's resolution to go to the gym and get healthier, it requires a ton of personal discipline. In the United States, only eight percent of the population exhibit the ability to be that disciplined[14]. Which, for the same reason as dieting fails, means that 92 percent of us will never be able to budget effectively even with a digital tool. Fitbit style bands, calorie and step counters, and a quantified self approach to fitness, on the other hand, have generally had greater statistical success in improving health. The same will undoubtedly be true of AIs that aid us in gaming our financial behaviour. Whether that is via raising awareness, limiting our spending or simply increasing moments we think about saving.

The reason our smart bank account, or AI smart assistant that is linked to our smart bank account, will be great at advice is that it will *stop us from making stupid decisions that today our bank allows us to do.*

Think of how banks promote debit cards and credit cards today. Cash back, airline miles, discounts on shopping are all used as methods of stimulating card usage in banking, but they inevitably lead to increases in spending (by design), which lead to debt[15]. But imagine an AI with smart banking that you've tasked with helping curb your spending.

"Alexa, order me a new XBox One X for Christmas."

[In Alexa's best HAL impression]: "I can't do that, Dave. You're already well over your suggested spending limits for the month. You can override my advice and continue the purchase, but if you do, you won't be able to afford the holiday you're planning for the new year."

If you are banker, you might be disappointed learning that personal AIs will discourage you from spending or using a credit card; but consider the fact that a behavioural-based AI money coach will promote much stickier behaviour for day-to-day banking relationships than your advisor in a bank branch would ever do. Credit card rewards won't be enough to get you to change your linked account for Apple Pay/Siri, Tmall Genie[16] or Alexa voice-based transactions.

Today Starbucks[17], Dominos Pizza, Tescos, Expedia, Amazon and a host of other retailers are enabling voice-ordering capability. Some estimates reckon that by 2025 we'll be doing around 50 percent of our e-commerce transactions based on voice[18], which would be about the same rate at which the world adapted to e-commerce after the commercial launch of the web in the mid 90s. It is logical we'll wrap advice into this ecosystem in real time, adapting to our behaviour. But it is mixed reality that's really going to change the context of bank accounts over the next decade, and where we have to think beyond channels and products.

Mixed reality and its impact on banking

In September 2017, Apple launched their new iPhone X, beginning its decade-long augmented reality or AR strategy.

I think it is profound. I am so excited about it, I just want to yell out and scream...Can we do everything we want to do now? No. The technology's not complete yet. But that's the beauty to a certain degree. [Augmented reality] has a runway. And it's an incredible runway. It's time to put the seatbelt on and go. When people begin to see what's possible, it's going to get them very excited—like we are, like we've been.

Tim Cook, Apple CEO, Bloomberg Businessweek,

15 June 2017

Apple is betting that consumer technology experiences become more and more integrated into our life, and they're betting that both voice and augmented reality will be big, big parts of that. Just as we all carry around smartphones today, commentators like Robert Scoble and Shel Israel predict that in 10 years we will be donning smart glasses in the same way that the iPhone took off in 2007–2010[19].

What this means for banking is that the two most influential future channels for day-to-day banking use are both designed to be real time and experiential in nature, not transactional or product-based in nature. You won't choose a traditional credit card or mortgage through your head-up display or using voice, but you will use these tools to assist you in determining if you can afford to buy a home, or how much you can spend out shopping, or if there's a better approach. The tech will help you buy the home, not a mortgage.

The key problem for banks is that based on our history around technology adoption, we will simply view voice and augmented reality glasses as a new channel to push branch-style engagement and products, and if we do, we will fail miserably. Let me illustrate. Capital One was the first bank to take to market their Alexa voice capability in the United States, and while it has since added more conversational money moments, their first attempt looked just like design iteration.

The first skills on Alexa that CapOne launched included: "Alexa, ask Capital One when is my credit card payment due?" and "Alexa, ask Capital One to pay my credit card bill."

That is design by analogy thinking, and it won't be enough to make the transition into the Bank 4.0 world.

Endnotes

1 Commentary on bKash inclusion: "More than Tk1,000cr transacted on mobile phones daily". *Dhaka Tribune*, 25 July 2017—http://www.dhakatribune.com/business/banks/2017/07/25/daily-mfs-transactions-cross-tk1000cr-mark/.

2 Source: PWC Report—Disrupting cash, accelerating electronic payments in India (Oct 2015)—https://www.pwc.in/assets/pdfs/publications/2015/disrupting-cash-accelerating-electronic-payments-in-india.pdf.

3 January 2018, 280 million users—https://blog.paytm.com/looking-back-at-2017-top-10-interesting-facts-from-paytm-7bc59e08683f.

4 "Uber is trying to lure new drivers by offering bank accounts", Quartz online magazine, Ian Kar, November 2015—https://qz.com/533492/exclusive-heres-how-uber-is-planning-using-banking-to-keep-drivers-from-leaving/.

5 NPR story: "Is it time to write off checks?" 2016 shows 66 percent decline in check use between 2000 and 2014—http://www.npr.org/2016/03/03/468890515/is-it-time-to-write-off-checks.

6 See "Banking needs an Amazon Prime mentality", by Jim Marous, The Financial Brand—https://thefinancialbrand.com/66545/amazon-prime-digital-banking-loyalty-experience-strategy/.

7 Barclays is credited with the first use of a "cash machine" at their Enfield Town branch in North London on 27 June 1967.

8 See https://www.wellsfargohistory.com/internet-banking/.

9 APR or Annual Percentage Rate, is the standard moniker for the interest rate paid against a savings account annually, or in the case of a credit card the annual rate charged for balance carried on the card.

10 See "This is the end game for autonomous cars" by Marc Hoag—https://www.linkedin.com/pulse/end-game-autonomous-cars-marc-hoag.

11 Source: *The Guardian*, Stuart Dredge, 18 March 2015; "Self-driving cars could lead to ban on human drivers"—https://www.theguardian.com/technology/2015/mar/18/elon-musk-self-driving-cars-ban-human-drivers.

12 Source: "The Precarious State of Family Balance Sheets", Pew Research, January 2015—http://www.pewtrusts.org/en/research-and-analysis/reports/2015/01/the-precarious-state-of-family-balance-sheets.

13 Source: Press Release—https://www.moneyadviceservice.org.uk/en/corporate/press-release-65-of-consumers-are-exposed-to-unplanned-financial-shocks.

14 Source: University of Scranton Research, 2013.

15 Source: *Wall Street Journal*, Conor Dougherty, December 2010, "Reward Cards Lead to More Spending, Debt".

16 Alibaba's voice system.

17 Source: Retail dive, Starbucks enabling ordering via voice in Alexa-enabled Ford vehicles, March 2017—http://www.retaildive.com/news/starbucks-enabling-ordering-via-voice-in-alexa-enabled-ford-vehicles/438730/.

18 Source: https://techpinions.com/there-is-a-revolution-ahead-and-it-has-a-voice/45071.

19 *The Fourth Transformation: How Augmented Reality and Artificial Intelligence Will Change Everything*, by Robert Scoble and Shel Israel, Patrick Brewster Press (December 2016).

Should design have to wait for AI and device capability to catch up, or should we rethink design in a contextual world, where banking is embedded in our day-to-day life? Are banks even capable of evolving the role of data in decision-making and consumer engagement, such as categorised transactions, geolocation and behavioural triggers?

Are banking chatbots the future?

According to a report released by Juniper[1], chatbots will be responsible for over US$8 billion of cost savings by 2022. Are these savings to the consumer or for the bank?

I think clearly we would have to answer, the bank. Today, chatbots are regarded by most banks as a potential cost savings mechanism designed to replace call centre personnel. Yet worse, the companies developing chatbots have market and investor pressure on product, preventing them from reimagining customer interactions through the prism of human emotion and real customer needs.

Investigating how a consumer truly feels, what drives them and makes them happy is time- and resource-intensive. Most of the FinTech providers working on chatbots generally cannot justify undertaking that sort of research either. Instead, they plough ahead, developing incremental AI that tends to focus on product-based and marketing-heavy advice, rather than something more valuable to the end consumer.

As per Brett's earlier chapters, the problem here is that most chatbots are derivative of branch-based banking or call centre interactions, thus most of the scenarios or use cases resemble current call centre type support questions or cross-sell marketing offers. A first principles approach to a chatbot would start with the day-to-day problems that plague customers around money, and the role of banks in facilitating solutions.

Over the past few years, with the emergence of Human Centered Design practices, industry press and research organisations have repeatedly shamed incumbent banks for not investing enough time and effort into reducing friction in engagements. Brett makes a strong case at the start of his book for kick-starting the design of banking from scratch using first principles design thinking. A strong argument in support of this proposition is that when we research products designed with the insight of consumer's needs, they tend to be significantly more profitable than those built without those considerations. Despite it making good business sense, banks have been unable to deliver on that, hampered by compliance issues and heavy legacy in terms of organisational culture, process and technology.

The FinTech companies that are building AI-powered voice banking or chatbot applications have none of those cultural legacy problems, yet all too often they put immediate operational functionality ahead of designing a product that recognises and acts on emotion.

"Financial chatbots" are a worrying subsection of AI that is on the rise. The separation between a real, intelligent assistant that makes meaningful contributions to our lives, and a dumber version that can simply infer we mean "interest rates for savings" and "potential gain/loss scenario" when we query, "How much will I get charged if I leave my overdraft in the account", should not exist.

To become truly relevant and make an impact on behaviour, AI will have to become a day-to-day companion. It will have to be an entity that understands not only the client's actions as inferred by location or spending patterns, but their intent, their overall emotional state and even their deepest secrets—and be able to steer their state of mind towards where they are inclined to make better financial choices, instead of solely offering dry, meaningless information. Obviously financial coach will be only a subset of the capabilities that a voice-based AI or companion from Apple, Amazon or Google has, and yet banks treat chatbots like apps today. They think that people will come to their chatbot to interact instead of Siri or Google Home. That's the height of arrogance if you ask me.

The builders of chatbots shouldn't be asking themselves, "How do I implement geolocation push alerts this month?" but "When and how do I use the notifications based on location, ensuring the client gets a sense of gratitude for having been notified contextually of a potential gain, instead of just annoyed if they perceive it as mindless marketing?" They should consider how to become that trusted and invaluable advisor that the consumer turns to when needing help with their money.

AI with this capability is still a few years away. In the meantime, banks could tighten their game in bringing something that has been well within their reach since the advent of PFM in 2009: notification-banking, also known as "Contextual 1.0". Irrespective of the nuances, the overarching principle of this involves offering the consumer relevant financial information at the right time or place through the form of notifications on their mobile device. As the platforms mature, voice and augmented reality will provide further reach for contextual notifications.

At its core, being able to provide contextual money advice has one major prerequisite: that the bank has the information to both trigger the notification and provide the right advice. There is a substantial—and in this case, defining—difference between "data" and "information". Banks do capture consumer's financial data (and could capture much more of it). Whether they process it in any way to extract meaning, inference and relevancy and turn it into "information" is another matter altogether. An overwhelming majority of banks do not.

In my Emotional Banking™ method, I spend a lot of time studying why this happens, why banks do not explore the psyche of the consumer enough to understand how paramount the need for financial information is. The reasons are complex and are chiefly rooted in the culture of the organisation. But this also gives rise to practical impediments, such as the fact that most banks today are not equipped to either collect or collate data in a fashion that would allow them to turn it into relevant information that they can serve the consumer through well-placed notifications.

While being notified of an amazing opportunity to save on a favourite item as you pass a shop would be great, today the bank has no idea that item is a favourite—or if you're passing said shop. While being informed that by forgoing the mythical cup of coffee you'll be a week closer to your savings goal would be potentially useful, today the bank has no idea you're about to have that cup, or what your savings goal is. The bank simply can't advise you in respect to spending less on a certain type of expense or for thinking of retirement by starting direct payments to a private pension plan, because it doesn't actually know what your current situation or drivers are today.

Transforming "data" into "information" requires not only storing it, but having an ability to effectively, efficiently and accurately analysing it—with the ability to categorise transactions and behaviour being at the core of financial data analysis—and then having a way to access and transmit that information as close to real-time as possible. Each of these steps is a *sine qua non* condition to achieving effective notifications that offer relevant information that make a real difference in someone's financial life in lieu of meaningless, ill-timed tidbits of data.

Once banks learn how to slice and dice data and realise the promise of Contextual 1.0, real advice will follow shortly thereafter (2.0)—and it will be based on an ability to tap into other IoT-related data sources to infer wider behavioural cues for increasingly meaningful context.

Timing: Information is not received and consumed the same way at all times, so notifications about finances will have to become sensitive to that factor, in addition to location. Delivering an encouraging message about one's savings is immensely more efficient when the consumer is particularly receptive and ready to receive it, such as a weekend morning, as opposed to an inconvenient time in the middle of their commute. Taking into account the consumer's psychology and style will also be critical in terms of messaging.

Wider life context: Smart devices hold and are able to access data that goes far beyond mere transactions such as health parameters and emotional clues. In Contextual 2.0 and its AI component, banks will have to understand how to use this data to build addictive relevance in outlining and assisting *Money Moments* for their consumers.

Which of the following seems more efficient?

Notification	Contextual Notification	Wider Life Context	Next Gen AI
"You spent 10 USD less this week." —Delivered at 9 am on Mondays, location blind	"Congrats, you spent 10 USD less this week on sweets! Someone is smart about their carbs, keep it up!" —Delivered as you approach an area where the consumer's local Dunkin' Donuts is	"Wow, look at you, being 10 USD richer and two pounds lighter this week! At this rate you'll be beach body ready for Mexico and will afford twice the shopping you normally do on vacay! Way to go!" —Delivered on Saturday at 10:14 am, right before the weekly grocery shop order from Alexa and before answering an email with an invitation for a weekend party	";)" —A tap or a wink followed by a gif of the consumer 15lbs lighter, beverage in hand, head thrown back with laughter, having great fun shopping in Mexico— delivered every time there is temptation

Figure 1: Examples of smart device engagement.

Consumers will receive this type of financial companion within the next few years, whether it will be from their banks or, most likely, other technology companies that have developed the capacity to aggregate financial data and make wider, relevant, contextual sense of it. If you want to be part of the Bank 4.0 revolution, you need to start working on the broader data requirements that will power this type of emotionally sensitive and relevant banking.

Endnotes

1 https://www.juniperresearch.com/press/press-releases/mobile-banking-users-to-reach-2-billion-by-2020.

4 From Products and Channels to Experiences

> We still have one million people coming to our branches every
> day, and they need that channel. Some need it to transact, but
> a lot of them come in for advice and we want them to do that.
> So, we need a certain footprint of financial centers.
> —Paul Donofrio, CFO at Bank of America

The new "network" and "distribution" paradigms

Let's propose a binary question for the digital age. In 10 years' time, who do you think will have a greater chance of survival—a bank wholly dependent on branches for revenue and relationships, or a digital pure-play, challenger bank wholly dependent on digital channels?

If you answered a branch-based bank, I think the facts suggest a different reality[1]. While branches aren't going to disappear in the next 10 years, the relative importance of a bank branch for day-to-day banking is most certainly in decline. In December of 2015, Bankrate.com reported that 39 percent of Americans hadn't visited their bank branch in the last six months, and a report from CACI in 2017 predicted that visits to branches are set to decline by another 40 percent over the next five years. This is a global phenomenon in developed nations.

> We've seen drops of 30 to 40 percent happening over a few years,
> and in some of our traditional bank branches around Australia in
> some areas we see as little as five or ten people [visit] a day, and the
> economics are very difficult...But what's happening is the growth in

digital interactions is phenomenal. So we've gone from zero to 11.5 million transactions a month on a...smartphone.

—Michael Cameron, CEO Suncorp Bank,
The Courier Mail interview, November 2016

The reality is that by measuring just one simple metric, it's very easy to tell the future of the bank branch and how its importance is diminishing over time. That metric is the *average number of visits per customer per year to a bank branch* in your network. If you don't know how to get that metric and you work in a bank, it's easy—take the number of products sold, applications lodged or transactions made per customer per branch over the course of a year, but count a maximum of one interaction per day as a "visit"[2].

You'd be surprised[3], but the majority of banks I've worked with not only don't give out this number, but they neglect even to measure this internally, relying instead on the number of product applications per branch per year as their core distribution effectiveness KPI. The data, though, is irrefutable. My bet is in every bank in the developed world when measured between 1990 and today you'd see a decline of somewhere between 60 and 80 percent in respect of that single metric annually. Meaning, that if you expected to see a customer visit your branch 10 times a year back in 1990, today on average they're visiting less than two or three times per year. I'd also argue that a large percentage of those visits would be *false positives*, where the bank or compliance requirements mandate a customer visit the branch versus using an alternate channel; for example, where you only allow mortgage applications for new customers through a branch, or where a bank requires you to visit if you want to restore access to internet banking[4] after forgetting a password. Recently, Chase required me to visit a branch in the US to do an ID check because I tried to do a wire transfer on my account for the first time in some months.

These examples I've given are all false positives—they certainly do not represent an argument for continued viability of the branch. Why? Because as soon as a neo-bank competitor establishes a benchmark competency for these same capabilities without requiring a visit to a branch, then your bank will eventually be measured against that standard. Keep in mind that none of these examples I've given are required by regulation either, but they are in place because of an overly conservative internal compliance process.

For many banks, however, their distribution platform is their branch network: it's their access identity; it's the way they are embedded in the community; it's where their branding sits; it's how they measure customer excellence, experience and engagement. When bankers used the terms "network" or "distribution" in the 80s, 90s and 2000s, they knew internally they were talking exclusively about branch network and branch distribution. From a strategic perspective, while that has obviously shifted in most large retail banks today, it's a very hard habit to kick—all that revenue from the branch. As Michael Cameron alluded to above, if visits per customer to your branch network continue to decline, branch economics for all but the most active branches will fail, as will revenue.

Now, for those that really get upset when I talk about changes to branch networks, let me state this for the record: I don't think branches are completely dead, nor are they ALL going away, but by 2025 most branches will become much more difficult to sustain economically as we see alternative approaches to banking gain traction. These alternative approaches will consistently demonstrate that branches don't deliver revenue and relationships at the same scale or cost effectiveness as digital. Once the market starts to regularly compare a neo-bank like Moven or Monzo, a tech giant like Amazon or Alipay, or a FinTech like Acorns or Betterment with an omni-channel bank with massive real-estate investments side-by-side, branch networks will come under huge pressure to close because of climbing acquisition costs and reducing differentiation. Within a few years stock market analysts will simply ask whether branch networks are a sustainable way of doing the business of banking. Once that happens, it won't be long before analysts are discounting bank stocks for their excess real estate. Right-sizing branch networks will be forced upon publicly listed banks. Banks reliant on branches will have nowhere to go, they'll just continue to argue branch relevance while they shrink. In the same way that retailers argued people still wanted to come to their stores, while retail stores were closing by the thousands.

The problem for banks is that in this new experience world, network is a function of technologies that deliver capabilities in real time at scale, that anticipate or predict your needs, that are embedded in your world, that reframe the utility and import of banking in your day-to-day life. This has very real consequences for the future of banks.

In July 2017, Kakao, a Korean internet platform that has the largest messenger app in the country and runs a service like Uber called Kakao Taxi, launched their own internet-only bank—Kakao Bank. In just five days Kakao had opened more than one million accounts[5], attracting over half a billion US dollars in deposits, and they claim they would have been able to open more had their technology not been overwhelmed by the demand.

This is increasingly the standard the new internet banks are being held to, but Kakao, Tencent, Amazon, Uber and Alipay have advantages over digital pure play and incumbents alike. They can apply network effect from their existing platforms to functions like deposit taking and payments. It's not just that they have access to millions of customers, but that those customers will use their networks for payments, commerce and other bank-like stuff. When those platforms start to offer banking utility, it's an obvious evolution of their network utility.

> In 2004, whenever I had to pay my rent, I would go to my bank, queue, withdraw my rent as cash, walk it across the street to my landlord's bank, take a number and queue, and then eventually deposit the money into his account. Today, I pay my rent using Alipay from Alibaba. I invest using WeChat from Tencent, and I bought a mutual fund from Baidu. The landscape has completely changed.
>
> —Kapron, a Shanghai resident talking banking in China;
> Bloomberg Markets[6]

Changes in day-to-day bank utility as a result of the underlying technology we use daily also changes the way banking effectiveness will be measured. In China where Alipay and Tencent's WeChat dominate the payments landscape, banks there have had to rapidly retool to build their own mobile capabilities as their deposits and fees were increasingly at risk.

Distribution of financial services in China has fundamentally changed because of TechFin. But no matter where you are based, if you don't have a revenue or relationship strategy built on real-time delivery, you are going to be severely hampered in the near future. If you have a product or service that still requires a signature in five years, you are going to be struggling for any cross-sell and upsell. You simply won't be able to survive as a bank with revenue from the branch alone. No way. Friction will be the biggest killer of bank revenue in the next 10 years. The lowest friction experiences will win the highest network adoption rates. We can already demonstrate that in China, India, Bangladesh, Kenya and elsewhere.

Ask ICBC, the biggest incumbent bank in the world, based in China. Because of the massive dominance of Alibaba and TaoBao, they were forced to launch their own Alibaba e-commerce competitor in recent years called Rong E-Gou ("融e购" roughly translates as "buy easily")—today, more than 10,000 merchants sell their goods and services across this platform, generating more than 1.27 trillion yuan (US$184 billion) in sales in 2016[7]. In 2015, Rong E-Gou sold more than 100,000 iPhones, the trick being that ICBC also offered financing for these purchases online. One needs to ask, how many banks have the resources necessary to build an Amazon or Alibaba competitor in their home markets to stay connected like this to their customers?

ICBC added business services to Rong E-Gou in 2015, and today 3,000 companies have sold US$218 billion of products, with things as varied as office supplies through to manufacturing robotics. More than a quarter of a million buyers have used the platform. In this case, ICBC is not building bank platform or channels, they are building ways to incorporate banking utility into everyday commerce. Why? Because they realise that banking is quickly becoming embedded in their competitors' platforms, and customers who have a low friction choice will choose the same financial services through a platform provider rather than "go to the bank". I really can't imagine ICBC launching this e-commerce platform if not for the success of Tencent and Alipay these last few years. How much do you think ICBC spent on launching Rong E-Gou—$200 million, $400 million? At least. That sort of investment in retail commerce would have been considered untenable in years gone by, especially as it is not core to the banking business.

But it was a smart move.

Emirates NDB entered the retail e-commerce fray in May this year with the launch of SkyShopper, a platform through which merchants from around the world can offer special deals to Emirates NDB customers. Why are banks like this looking for more commerce action? Primarily because the data and behaviour that drives use of banking services is increasingly shifting online and to mobile—and advertising on billboards, TVs and newspapers just doesn't cut it anymore. Today, if you want to get a customer to use your banking services, increasingly it has to be wrapped around some other sort of transaction or interaction where they need credit available to complete a purchase, for example. Additionally, once a consumer is using banking embedded in another platform, banks lose visibility on what customers are doing.

In a survey conducted by a Beijing newspaper in March 2017, 70 percent of consumers in China's urban centres said they would be comfortable leaving home without cash or cards today. *The New York Times* reported in July 2017 that there are large sections of urban China that are virtually cashless and cardless because of the huge popularity of mobile payments[8]. In August 2017, the prime minister of Singapore said in his national address that Chinese tourists to Singapore are asking why it is so backward that they still have to use physical cash. It was then that he stated that Singapore had to go cashless fast, and announced a government-backed initiative to achieve that.

Commercial banks, Mastercard, Visa and Union Pay are just not leading players in the mobile payments game in China. Why? Because plastic is not in the mobile payments game in China, neither are POS terminals or even, God forbid, ATMs. New ecosystems have taken over the economy. If you are a bank still using debit cards in China today, you're probably scratching your head wondering how you can get people to use their plastic cards again if it's not for online purchases. If your latest innovation is opening a bank account in a mobile app and shipping cards to your customers, you're still behind the eight ball in China.

This is a world where issuing plastic, or applying for plastic, is no longer of any significant value. In 2016 mobile payments overtook card payments in China. In 2018 China's mobile payments volume will overtake the rest of the world's credit and debit cards transactions. The decline of plastic in China is just the beginning.

Uber made waves in the auto-financing market launching its Xchange Leasing program. At one Nissan dealership in Chicago last year, Uber Xchange accounted for 41 percent of their sales[9] and contributed to a 200 percent increase in year-on-year Q1 sales figures. Didi Chuxing, Uber's equivalent in China, launched its own leasing business in 2016 also.

You may have heard of small business lenders in the US such as Kabbage, OnDeck Capital, or in the UK Funding Circle, but platforms like Amazon, Square and PayPal are increasingly active in the space as well. Amazon lent $1 billion last year and has lent $3 billion to more than 20,000 small businesses since launching their small business lending initiative in 2011. Alibaba also has a rapidly growing loan book, extending 50 billion yuan (US$7.5 billion) of loans to businesses and providing credit lines to over 100 million individuals for customers on Singles' Day alone.

In a strategic move designed to gain access to Chinese tourists, even Marriott got into the Alipay game when they announced in August 2017 that they will accept payments from Alipay's digital wallet across their global properties[10]. As did New York's yellow taxis.

These examples are all illustrative of banking becoming more and more embedded in non-bank networks and platforms, where many of those businesses are starting to offer financial services in context. The big shift is this: in the world of banking from the 1400s to 1995, every bank transaction or product was issued through a bank-owned and operated channel—a branch, call centre, broker or ATM network. Today, *non-bank channels* clearly dominate day-to-day banking access and transactional activity (mobile app, web, and voice as examples). Within a decade, non-bank channels will dominate revenue also.

Bye-bye products, hello experiences

Tencent's WeChat, Alipay, GCash, Kakao Pay, Paytm, Venmo and M-Pesa all offer day-to-day payments capability that don't require a plastic card to transact—they are platforms that have created differentiated payment experiences. Alibaba and Amazon offer small business loans and Uber offers car leasing to entrepreneurs on their platform that don't require application forms, traditional credit approvals, or credit scoring. Digit, Acorns, Qapital, Moven and Stash are all examples of apps that stimulate savings behaviour, but don't have a traditional savings or investment account structure—you don't even apply for a savings account to start saving, you just apply for access to the service or app.

Now bankers might argue this is semantics, that at the end of the day it's still a bank that is holding the money. But if that was your first thought, you are missing a larger trend at play here.

To illustrate. Think about payments evolution and where technologies like voice and augmented reality smart glasses are taking us over the next decade or two. If you lived in the US or UK at the start of the 20th century, you more than likely got paid in cash, and did all your payments in cash. But 50 years later cheques were the dominant form of payment for large items, and people would even use cheques to pay for groceries. Then in the 1980s cards became increasingly popular, and were adapted to be used for online when e-commerce came along.

Cash was instant, but required you to carry it and to visit a bank to get more of it.

Cheques took three to five days at a minimum, were processed through bank clearing houses, and required you to carry a paper booklet that you were suggested to "balance" regularly. Until cheques started to bounce, they had pretty high utility.

Cards were super-convenient and once we dispensed with knuckle-busters and moved to electronic point-of-sale terminals, payments were effectively instantaneous.

In China, India and Africa today, Alipay, M-Pesa, MTN mobile money, Paytm and WeChat Pay wallets are all instantaneous, but don't require plastic or POS terminals, or going to a bank branch to sign up.

Venmo, PayPal, Zelle and others are the equivalent in the US. While most of these services enable you to link a debit card or bank account for top-ups, activity within these networks does not require going through your bank account.

If you trace these developments over the last 50 years, you have an accelerating emphasis on low-friction, payments immediacy and consistent erosion of complexity. The future of payments is clearly based on this trend: real-time, frictionless payments from one value store to another, independent of a physical payments artifact (like a cheque or card), with the greatest network effect.

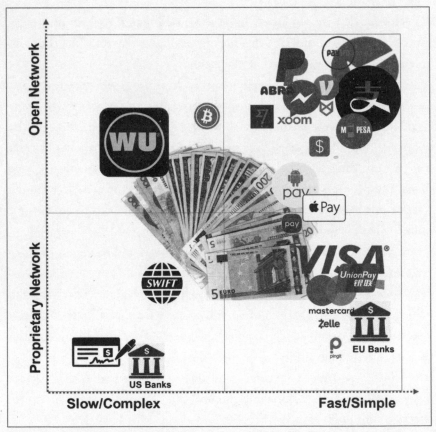

Figure 1: Emerging payments experiences appear to be getting simpler and more inclusive over time.

As payments have evolved the tendency is to move away from both the closed, proprietary nature of bank owned and operated payment networks and from complex slow systems towards instant or near real-time payments that sit on open networks, because network effect allows greater payments utility.

Cash is fast but requires going to a bank periodically to get access, while it is generally slow in a foreign geography and can't be used online without a ton of friction—so that's the baseline. Bank-to-bank networks in the EU and card networks are fast, but are also not inclusive generally. Cheques might appear simple to those that have used them for 40 years, but ask a young working professional to write a cheque, or try using a US bank-issued cheque outside the US or online, and you might be laughed at.

The reality is that networks like PayPal, WeChat Pay and Alipay have greater utility within their networks than bank-to-bank transactions or cash today due simply to the scale of those networks. Yes, they are closed-loop systems in many respects, but the scale of those systems is based today on social media metrics of hundreds or millions or billions of users, so that they may as well be open. JPMorgan Chase has 80 million customers, AliPay 650 million, WeChat one billion, Facebook two billion.

Emerging market digital wallets are built for broad inclusiveness, low barriers to entry, and are real time by design, because they've been built on the IP layer. The trend seems to be a clear indication that future payments will be simpler, more inclusive and built into the digital ecosystem as seamless and experience-optimised. The best retail experiences in the future will be walk in, grab the goods you want, and walk out. The best online retail experiences via voice or augmented reality will simply know who you are and how you pay, taking any transactional friction out completely. The fastest way to pay your friend will be to use a simple gesture to swipe money from your mobile wallet to his, or when you say "Siri, pay Mark $50".

The future of payments is unavoidably experience-rich and friction- and artifact-poor.

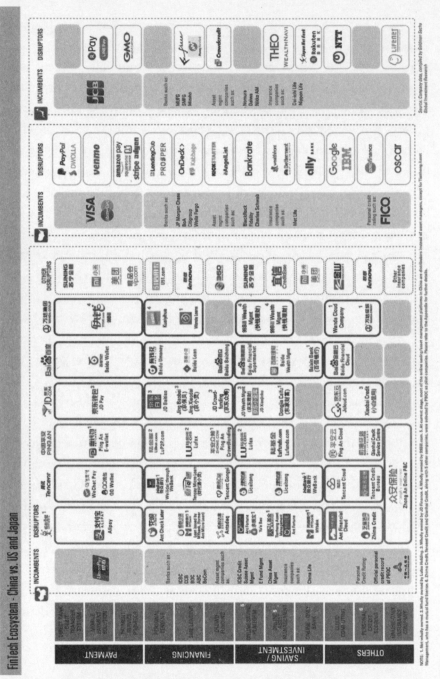

Figure 2: China versus US versus Japan FinTech ecosystems (Image Credit: Life.SREDA).

Examining savings, credit and lending, and other aspects of finance, will demonstrate the same trend. Online and mobile experience design is leading us toward rapid utility and fulfilment. The fastest, most seamless credit experience is not an application for a credit product on your phone or laptop while you're in a store, but simply a provisioning of credit based on a preferred or enabled relationship. The product (credit card, overdraft, personal loan, line of credit, etc) structure disappears to simply enable you to get access to the utility of extra cash when you need it the most. You don't need the card, you just need the cash. Applying for a card is simply unnecessary friction.

From a first principles approach, we should see new technologies like voice-smart assistants[11] and augmented reality smart glasses as ways to explore entirely new ways of leveraging bank utility on an experience basis. Innovation with a bank is often very much thinking inside the box, restricted by compliance, legal and legacy systems behaviour. Iteration on these processes and systems doesn't produce the same innovations as someone starting without those restrictions, or setting up based on completely different assumptions.

The end game with these technologies is *contextual banking services and utility*. So instead of paying your credit card with Alexa using your voice or going to a bank branch to apply for a physical credit card, we can use first principles to think very differently about credit access itself. First principles asks: if you have access to a personal AI capability while you are shopping, how would you design access to credit based on who the customer is and what they are doing?

A first principles approach might be illustrated using grocery shopping as an example. Using first principles thinking I look to predict your need for credit (your balance of your value store is lower than usual when grocery shopping) and when you walked into Whole Foods or Tesco, I'll then offer you the extra cash you need to do your shopping, with a simple and transparent fee structure. Remember, in the grocery store of the future there won't be a checkout cashier, either—you just take the goods and exit, with payment occurring automatically[12].

Figure 3: Credit and payments are increasingly contextual and extremely low friction.

Design by branch analogy would still require me to apply for a credit card in advance (even if via my mobile or via Alexa), just in case I needed the money one day. First principles mean new financial service networks wouldn't build credit scores that punish you for missing a payment on your card. First principles organisations would design systems that predict your behaviour, only encourage credit use when you really need it, and help you manage that credit line reactively, including influencing new spending decisions so you don't compromise your ability to pay back your credit line.

First principles design in credit means that a provider will likely have a much stronger relationship that encourages incredible loyalty, instead of like today, where it might lose out to another bank's plastic card at the checkout line—because it's integral to your life. A bank's ability to understand my behaviour and present to me a solution of the greatest relevance will reinforce their brand. Design by analogy might seek to present a credit card offer via your smart assistant (Alexa/Siri/Cortana) and streamline the application process. First principles design thinking means you don't need a plastic card or application process at all.

Context is the new experience battlefield because it brings the utility of banking to you when and where you need it, instead of relying on the customer asking to be approved for a facility. This is the key switch that is being made—*Bank 4.0 experiences will be an attack on the entire onboarding and application process banks have designed today.*

So here is a list of typical bank products that could disappear over the next 15–20 years as a result of friction and channel obsolescence, to be replaced by real-time, responsive experiences surfacing bank utility:

Financial Product or Service	Replacement Embedded Experience
Credit Card	Predictive and contextual credit access
Overdraft	Emergency credit access (grocery and healthcare optimised)
Checking, Current Account or Debit Card	Cloud-based personal value store linked to a mobile wallet
Savings Account	Behavioural savings tools and prompts
Personal Loan	Payment options advice in-store or contextually
Mortgage	Home purchase assistant
Car Loan/Lease	Autonomous vehicle access subscription
Small Business Bank Account	Intelligent business value store (with accounting, taxation and payments AI)
Business Line of Credit	Predictive cash flow analytics and smoothing
Life Insurance Policy	Longevity and after-life management
Health Insurance Coverage	Health optimisation and monitoring service
Term Deposit, CD, Investment or High Yield Savings Account	Wealth builder robo-assistant
Mutual Fund or Investment Product	Robo-advisor with net worth manager
Foreign Exchange Service	Global wallet add-in

Table 1: List of typical bank products that could disappear.

If you consider some of the emerging technologies that might have a marked effect on access to banking services (in the same way mobile and web have), here are some design-by-analogy versus first principles approaches to innovation in the space:

Emerging Technology Layer	Existing Product or Service	Design by Analogy Examples	First Principles Thinking
Voice Smart Assistant, Cloud-based or Device-based Personal AI	**Credit Card** • Application • Payment • Limit	Pre-approved credit offer Card payment via voice Limit change request	Emergency cash access <<Fully automated>> Behavioural based, responsive credit limit and coaching
	Mortgage • Application • Refinance	Mortgage via voice Ask for refinance options	Home buying assistant Payment variables advice for cheaper annual cost (embedded)
	Checking Account • Opening • Savings	Rapid account opening Special offer savings rate	Enable wallet service Crowdfunding your purchase
Augmented Reality Smart Glasses	**Credit Card** • Merchant offer • Rewards promo • In-store financing	Pop-up discount offer Pop-up rewards multiplier Available finance alert flag	Price alteration in visual feed Ghosted reward products Visually tag product with monthly cost (based on best financing option)
	Auto Purchase • Personal loan • Leasing options • Insurance	Available auto credit line Lease calculator app Policy finder tool	Affordability mode overlay Sharing platform options Self-drive protection plan
	Health Insurance • Application • Co-pay costs • Claim process	Instant approval alert Co-pay alert flag Claim helper	Hospital "Prime" subscription Authorisation notification Reimbursement alert
	Home Buying/ Rental • Mortgage • Real estate search	Monthly payments display GPS property finder	"Visual" budget home isolator Visualise your furniture app

Autonomous Vehicle	Payment options	Tesla wallet setup	Enable car pay alert
	Debit card	Payment configurator	Automated charging configuration
	Fuel card	Mobile wallet configuration	Autonomous network options
	Uber AI driver mode		

Table 2: Design-by-analogy versus first principles approaches.

Designing experiences in the Bank 4.0 age means that the previous product and channel structures offer almost zero benefit in this new world. In fact, they may bias you towards experiences with unnecessary friction and limit you in terms of scale.

The trick with first principles is that you need to start from scratch. Think of how to optimally solve a problem within the bounds of the new technology—how best to buy a home, how best to buy something like groceries in a store when you don't have enough cash, how to deal with healthcare costs in an emergency while you're at the hospital, and simple advice like "How can I afford to buy this new dress for a friend's wedding?" You don't begin by thinking how you can stick an existing bank product on a new channel. That is design by branch analogy, and means by virtue of the competition that you're slipping further behind in terms of *experience competitiveness*.

Platform owners like Alibaba, Amazon, Apple, Google, WeChat and Facebook may have some considerable advantages here. It's why there are way more mobile and augmented reality payments patents owned by technology manufacturers than banks. Think about that—if patents are a measure of innovation in a technology field, then why wouldn't banks and financial services players today own the vast majority of patents emerging in respect of payments?

This begs the question: if products have to make way for contextual experiences what does a bank organisation chart look like? Where do all the products and channels go?

> BBVA will be a software company in the future.
> —Francisco González, Chairman and CEO BBVA,
> Mobile World Congress in 2015

The Bank 4.0 organisation chart looks very different

If you want to truly understand the impact of first principles you need to look at the step-change effect that first principles thinking has on ecosystems.

When the automobile was invented the dominant form of urban transportation was horses—within 30 years that had all changed, along with it the shape of cities, manufacturing, and support systems around cars. When the telephone was invented, it rapidly changed communication. The same is patently true with the impact of the iPhone—not only has it changed the way people think about their "phone", but it created entirely new ways of doing business via apps, it changed the music and taxi industry markedly, it changed the hours we spend on our devices, and it changed the way people consumed and created content. The businesses that emerged on top of mobile didn't look like those that came before them, and some of those businesses are now worth billions of dollars, and yet they wouldn't exist without the smartphone.

Just take one small area of the smartphone's impact—photography. Prior to commercial cameras only a few million photos had ever been taken. When Kodak introduced the Brownie in 1900, it rapidly changed photography, with over a billion photos a year being taken by 1930. The emergence of digital cameras meant that by the year 2000 we were taking about 86 billion photos a year across the planet. But then the smartphone arrived. In 2017 it is estimated[13] that 1.2 trillion photos were taken, and we'll be storing 4.7 trillion photos through our smart devices and on the cloud. Of the 1.2 trillion photos taken in 2017, only 10.3 percent of them came from digital or conventional cameras; 85 percent of those photos came from smartphones.

Welcome to the broader impact of first principles thinking. It's why Tesla is not just about building electric vehicles, but also about supercharging networks, solar-charging stations, and autonomous systems.

When we think about the impact that the smartphone has already had on banking, it is clearly significant. 2015 was the first year that more people used their smartphone to bank than visited a bank branch, call centre, ATM or bank website. It took just eight years for the smartphone to become the dominant form of day-to-day banking access[14]. Despite that, we've not really made major changes to the bank organisation chart to cater for this behavioural shift. Today, heads of mobile, CDOs (chief digital officers) and the tech guys have moved up the organisation chart hierarchically (sometimes), but structurally the rest of the bank has not significantly changed. But as indicated by Francisco González's quote above, as technology comes to dominate the banking experience landscape, the organisation chart must change to reflect entirely new operational competencies.

What's missing?

When I'm asked by bankers who they should hire for what's coming next, I always begin with "Stop hiring bankers!" The skills needed to be competitive in the future won't require any banking experience, but these new skills are what banks could live and die on. Over the past few years I've been surveying my FinTech friends on what hires will be most critical to the growth of their businesses and watching job boards and the like. The qualitative research I've carried out has come up with just a few of the jobs that will be considered critical in revenue and capability growth in financial services over the next five years or so.

1. **Data Scientist**
   Data scientists are a new breed of analysts and data architects who have the technical skills to solve complex problems and to answer big questions. More often than not, data scientists find themselves exploring exactly what problems need to be solved, based on where the data takes them. They're part mathematician, part computer scientist and part trend-spotter. They sit between the business and IT worlds.

2. **Machine Learning Specialist**
   Machine learning or algorithm specialists are specialist programmers, architects and modellers that built the systems that use cutting-edge artificial intelligence. They design machine learning (ML) algorithms, source data, train, evaluate and deploy ML models, and work to develop predictive and

cognitive processing capabilities. The ability to test systems quickly and deploy at scale rapidly are key.

3. **Experience Designer/Storyteller**

   Experience designers and/or storytellers can place the bank and its utility in customers' lives through technology in the most frictionless manner. They look at aspects of design like interaction and interface design, rapid prototyping and usability to develop highly compelling, low-friction engagement. The ability to think differently, circumvent existing processes and policies and challenge the organisation are key.

4. **Behavioural Psychologist**

   When it comes to designing interactions and new systems, the capability to understand how someone will react, what behavioural models they will apply in certain scenarios, and the use of conscious and subconscious triggers to gamify behaviour will soon become levers for short-term and longer-term engagement and loyalty.

5. **Blockchain Integrator**

   As blockchain becomes critical to money movement, IoT wallet capability, identity passporting, trade finance, etc—the core systems of today will not cope with the level of change thrust upon transaction banking. Thus, as banks can no longer afford the time for full core replacements, cloud integration of blockchain capabilities that extend the bank platform and allow integration into new plumbing will be critical.

6. **Compliance and Risk Programmer**

   All compliance, law and risk will be embedded in automated processes before long. This will shift the functions of compliance and risk away from human processes and bank policy, to a system of monitoring, alerts and action triggers. Within 20 years most regulators will also have moved to similar systems—so the bank AI will talk to the regulator AI.

7. **Community Advocate**

   Community advocates look at placing the new experience in

the best places to get the fastest traction and scale. Community advocates look at consumer trends, network effect and emerging technologies to see where the bank needs to be most active in the future to engage customers, just like planners used to look at foot traffic and vehicle flows in a city to decide where a branch needed to be physically situated.

8. **Identity Broker**

In the future non-bank entities will have much, much better identity, heuristics, biometrics and behavioural information than that of banks, so we'll need brokers to identify customers accurately and in real time. Identity brokers will construct the new IDV (identity verification) systems that replace our current KYC (know your customer) processes. This will be about real-time customer profiling and verification, not onboarding through a process.

I refuse to add Robot Psychologist, Emoji Translator and Customer Experience Ninja to this list. However, I might be tempted to add an AI Ethicist, for example.

Some roles I've left out that are critical for future development already exist in numerous banks, but they will become increasingly important in building a bank platform that is competitive. They include business analysts, venture capital teams for investing in FinTech, those that manage and grow technology partnerships, hackathon and incubator labs, etc—basically the ability to rapidly grow the bank's technology capability without building it internally. The real challenge for banks, of course, is that if you're a tech graduate coming out of a university looking for a job today, would you be looking to work for a startup, a tech major like Facebook, Apple or Google, or would you want to join a bank? Recruiting these skills will surely be a challenge for financial services organisations culturally, as we'll discuss in later chapters.

Technology partnerships with organisations outside the bank will become increasingly commonplace as banks realise that they no longer have the technology expertise that outside actors do, and that to build it themselves will cost much more and take much, much longer than simply partnering with a FinTech or tech firm that excels at that same competency.

At Moven we call this the ability to *bend space and time* for our partners[15]. To deliver the same or better technical or customer experience capability the bank requires, but at a fraction of the time and cost it would take to deliver using internal resources. I know there are bankers who will remain sceptical about this assertion, but let me throw down some home truths here using Moven as an example.

After we launched Moven in 2013 we had an approach from one of the big four Australian banks. They engaged with us multiple times, we presented to them in Australia, they flew to New York twice to meet with us, and they even looked to engage us offshore in Asia on some specific projects. They visited our partner bank TD, to check out Moven's white label product we launched for them branded "TD MySpend"—one of the most successful product launches in TD's history, according to their CEO[16]. But over time it became clear that even after two to three years of engagement they were tyre-kicking, trying to glean as much technical detail as possible about our product roadmap, but they had no real intention of buying our services or partnering.

Then in 2015 things got interesting when they recruited our chief product officer, offering him in excess of US$500k per year to leave Moven. Over the next two years they proceeded to spend a reported $20–30 million to finally launch their own "financial wellness" capability called...yes, you guessed it MySpend—very original fellas.

Yes, in two years at a cost of $20+ million they launched their own version of Moven's financial wellness, which they could have launched in three months for under $1 million if they had partnered with us rather than going it alone. Not only that, but the features of MySpend reflect essentially the capability Moven had in 2015, and today we've advanced features on our product for behavioural savings and contextual credit that will likely cost them another $20–30 million to develop and take another two to three years. Partnering with us could have given them that capability today.

Now I'm sure a player at that leading financial institution will have a very sound explanation for why they went down this path, and they'll talk about how agile they've become. But at the end of the day, it cost this bank 20 times more and took them 10 times longer to build it internally than if they had simply partnered with us. Now I'm not telling you this story because I'm upset they didn't partner with us, they had that right. I'm telling you this because in hindsight it was clearly a poor economic decision. Should this sort of case really be a surprise, though?

Who is going to be faster and cheaper at building new tech for financial services? A company that only focuses on tech, has a smaller more agile structure, works with multiple financial institutions around the world and has to answer to a board full of venture capitalists? Or a bank that has to deal with legacy systems, compliance and risk issues, and significant challenges with recruiting the right skills to build these new technologies in the first place?

More and more this will be a question that the CEOs of major institutions are going to have to answer. Do they retool to become an agile, technology organisation, or do they look increasingly to partner with those that are technology-first, and are cheaper and faster at innovations?

Anecdotally a story is doing the rounds right now that Jeff Bezos is big on AI and data science, so big that he told his team he wanted to recruit a thousand new data scientists and to do whatever it took to get them. Reportedly, this effort gleaned only 600 new recruits, working for one of the hottest companies on the planet in this arena, paying better than average salaries. Now think about a bank trying to recruit just 20 or 30 data scientists, and tell me they're going to be more effective than Amazon. Tough problem to solve—and one that may require even sponsoring university scholarships or creating internal training programs to home-grow those skills.

This all speaks to the broader capabilities of a bank. How do you organise these new competencies in a 21st century, Bank 4.0 bank? Do you simply create new roles in the existing business, or does it require reorganising the business to be more effective?

An exercise like this in organisational design theory could take many years of rooms full of academics to crack. Explaining this is beyond the parameters of this book, so instead let me try to take a shot at it in simple competency terms. Let's start with what a typical bank organisation chart might look like today, in very general terms.

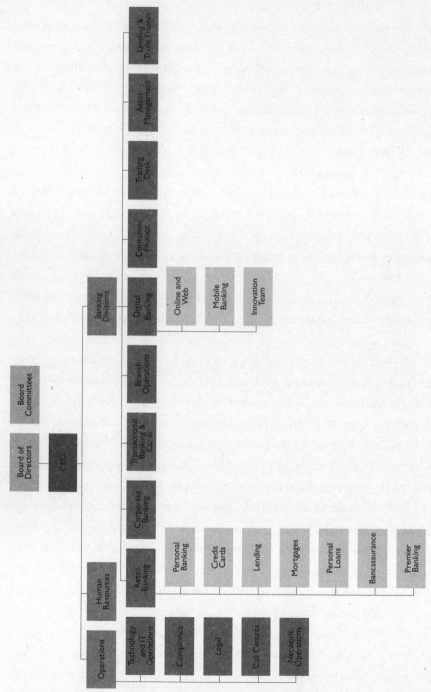

Figure 4: Representative organisation chart of a commercial bank today.

An organisation chart in today's modern bank reflects an evolution over decades—incremental change as a result of market focus, increased regulation, and technology impact. In reality it's not all that different from an organisation chart you might have seen 30 or 40 years ago in banking, but there have been new competencies and capabilities inserted into the structure. A first principles approach to banking is necessarily going to have a significant impact organisationally.

What is most noticeable about an organisation chart of a bank in the future is that the bank functions as a "platform"—it has the ability to surface the underlying utility and capability of the bank. In a Bank 4.0 organisation it is not omni-channel capability that is the key, it's complete channel agnosticism, engagement and revenue-pragmatic focus. In a world where you compete on utility, product structures and channel capability are what lie under the surface, whereas the tip of the iceberg is all about experience mechanics. In an experience world, the whole business is geared towards great banking experiences—it's not a channel-based afterthought where you retrofit a credit card into Alexa so a customer can make a payment on time.

When it comes to AI, which will by nature seek to automate much of what we have hard-coded in legacy architecture and process today, this won't just be a department that sits under IT. Artificial intelligence will likely eliminate whole swathes of the organisation chart as it stands today, but AI and data mining and modelling will power elements of almost every interaction. If you are tempted to think of AI like you do your bank's website (a piece of tech), then iterative thinking (design by analogy) will dramatically limit your ability to compete because you'll end up with competing AI projects, data silos, competing teams, fractured budgets, and inconsistencies in process approach. You'll have highly automated processes in retail, but tons of retained friction in corporate banking, because the retail guys will get more budget.

The table on the next page breaks it down into potential core competencies by functional area, showing how revenue might be delivered and people and resources managed in the near term:

Corporate Function	Core Competency	Outputs
Delivery	Data Modelling and Behaviour	This is the core discovery capability that replaces the segmentation and targeting typical today—data science, psychology, gamification, etc
	Core Capability	Interface to core utility in the bank. Reframing what we used to call products into utility and the rules associated with lending, etc
	Brand and Advocacy	Core branding will be tied less to physical and more digitally enabled. But branches that remain will be a key brand presence
	Experience Design and Technology	This is where it all comes together in terms of customer expectations, data and observation, behavioural science, predictive analytics, design competency, engagement and delivery
	Support, Engagement and Retention	Tactical customer retention and engagement planning happens here, along with call centre and human frontline support
Technology	AI, Machine Learning and Modelling	Core AI assets, machine learning capabilities live here
	Technology Stack (Network, Core, Cloud, Platforms)	The entire tech stack is managed here, including internal core systems, cloud-based modules and other IP/network based platforms
	Internal Systems	This is the operational capability for internal systems and leveraging tech within the organisation
	Identity, Security and Risk Management	Cyber security, fraud, identity management and IT risk is managed within this team, with links to external capabilities and platforms where necessary
	Emerging Technologies	This is where the team explores emerging technology capabilities, with a heavy focus on prototyping and testing in market

Business Operations	Partner Management and Operations	Increasingly as technology and FinTech partners exceed the bank's own capability, partnerships and collaboration become essential
	Compliance, Legal and Algorithms	This is the codification of business rules that encompass compliance, legal and risk requirements for the business—from process and laws, to code and algorithms
	Research, Strategy and Development	The strategy team look at trends, competitive differentiation and emerging business models threatening typical bank products and services
	Finance and Control	Corporate finance, cost control and accounting function
	Communications and Organisational Development	Corporate communications, investor relations and organisational development
Banking	Credit and Lending	Core credit and lending competency, with credit risk function, application of behavioural models, and experience design outputs
	Stores, Investments and Savings	Core value store engine with extensibility into various savings modes, wallets, and robo-advisor systems, etc
	Payments, Networks, Trade Finance	Money movement across open and closed payments networks, bank-to-bank payment schemes, etc

Table 3: Corporate function versus core competencies by functional area.

The organisation becomes less hierarchical and more collaborative as product structures and channel capabilities don't compete for budget, but are just levers for engagement, relationship and revenue. This approach, in theory, allows for much greater leverage of technology agnostically across the utility spectrum and allows for use of distributed technologies like blockchain or IP-based solutions from partners, without running into sacred cows or silos. There is a much more agile banking organisation structure, one that can compete side-by-side with technology pure-play competitors. The modern banking organisation is focused around customer delivery, whether retail, SME, corporate or otherwise. As such, the organisation becomes much more mission-focused when it comes to revenue delivery.

When you look at the likes of Ant Financial and others attacking this space, they have business units around core competencies, but not organisation charts focused on product. Their organisation chart is unconventional, focused on KPIs that measure active users, daily engagement, cumulative actions such as borrowing over the lifetime of the customer, and year-on-year growth. Their collective business unit growth is designed to speed up the reach of their network as it grows[17].

This leads us to think of the new Bank 4.0 organisation structure not as a chart showing strategic business units, but as core competencies across the organisation that can share missions, customer goals and so forth in a matrix form that a typical bank today would encounter huge challenges to accomplish.

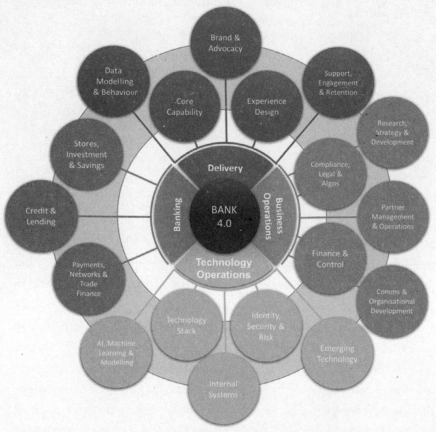

Figure 5: The Bank 4.0 core competencies chart (circa 2025).

In terms of competencies, we see that "banking" per se just becomes one of the competencies of the bank, and in equal terms Delivery, Business Operations and Technology Operations are just as critical.

While we might see today that AI and something like Amazon Alexa or the latest mobile app would sit under the purview of the information technology or digital team, in this new world delivery capability becomes a customer experience and engagement platform that is far reaching—essentially the new driver of revenue, relationship and reach. In this new model, technology operations become the underlying platform capabilities that are needed to surface utility and experiences in real time. Instead of traditional operations, we have technology and business operational competencies, as both are just as critical, but require very different skill sets and division of labour.

A few new areas emerge that you wouldn't find on an organisation chart today. Namely, Research & Development, Partner Management & Operations, Data Modelling, Experience Design and, of course, Artificial Intelligence. Many of these functions are counter-intuitive for the banks that have iterated from the Bank 1.0 world—their immune systems of internal core systems, legacy process, compliance, and entrenched product teams are extremely likely to push back against these new strategic business units. If these competencies aren't built, however, the ability to deliver revenue in a real-time tech-first world will be tough.

> Banks that still require signatures on a piece of paper to onboard a customer should be very, very nervous right now. FinTech [startups] are built to deliver every product imaginable in real-time, without a signature.
>
> —Accenture Perspectives, 2016

Onboarding and relationship selling in the new world

In a world of experience-based banking, there's no such thing as cross-selling as we'd describe it in today's world. Given the dramatic shift in behaviour regarding preferred banking access, the likelihood is that banks are going to have to adapt to this new normal. In the short-term, if you can't deliver a product or service in real time over digital, you will be losing customers and revenue by 2020. By 2025, there's a better than even chance that you'll be hunkering down in survival mode.

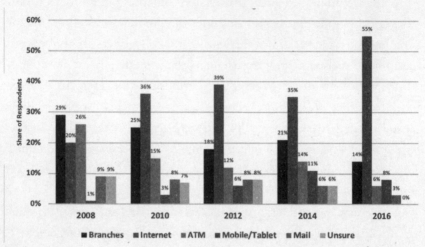

Figure 6: Preferred banking methods in the USA (Source: ABA 2017).

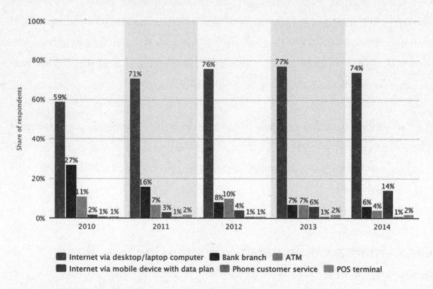

Figure 7: Preferred banking method in Latin America (Source: Statista 2015).

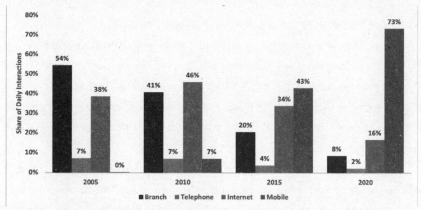

Figure 8: Preferred banking methods in the UK by # of interactions, 2010–2020 (Source: BBA).

If you look at this data from different geographies, while the timeframes are slightly different, the trend is the same—branch as a preferential day-to-day channel has *declined* between 50 and 80 percent since 2008. Surveys from Novantas, Statista, CACI, BBA and others all suggest that this trend is likely to continue or even accelerate over the coming years.

Again, this data doesn't suggest every branch is going to close—that's not what I'm getting at here[18]. The data, however, absolutely shows that preference for branch interactions on the whole is continuing to decline (as it is in retail storefronts broadly). Therefore, multi-channel revenue capability is not optional anymore, it is a matter of survival for a retail bank beyond 2020. FinTechs are already onboarding new customers at 1/20th and even 1/50th of the price of their forebears with non-branch acquisition. So it can and is being done. We'll talk more about this shortly.

The addition of voice-user interfaces (from 2016 to 2022) and the representation of advice and feedback in an augmented reality head-up display (estimated from 2025 to 2028), are both technologies that will further detach the branch process from daily engagement and sales. The more serious issue is that acquisition, cross-sell and upsell capability in this new world is based on an entirely different competency to that before.

"Alexa what are my options to invest this money?"

There are no demographics in Kansas anymore, Toto

Today we measure key segments based on demographics and behaviour that is exhibited amongst their peers. In today's banking world when someone measures that a segment like "Mass Affluent" can achieve a ratio of, for example, three to five products per customer, we aim for that average as a proficiency benchmark. It mostly comes down to sales targets and marketing spend, rather than platform capability.

In tomorrow's world, your ability to upsell or cross-sell to a customer will be based on actionable data and customer behaviour intelligence. Your ability to anticipate when and where a customer needs your bank to solve a problem or fulfil a need will be the trigger for a real-time, or near-time, highly relevant cross-sell or upsell engagement. Differentiation will be based on your data pools, partners and sensors that lead to the right trigger at the right time, and your ability to deliver that contextually with the least friction.

While some might be tempted to see this as an evolution of database marketing, the key here is going to be behavioural models and not segmentation and targeting. It is a pretty significant shift in underlying capability, because most marketing departments don't have that skill. It's a data modelling problem, not a targeting problem. It's data science, not market research.

And yet…this is where the relationship revenue is coming from in the future. If you only have branches and traditional marketing capability trying to pull customers into a branch to sign a piece of paper, you are massively hampered in this experience-led world, and you simply won't survive.

Endnotes

1 And I think you're probably a resident of Colorado, Oregon or Washington State smoking legally.

2 That is, if they visited a branch, withdrew cash, applied for a credit card and for a CD or term deposit on the same date—it still just counts as one visit for that day.

3 Maybe you wouldn't…

4 I have a banking relationship in Hong Kong where this is still the case today.

5   See Pulse news, "Kakao Bank attracts more than one million accounts in its first five days", 31 July 2017.

6   "A Hundred Apps Bloom in China as Millions Bank on Their Phones, Bloomberg Markets", August 2015—https://www.bloomberg.com/amp/news/articles/2015-08-19/wechat-baidu-and-alibaba-help-chinese-embrace-digital-banking.

7   Source: Industrial and Commercial Bank of China —Annual Reports.

8   "In Urban China, Cash is Rapidly becoming Obsolete", 17 July 2017, *The New York Times.*

9   Source: Fox Business, June 2016—"Uber's Leasing Program Is Changing the Auto Loan Market".

10 Source: Marriott Press Release—http://www.digitaltransactions.net/news/story/Marriott-Will-Accept-Alipay-As-Part-of-an-Ambitious-Joint-Venture-With-China_s-Alibaba.

11 See article below: "Future Vision: Your Personal Voice-Based AI Banker", by Brian Roemmele.

12 See Amazon Go.

13 Source: InfoTrends Worldwide Consumer Photos Captured and Stored, 2013–2017. See also: http://mylio.com/true-stories/tech-today/how-many-digital-photos-will-be-taken-2017-repost.

14 See ATM Marketplace "Mobile vs. branch: Beyond the tipping point", March 2016.

15 Shout out to Greg Mitdbo who came up with this one.

16 Source: TD 2016 Q4 Quarterly Earnings call with CEO. MySpend had the fastest ever growth to one million customers of any of the TD products/platforms in their history. MySpend was also the only TD app ever to hit #1 on the Canadian Apple iTunes and Google Play app stores.

17 See Ant Financial Investor Day Report—http://www.alibabagroup.com/en/ir/pdf/160614/12.pdf.

18 Settle down Ron Shevlin and Kevin Tynan.

FEATURE
Future Vision: Your Personal Voice-Based AI Banker
By Brian Roemmele, Voice-First and Apple Pay Market Analyst

From the introduction of the ATM machine in the 1970s to the web-based interfaces of today, banks have been famous for their love/hate relationship with technology. The early days of the ATM was nearly curtailed by the insistence of banks to charge patrons for ATM usage, even though there was ample evidence that many basic functions would save the banks money and serve patrons faster. When the ATM was finally adopted, it started a trend away from full service branch visits, offering the opportunity for the local banker to become closer to regular patrons, to know them personally and their financial needs and goals. The technology began to push bank patrons away from their bank, and this started a break in the relationship.

Today the chasm is wider than ever, most people under the age of 35 could, perhaps, count the painful times they have ventured beyond the ATM lobby of a bank. Those older customers remember the bank visits, but it falls into the category of a post office visit, or worse—a Department of Motor Vehicles visit. Much older people may be able to remember buildings and loans and savings and loans, with the essence captured in the classic movie, *It's a Wonderful Life*. In these memories of the past we can see the arc of the future.

There is now a generation that has been raised with financial services that are 100 percent self-service. Of course, some of this was needed, yet what now appears elusive is a personal, almost human connection. In the old days of banking, in most medium to small towns the banker knew the customer, they watched them grow up and meet the milestones from first savings account, college loan, car loan, wedding ring finance, first home finance and so on. In between all these banking milestones there are thousands of points of guidance and advice. The relationship with the banker was almost raised to that of a family doctor. The advice was welcomed, there was trust and confidence and the patron was more friend than customer.

This may all sound old fashioned and quaint, yet today we have a generation of younger people coming into the financial system with no real trusted confidant from which to ask financial advice. Certainly, one could search the internet or call a toll-free number and get simple answers read off a screen by a person that might be mildly interested in helping you, or who wants you to apply for their product so they get a sales commission. The rise of the smartphone app has, however, started a trend that now allows for a deeper connection of personalised services with banks. The app ecosystem evolved us from the isolated ATM days and set up a foundation for the next shift, voice-controlled AI.

As it stands today Alexa, Siri, Google Assistant and Cortana are already becoming very useful question and answer (Q&A) systems. Q&A systems are limited in that they do not recognise a continuity and a context between you and the AI system. Continuity has many elements, but the most simple element is that at the very minimum it understands the questions you asked before and is able to establish how questions are connected with previous conversations. Context has even more elements, but the simplest element is recognising who you are and what you are trying to achieve during this moment of interaction. This is the next stage of what I call the "Voice First Revolution" and it sets the stage for even more advanced interactions we can truly call a dialogue or conversation.

This is all mediated by a contextual form of AI that rests upon knowing the user to a degree not achieved by current AI systems and voice-first platforms like Alexa. This will change in a remarkable way. There are many new and innovative techniques and protocols we can use to achieve continuity and context. It will form the basis of a true digital personal assistant, something that will become more useful and more powerful over time. There are many things our true personal assistants will do; one of them will be financial advisement custom-tailored for you, based on your deep context and your goals.

Your personal assistant will be a voice-first AI system that never leaves you. Over time the context it establishes will be with your clear permission and with the highest security. You will also form an alliance with your personal assistant in a way previously unseen in technology. This will allow for the rise of the new automated, personal banker powered by your personal assistant and integrated with your banks and other financial companies.

The interactions will even surpass the advice one would have received from a family banker in 1950s United States. The tremendous ability to compare your current context and continuity with proactive interactions on your behalf will form the new voice-first AI personal banker. This personal assistant will know all past, current and potential future financial events down to the minutest detail. Your AI-powered banker will know details that cannot be found in banking statements, investment statements or credit card statements. It will ultimately know it all.

Here is an example of a typical interaction with your personal assistant AI: "Lesley, can I afford this new VR system? Is this the best time to buy it? Is it the best price?" Your AI banker can respond based on how you have curated "afford" over time against the other purchases you have made or plan to make, and create a contextual insight specific to you. You may not be able to afford this purchase; however, there may be many other suggestions and options. Let us assume for this purchase that $2,000 is the best price and the best time to buy. The next question is: how do you pay for it? Your AI banker can establish on-demand credit to be issued or a payment plan. There can also be a real-time banking auction that can use your current financial context and type of purchase to be bid on in a private way, giving you far more options than ever before. The system can also establish the best possible loyalty and bonus points.

Consider this interaction: "Lesley, when can I afford to buy my first house? What can I do now to shorten the time it will take to get a deposit ready? What investments will help me get there?" Today, answering these types of questions would require the insights of financial planners, as investment advisors and bankers working together. Yet with your new AI banker—a single point of contact that understands all of your context—a simple conversation will give you a useful answer that would otherwise have taken hours to derive. Your AI banker won't be selling you a mortgage, it will be helping you understand what you have to do to buy a home. This is already an improvement on a mortgage advisor who can only really suggest different types of mortgages.

With our ever-persistent AI banker working for us 24 hours per day, seven days a week, this will form a dedicated intermediary between you and the financial world. In this world "advertisements" will not be aimed at you directly, but at your AI banker. Banks and financial service companies will develop technologies that will allow them to become the service your AI banker chooses and prefers. All of this will be performed with your oversight; however, at some point you will forge a trust with your AI banker to always do the best thing for you.

The power of voice-first AI allows for the rise of this new personal banker that can be summoned by voice whenever we need it. The deep knowledge and deep context will create a "relationship" that would rival that of a personal banker for the very wealthy. The ability to have an ongoing, perhaps life-long dialogue with our personal AI banker will create a relationship that may become the single most important business relationship we form in our lives. This relationship will weave into just about every aspect of your life. Once you have the power of a personal AI banker, there is no chance that you would want to contemplate a world without it. There's also no reason to go to a branch to speak to a human either.

5 DLT, Blockchain, Alt-Currencies and Distributed Ecosystems

Dubai is a frontrunner in adopting the latest technology
and has set a goal to become the world's first
government to execute all implementable transactions
on the blockchain by 2020. The government initiatives
in this direction present tremendous business
opportunities for the private sector in the UAE.
—Ahmad Al Mulla, chairman of CIOMajlis, 24 July 2017

Now before I start, I'll make the obvious observation. By the time this book comes out, whatever I've written here about blockchain and cryptocurrencies will be out of date. News about China and their Bitcoin exchanges, regulatory responses to initial coin offerings (ICOs), bankers talking about a bubble or Ponzi scheme are daily occurrences. But that should also tell you something. I'll also be clear that if you're looking for an exhaustive essay on how blockchain works, consensus versus private versus public, etc—you'll be disappointed—this is not the book for that. What I want to discuss is how technologies like blockchain will force banks to evolve and how cryptocurrencies and ICOs may signal an evolutionary change in the way we think about capital markets, commodities and capital flows themselves—a futurist's perspective on the whole ecosystem if you like.

Prior to 2008 we hadn't heard of Bitcoin, blockchain or distributed ledgers. There was scattered talk of digital currencies, like the early QQ coins and Linden dollars from SecondLife™, but DLT[1] was nowhere to be seen.

Today the total capitalisation of cryptocurrencies is measured in the hundreds of billions; ICOs are exceeding early venture capital investments in startups; while major banks, governments and firms are deploying blockchain technology. Blockchain, Bitcoin, altcoins and ICOs are hot.

This shouldn't be news. Neither should it be all that surprising. Today, five of the top six stocks in terms of market capitalisation in the United States are tech companies (Apple, Alphabet, Microsoft, Amazon and Facebook). It wasn't that long ago people were debating whether Facebook's IPO was a total bust. And before that people were debating if the internet was a fad. Technology is transforming every sector today, from EVs and solar that are obliterating the future of fossil fuels, to Apple's app ecosystem that has created some of the fastest growing companies in the world today (such as Uber and Airbnb). We've even had to invent new language to describe these shifts, like the "sharing economy", the "gigging workforce", "unicorns", "social media", etc.

If you can step back from the heavy regulated banking sector and observe the changes taking place in the world writ large, the view from the bleachers is that we are simply replacing all the old infrastructure and value chains with technology-first constructs. In the world we are moving into, old regulated systems on old rails can't survive—even with protectionism— because they simply aren't fast, flexible and scalable enough in a world where 200,000 internet-enabled smartphones are sold every hour of every day[2]. If you can look out from the tree branch you're sitting on, you'll see a forest of change that is inexorably forcing a rethink in the way we do things: how we send money from point A to point B, how we grow businesses, how we create brands, how value is exchanged, and more.

Emerging digital currencies

Bitcoin, and the blockchain it sits upon, is what inevitably emerges when you have to retrofit money, value stores and payments systems to a real-time world sitting on the IP layer, directly accessible by the user rather than through a gatekeeper. This sort of solution emerges when you realise that a single banking core system sitting in a single data centre somewhere can't possibly deal with "deposits" and transactions happening simultaneously everywhere in the world where a mobile wallet might exist. It emerges when you realise that a single database accessed by potentially millions of computers simultaneously couldn't possibly handle the security requirements you need to keep secure custody of digital money. When you realise that having to first jump through KYC hoops just to get access to a payments system doesn't work when the transacting device is an AI or an autonomous vehicle with its own autonomous payment capability for road tolls and charging stations. When you realise it's no longer just a transaction you need to execute, but all the other data (geolocation, biometric, behavioural, heuristic) that goes with the transaction, that will be just as critical for building the future of your business.

Those involved in cryptocurrencies like Bitcoin and distribute ledger technology will often tell you that it's going to change the world. Not because they are all "true believers", but because they've seen the possibilities of a world that isn't constrained by regulation built for 19th century banks on top of legacy systems built decades before the internet existed.

As discussed in earlier chapters, the first layer of changes we saw in banking were channel-led. We first talked about internet channels, then mobile channels, then omni-channel banking. As users started to get frustrated with bank speak and bank interfaces we started to talk about usability, the premise that we could design better user experiences, make screens easier to read and apps easier to use. This led us to understand that emerging technologies might change access to banking in fundamental ways. Suddenly the fastest growing financial institutions in the world were based on technology interfaces and experience design. The rules around financial inclusion were being completely revolutionised by simple value stores accessible through a basic mobile phone. Next, just as the FinTech world seemed to be stabilising around best-practice user experiences, a second stage of innovation kicked-off—FinTech and technology startups focused on rebuilding the core infrastructure and back-end upon which banking operates. Upgrading the pipes and rails. Finally, we started to realise we might remove traditional interfaces all together.

In July of 2017, the then largest ICO to date raised an incredible

$232 million in funding for Tezos[3]. Tezos used both BTC (Bitcoin) and ETH (Ether) for its raise. Tezos, reportedly, wasn't aiming to raise $232 million in funding, it was aiming for $30–50 million, but they took in 65,693 XBT/BTC and 361,122 ETH in just days. As I write this chapter, Bitcoin has been on one of the biggest rollercoaster rides we've seen, rising to top out at US$20,000 before Christmas 2017, then hitting a low of around $6,000 at the end of January 2018. At those prices the value BTC contributed to Tezos is still well over $400 million.

Truth be told, Tezos raised so much money with their ICO they didn't know what to do with all the crypto-cash. So they started their own VC fund[4]. Since then they've gone into a bit of a meltdown—I guess an unexpected windfall of $230 million cash will do that to some founders.

Today Tezos is old news. They no longer hold the record for the fastest $200 million ICO raised in history. In just 60 minutes early in August, Filecoin's own ICO raised more than $250 million[5], and then in December 2017 EOS followed with a $700 million ICO trebling the previous record. As I write this I'm painfully aware of the fact that I'll be updating the figures in this chapter right up until the point it is published. Then, as soon as the book is published, these figures will all be out of date. We live in a very dynamic world in all things cryptocurrency- and ICO-related.

For the first half of 2017, CNBC reported[6] that ICOs accounted for more than $1.2 billion in startup fund raising, more than the total VC-based early stage funding for the same period. That is an incredible statistic. Why? Because that $1.2 billion in funding is up from just $78 million in 2016 (excluding the DAO's failed $150 million ICO), and in the United States, as mentioned earlier, for many of the startups that have raised capital via an ICO, it might all soon be considered illegal thanks to an Securities and Exchange Commission (SEC) ruling. Why? Because as with any technological advancement that allows rapid returns, there are numerous bad actors out there that will inevitably give a bad name to the honest guys trying to use an innovative method of raising capital to start their businesses.

Imagine that a friend is building a casino and asks you to invest. In exchange, you get chips that can be used at the casino's tables once it's finished. Now imagine that the value of the chips isn't fixed, and will instead fluctuate depending on the popularity of the casino, the number of other gamblers and the regulatory environment for casinos. Oh, and instead of a friend, imagine it's a stranger on the internet who might be using a fake name, who might not actually know how to build a casino, and whom you probably can't sue for fraud if he steals your money and uses it to buy a Porsche instead. That's an I.C.O.

—NY Times, "Is there a cryptocurrency bubble?
Just ask Doge",
15 September 2017

All-time funding by ICOs hit $5 billion in December 2017, with a big surge in Q4. To put that in perspective, $4 billion of that total cumulative funding was in 2017 alone. Despite the SEC's Investor Bulletin on ICOs in July 2017 and various governments cracking down on ICOs, things don't seem to be slowing. If anything, they would appear to be speeding up.

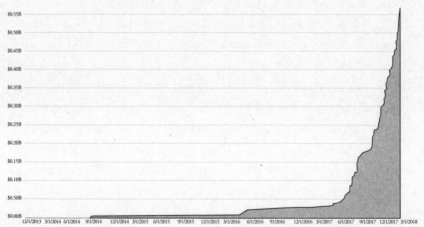

Figure 1: ICO funding exploded in 2017 (Source: Coindesk ICO Tracker).

Despite this flurry of activity and massive growth in funding, not all ICOs are successful.

In 2017, Bitcoin Market Journal's analysis showed that of approximately 600 ICOs evaluated by their team, only 394 of these completed their ICOs reaching their end date. About 35 percent of these reported or published funding details. Thus, the assumption in that data is that almost two-thirds of ICOs in 2017 failed to reach their intended funding target. It doesn't mean they failed completely, just that they didn't hit their numbers. That is one explanation. The other explanation is that in an unregulated market, auditing of financial results is simply *optional*.

There were some spectacular failures, though. Whether via failed technology, poor execution or outright scams, ICOs generally got a pretty bad rap as an asset class, primarily because they rely on self-governance, and there are enough bad actors that negative stories are not isolated instances. The most publicised failures of 2017 included:

1. **OneCoin**—A textbook scam of the multi-level marketing Ponzi scheme variety. $350 million lost and 18 founders jailed by Indian authorities.
2. **Enigma**—Poor execution failed this cryptography and security service. The CEO was hacked losing $500k, which killed their security imprimatur.
3. **Droplex**—A scam ICO that literally copied another company's whitepaper (QRL) by doing a global find and replace. Still, they made off with $25k of investors' cash.
4. **Coindash**—A hacker boosted $10 million off this Israeli startup via a phishing site. Rumours of an inside job continue to plague their team.
5. **Veritaseum**—YouTube ads pumped up this ICO before $5.4 million in coins were stolen and quickly converted to Ethereum. Claims that the Veritaseum team engineered the hack to pocket funds continue.
6. **Parity**—Straight-up hack of the multisignature wallet by exploiting a flaw in the code and two-step verification process. White hat hackers were able to recover most of the stolen Ether.

The one lesson learned from all this is that despite the promise of ICOs as a funding mechanism for startup, it is still "buyer beware" for now.

Bitcoin and cryptocurrencies on a surge

Bitcoin and Bitcoin Cash (BTC/BCH), Ether (ETC), Ripple Coin (XRP), Litecoin (LTC) and others were all performing at record highs at the close of 2017, with many traditional investors and traders looking on and shaking their heads. XRP was up almost 4,000 percent in the first half of 2017[8] alone, and today is listed on 30 exchanges around the world. But Bitcoin is the cryptocurrency that started it all.

On 22 May 2010, one of the first real-world transactions on Bitcoin occurred and will forever be memorialised as "Bitcoin Pizza Day", when a BTC user paid 10,000 Bitcoins for two pizzas from Papa John's Pizza in the Bay Area. At Bitcoin's peak pricing in December 2017, those pizzas would have been worth more than $200 million.

In February 2011, Bitcoin wrestled with US dollar parity, coming close numerous times before finally settling on the milestone on 9 February. In June 2011, Bitcoin was trading at almost $30 per "coin"; then on 19 June the famous Mt Gox hack occurred, with the price of Bitcoin plummeting to $2 in the months that followed. At the time, the Mt Gox hack represented a loss of more than US$2 billion assets (or about 300,000 Bitcoins).

For many, this was clear evidence that Bitcoin was subject to weaknesses due to its computer-based nature, and therefore doomed.

However, the nature of Bitcoin was changing—people were starting to talk about the future value of Bitcoin in lofty terms[9]. By 2013, Bitcoin had passed the $1,000 value mark, and topped out at $1,242 near the end of the year. But then all hell broke loose again as the Chinese government banned financial institutions from dealing in Bitcoins. The price of Bitcoin then steadily declined over 2014 and reached a level of trading around $200–250 throughout 2015. Many traders and analysts thought that Bitcoin had reached a stable point of trading and it was unlikely to revisit its heights of 2013. They were obviously wrong.

In 2017 all crypto-hell broke loose. One milestone after another fell by the wayside as Bitcoin grew and grew and grew. John McAfee, the crazy former resident of Belize, came out and said Bitcoin would hit $1 million. More specifically, McAfee made a bet that either Bitcoin would hit $1 million, or he would eat his male parts live on TV. The illusive Satoshi

Nakamoto's personal net worth climbed past $1 billion, then $10 billion and then $19.4 billion based on his[10] holdings of Bitcoin. You couldn't turn on a finance show without hearing about Bitcoin. Jamie Dimon said Bitcoin was the greatest Ponzi scheme in history, and the same day JPMorgan Chase traded millions of dollars in Bitcoins. Ransomware started to pop up globally, with the only way you could release your files being to send Bitcoin to the hackers. The world had gone Bitcoin crazy. Incidentally, if Bitcoin ever does get to $1 million per BTC, Satoshi would become the world's first trillionaire (if Bezos doesn't beat him to the punch).

Then in January 2018 Bitcoin crashed, spectacularly. The same traders and analysts that were saying Bitcoin had stabilised in 2015 were now saying Bitcoin was heading to zero. Nobel Prize winning economists were saying the bubble had burst and Bitcoin was going out of business[11]. At the time of writing, Bitcoin is slowly edging its way back up around the $7,000–10,000 range, while international markets have gone through their first series of corrections of 2018.

Calling Bitcoin volatile would be an understatement. Some analysts are calling Bitcoin a crypto-asset class these days, not a digital currency anymore. Others are still telling us that it's going to replace all the central banks in the world, while the predictions of a Ponzi scheme and bubble continues. The Bitcoin faithful even came up with their own term to describe the rollercoaster ride in Bitcoin valuations and volatility—HODL or "Hold On for Dear Life!"

How on earth did we get here?

Understanding Bitcoin's rise

If you haven't read Dave Birch's latest effort (*Before Babylon, Beyond Bitcoin*[12]) yet, please avail yourself of his comic and academic brilliance. One of the key points Birch makes in his review of the future of cryptocurrencies is that over time money has increased in both utility and function, and that money must become intelligent to retain utility and function in the medium term. Ultimately money is becoming a form of technology itself. Michael J Casey and Paul Vigna make similar arguments in their most recent book *The Truth Machine*.

While this might sound a little bit like science fiction, Bitcoin and ICOs are simply part of the digital evolution of our monetary and trading systems. But there's something else happening here beyond just the evolution of currencies or money.

Bitcoin has proved a number of things. Blockchain was a stable technology, and although evolving, it had stood the test of time. Numerous infamous wallet thefts had occurred, some famous wallet owners had lost an old hard drive years ago and had come to the realisation that they would have been millionaires had they not lost it. Mt Gox and other exchanges suffered spectacular thefts. But the blockchain never got hacked. It proved resilient.

Blockchain is a new architecture enabling applications like Bitcoin and ICOs. Some say ICO token sales are the "killer app" of blockchain. But consider this: these applications have become almost self-sustaining today, with enough market capital that total failure (going to zero) is becoming inconceivable—there's almost too much capital tied up for it all to disappear. Once Bitcoin surpassed the value of gold, from a trading perspective it had already became an asset class that many claimed would hedge against market changes. While volatile, its performance has made it a solid long-term bet, and if institutional investors continue to play in the space, it will just become a mainstream instrument.

Is this a global capital markets evolution?

The rise of Bitcoin needs to be seen in the context of the market as a whole. While stock markets around the world continue to reach record levels, there are signs of structural changes to capital markets and economies globally. Developed economies like the US and UK are not in sustained low-GDP increase territory. While not in recession, modern economies aren't capable of the higher rates of growth we saw in the 20th century because productivity gains are slowing. We celebrate a GDP figure of better than two percent like it's 10 or 20 percent today. The mainstream companies that fuelled economic growth, like GE, Exxon, and the banks, are still profitable, but compared with the tech giants like FAANG (Facebook-Apple-Amazon-Netflix-Google) and BAT (Baidu-Alibaba-Tencent), they aren't going to see results like they had in the 1980s ever again. Underpinning this are a few major macro trends:

1. **Productivity** is all moving to technology, and so traditional players are either having to become "tech" or see revenues, stock prices and returns enter a slow decline;

2. **Austerity** and multiple rounds of cost reductions are a road to nowhere economically;

3. **Early indications** are that Brexit[13] and Trump policies are slowing economies and industries (agriculture is the first to go due to immigration policy[14]), giving credence to the globalisation mantra as a prerequisite for growth;

4. **Energy markets** are undergoing deep structural changes, and this creates a shift where oil is no longer the foundation of commodities markets and futures;

5. **Capital flows** and market make-up appear to be transforming almost exclusively around technology ecosystems.

Prior to the big correction of January 2018, the US stock market had gained $3 billion in value in 2017 and saw gains of 17 percent. But fully one-fourth of that growth came exclusively from technology stocks, namely Apple, Microsoft, Facebook, Amazon, and Alphabet (Google's parent company)[15].

An age of digital commodities, technology infrastructure, smart economies and new value systems is rising. The economy cannot possibly function today like it did in 1960, and thus protectionist efforts like Brexit and the Trump administration's policies threaten to isolate their economies from the levers that will continue to create economic growth, namely investments in core technology advancements that underpin 21st century infrastructure and economies. I know this is debatable, but there are real structural changes here, and we've seen this before during the Industrial Revolution.

China has made massive moves towards solar energy in the last two years. Indeed, in 2017 alone China installed more than 60 GW of solar capacity—that's more than the entire US solar capacity—and China deployed it in just a single year. India is rushing to do similar, with both economies shedding reliance on coal as quickly as is viable. Coal is running at $40/st, at approximately the same price levels as it was back in 2001, and oil crude prices are at sustained lows. With renewables looking to overtake fossil fuels in the 2030s in terms of total generation capacity, and with solar this year becoming the cheapest form of unsubsidised electricity generation per kWh, we are looking at a slowly collapsing commodities market.

Despite Trump's efforts to bring back "big coal", the US created more than 350,000 jobs in solar between 2016 and 2017[16]. Coal jobs increased by 50,000 according to the administration, but the entire coal industry employs only 160,000 people in total according to Department of Energy figures—less than half the solar jobs just added in the last two years. Then in January 2018 Trump raised tariffs on foreign solar panels and started talking about levies on solar energy itself. This is one of the fastest growing industries globally and in the United States in terms of job creation, and the administration aims to slow it down to favour fossil fuels.

In 2016, energy-based commodities represented more than 50 percent of US trading volumes[17]. If those commodities are set to remain flat or decline, there will be a total decline in commodities trading and volume over the next 30 years in the trillions of dollars. Markets desire growth.

Figure 2: Oil prices are in for sustained lows given that solar's price is declining so rapidly (Graph: Brent Petroleum prices since 1987).

Clearly while the stock market is growing, commodities overall (largely because of fossil-fuel commodities' sustained slump) will not provide the growth opportunities they once did, save for perhaps rare earth metals. Hence it is reasonable to think that digital commodities and digital assets might move to fill the gap in available investment dollars or to make up a balanced portfolio for growth investors—especially with the strong returns we're experiencing. If you're an investor and you want growth, cryptocurrencies like Bitcoin are volatile, but they are going the right way in 3–5 year time horizons.

Think of it like this: in the 1850s and 1860s, the growth economies were investing in electricity, railways and telegraph lines. In the early 1900s it was roads, telecoms, and factory-based assembly lines. In the 1960s it was electronics, computing and business services. Each of these competencies were the core infrastructure and talent components for industrial and GDP growth over the next 50 years—the ability to stay competitive. Economies that failed to invest in that infrastructure found themselves significantly behind the competition within just a decade or two. Developed economies were those that continually invested in the infrastructure required to make themselves more competitive.

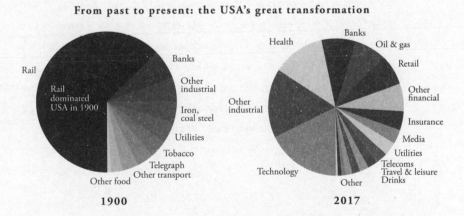

From past to present: the USA's great transformation

Figure 3: US Stock Market by sector, 1900–2017 (Source: Credit Suisse).

Are cryptocurrencies like Bitcoin part of the new, smart infrastructure the global economy is going to need to be viable in 2030, or could it all be a bubble, a Ponzi scheme and a scam?

The whole "Bitcoin is a fraud" argument

On 12 September 2017, Jamie Dimon, the CEO of JPMorgan Chase, proclaimed Bitcoin a fraud—and it wasn't the first time. The price of XBT plummeted overnight and it was reported that traders at JPMorgan Chase had initiated more than $17 million worth of buy orders on Bitcoin immediately after. Some said Dimon was involved in a dump-and-pump scheme. After that Dimon said he wasn't going to talk about Bitcoin anymore. But he did. In January 2018 he simply said he regretted making that comment—oh, and his daughter has some Bitcoin investment apparently.

In an internal JPMorgan report published on 8 February 2018, the leading US bank said that cryptocurrencies were "unlikely to disappear". The report analysed the future potential of cryptocurrencies in general, along with the incredible risk-adjusted returns that cryptocurrencies have provided as an alternative asset class over the last few years for investors, when compared with the S&P500 and stock markets in general.

> CCs [Cryptocurrencies] are unlikely to disappear and could easily survive in varying forms and shapes among players who desire greater decentralization, peer-to-peer networks and anonymity, even as the latter is under threat...The underlying technology for CCs could have the greatest application in areas where current payment systems are slow, such as across borders, as payment, reward tokens or funding systems for other Blockchain innovations and the Internet of Things, as well as parts of the underground economy.
> —"J.P. Morgan Perspectives: Decrypting Cryptocurrencies: Technology, Applications and Challenges"
> 8 February 2018

Some, like Dimon, have over the last nine years regularly asserted that Bitcoin is a bubble, like the South Sea Bubble of 1720 or the Great Tulip Craze of the 1630s. These bubbles are often created with investment vehicles that are highly subject to market speculation, often with the creators making the big bucks as the craze reaches the broader market. The South

Sea Bubble used network effect like Bitcoin and ICOs by giving British politicians, lords and even royalty access to a form of stock options, which encourage them to pump up demand for the stock (they could hold their stock without cash changing hands and sell it back to the company or to the public once the market price exceeded their option price). Ultimately, the claims made by the South Sea Company were found to be fraudulent, and an Act of Parliament helped introduce the modern stock exchange to protect the market from these types of frauds.

The total market capitalisation of cryptocurrencies today is fluctuating between $300 and 500 billion, or in the range of the value of Wells Fargo as a company. Bitcoin alone exceeds the market cap of McDonald's, CBS, 3M, Netflix[18] and others in today's terms, and it's closing in on Disney's current market capitalisation. However, rather than being purely an asset class in a speculative bubble, ICOs are now distributing Bitcoin's value across tokens that are linked to a wide range of companies—operating in a very similar way to the way securities are issued on an exchange.

The problem for regulators is that Bitcoin, altcoins and ICOs have become almost self-sustaining in the same way that the stock market is self-sustaining. As long as enough investors participate, and their exposure is limited or diversified, the likelihood of a complete collapse of Bitcoin or Ether is about as likely as the complete collapse of a secondary stock market today.

That's not to say that the occasional bad actors that issue their own ICOs won't affect the price of Bitcoin or ETH. There are plenty of stories of unscrupulous actors that have disappeared with their ICO "winnings", and the fact the SEC is gunning for them. The collapse of numerous token-based companies and funds are certainly more likely than the collapse of a publicly traded company. Despite all of that, the fact that tokens enable emerging startups to raise capital without listing, and without giving away equity, is simply too compelling an idea for many founders. Thus, it is likely more capital will flow into the ICO market over time, and ultimately in 10 years, the total ICO market will surpass some of the world's smaller stock markets in terms of market capitalisation.

Venture capitalists have been investing in innovation and disruption for a very long time, but as an industry they rarely innovate themselves. If you're in the blockchain or bitcoin space, our view is that we're trying to decentralize the world, we're trying to democratize the world in a way that creates a level playing field where everyone has equal access. Crowdfunding was the first major leap in the democratization of the world of early-stage finance. I believe the tokenization of it— what we're doing—is the next, even larger leap.

—Brock Pierce, Bitcoin Foundation and EOS

Some regulators will certainly ban ICOs, some will even ban cryptocurrencies altogether. But others will see this as a competitive differentiation in a globalised economy that is restructuring around digital assets and commodities.

The trick here is that the ICOs and cryptocurrencies represent a sort of systemic shift similar to what occurred *after* the South Sea Bubble collapsed, not during the South Sea Bubble itself. This is the formation of a new marketplace built without the legal and geographical hurdles of the stock markets that operate globally today. ICOs on top of cryptocurrencies are simply an IP-optimised system designed for value exchange in a real-time world, where the value is decentralised, based on computing power and network effect, not central banks and government legislation. ICOs are, like most FinTechs and technologies, an attack on friction—the friction of raising capital.

I personally believe the regulators who win will be those that enable a light-touch process for legal ICOs, encouraging investment, but with enough protection to weed out the bad actors. The investors who win will be those that invest in cryptocurrencies for the long-term and pick tokens that are clearly linked to the performance of the company they're invested in, and not designed just as a way to raise funds sans equity. As with the best markets, the best performing companies will win for both their investors and for their founders. Bad actors won't be able to kill this. But they will most definitely force us to regulate the ICO market, just like the South Sea Bubble created modern stock markets.

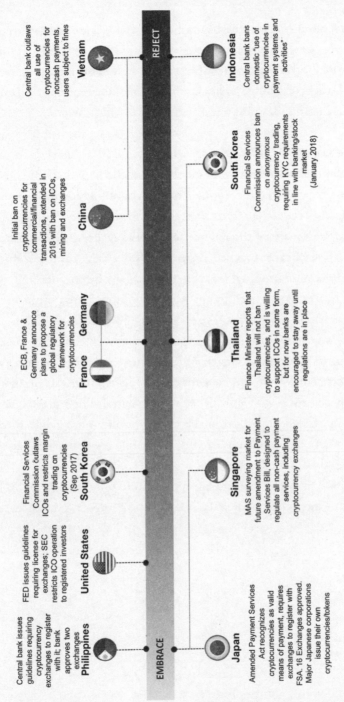

Figure 4: Regulatory responses to ICOs and cryptocurrencies over the last 12 months (Source: Nikkei.com, others).

It's not going to be a total crash with ICOs and cryptocurrencies disappearing—it's just going to be the formalisation of the ICO market by regulators, backed by cryptocurrencies as both alternative asset classes, alternative value exchange systems and payments networks. So maybe HODL on to those Bitcoins and Ethereum for a bit longer.

The structural implications of DLT

Hearing about the whole history of the blockchain tied to Bitcoin, the growing ICO market and the stories of banks scrambling to implement their own blockchain intiatives, you'd be forgiven for thinking that blockchain was solely the domain of the finance sector. The reality is that blockchain initiatives have already touched dozens of industries, from government through to diamond mining, from energy to smart infrastructure.

Distributed ledger technology (DLT) is now being implemented by banks around the world. We're starting to see trade finance and cross-border transactions moving to blockchain POCs. The types of blockchain, or distributed ledger, technologies are varied. In fact, some private blockchains may not be considered "distributed" at all, as Dave Birch's flow chart shows (Figure 6). A private shared ledger may be heavily restricted in respect of use, so in the classic public models like Bitcoin's blockchain, the restricted use of the ledger doesn't really lend itself to being called distributed at all.

There seems to be no end of applications for blockchain or DLT technology. And blockchain is having a direct impact on the banking sector.

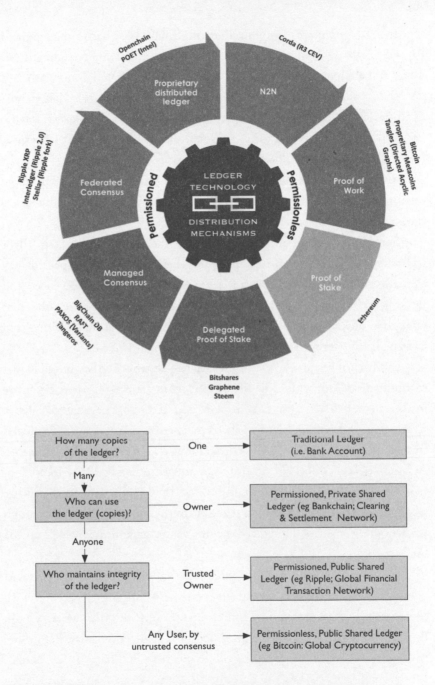

Figure 5: Different flavours of distributed ledger technologies by consensus mechanisms (Source: KPMG Research/Dave Birch).

In 2017, Ripple announced more than 100 banks had joined RippleNet to modernise global and cross-border payments transactions. That's still a far cry from the 11,000 banks using the SWIFT network, but it's 100 more than a few years ago and growing rapidly. In a 2017 report by IBM, "Leading the Pack in Blockchain Banking: Trailblazers Set the Pace"[19], 15 percent of the top 200 global banks said they had rolled out full-scale, commercial blockchain applications in 2017, and 65 percent were expected to have blockchain projects in production by 2020. Large institutions with 100,000 employees or more were consistently those leading the charge, according to IBM's research.

So what prompts banks to work on blockchain or distributed ledger technologies? Often it is future-proofing their business in respect of key elements of the back office, such as transactional flexibility and speed and interoperability with emerging networks, but in many cases it is because emerging blockchain technologies offer security and auditability that existing bank databases and payments networks don't have.

But it's not just banks that are seeing the benefits of distributed ledger technologies. Companies like the Sun Exchange are building their entire business smart assets, smart contracts, and ICO tokens on blockchain. Everledger is tracking diamonds from the moment they're extracted from a mine in Zambia, to the engagement ring sold in Tiffany's on 5th Avenue in New York. Hanson Robotics and Singularity AI are looking at managing emergent machine cognition on the blockchain. In the future a baby might have his identity tracked from the moment of birth through his schooling, his first bank account, his marriage and death—all on the blockchain.

In 2017 Vladimir Putin proclaimed that the Russian government would be re-engineered upon blockchain technology, starting with transportation services. This comes just a few months after Vitalik Buterin from Ethereum met with Putin at the St Petersburg Economic Investment Forum in a closed-door meeting. Dubai's ruler Sheikh Mohammed set 2020 as the date for all government transactions to be done on blockchain infrastructure. At the 2018 World Economic Forum, governments around the world announced that a globally recognised traveller and identity program would be implemented on blockchain, which could one day spell the end of physical passports. Brazil and Canada are also talking about national identity programs on the blockchain in line with this initative.

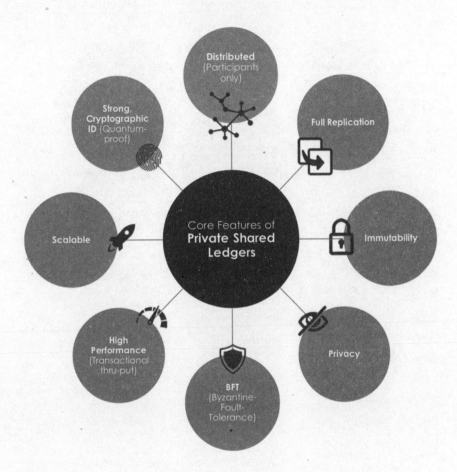

Figure 6: Core benefits of private blockchains compared with current transactional systems (Source: Gilbert+Tobin).

The world appears to be in love with the concept of the blockchain. Below are just a few of the areas where active blockchain implementations and startups are operating today in the non-financial space.

Figure 7: Blockchain applications.

If you thought blockchain was about cryptocurrencies, you're wrong. If you thought blockchain was a finance thing, you're wrong again. If there is a database somewhere in the world that needs a distributed presence, strong auditability, and/or automated management, then it's likely we'll see the blockchain become the foundation of those datasets over the next couple of decades.

Blockchain is still in its infancy, even in the banking world. If you step back from the present, you could envisage blockchain as an element of first principles thinking and as a redesign of basic transactional services that power the financial services market. It offers the potential to create broad interoperability across new identity systems, technology services, financial products and payments networks. It is a way to break through the current system constraints of legacy "pipes and rails" that the banking system has established over decades. While the likes of SWIFT and NACHA talk about their own blockchain attempts, the reality is that the fastest growing networks in financial services today are not connected to incumbents, but are new systems developing on top of mobile and internet protocols.

Why your core system has a shelf-life

Today the largest super-wallets in China, India and Africa are effectively closed loop systems that are holding deposits in the trillions. These mobile wallet value stores are essentially what we used to call a bank account. Even though we've had alternative value store mechanisms like airline mile programs, transport cards, etc for some years, the sheer scale of these alternative wallet ecosystems, and the fact that they are interchangeable with cash and card payments, make them extremely bank-like in nature. Just 10 years ago the only players in the very space that M-Pesa, Paytm, Alipay, Venmo, and WeChat Pay operated were bank-owned, with the one notable exception of PayPal, of course.

As we've already pointed out, however, Paytm, Alipay, M-Pesa and Tencent don't have banking core systems underpinning their mobile wallets. At least not for the ledger operations—they have to store all their cash deposits they take in accordance with local regulations in an actual bank account with a partner bank, but within the closed loop system they are core-less.

As IoT devices, ICO tokens, e-money licenses, cryptocurrencies and super-wallets become more and more common, a great deal of day-to-day banking activity, particular around deposits, payments and investing, will be core-less and bank-less. Now you could argue that this is just crying out for regulation, to force these organisations to become chartered or formal (licensed) financial institutions, but that still won't require them to put in place a banking core system. This is because their digital value stores aren't part of a universal banking model, they aren't replicating the products that banks, card networks or investment houses are built on today. They are surfacing the same utility as banks with core systems, but that only requires a strong experience layer, and not a core system.

Ultimately, as banks are forced to compete on utility and build more and more technology experiences to surface that utility, they'll be beefing up a middleware layer that looks more and more like blockchain platforms and the likes of Ant Financial or Tencent's WeChat. Essentially, they'll be stripping the core back to its very core (excuse the pun). Yes, the ability to offer interest rates will be there, the ability to store value will still be there, and access to credit will be there. But the core systems that reinforce branch-analogous products will be used less, and more of the middleware will be used to surface banking experiences across mobile, voice, augmented reality glasses and the like.

What do you get when the "bank" is not delivering any of the old products it used to deploy in the branch; when it is just a concentrated core of banking utility, its processes around capital adequacy still enforced by regulators; its identity outsourced to brokers and government blockchains; and its risk operations managed by artificial intelligence?

The core banking system will largely have disappeared, replaced by improved utility and ubiquitous banking experiences. At a minimum it will just be part of a much larger technology-and-experiences delivery stack.

I know we're talking about a decades-long shift here, but think again about the organisational structure, technology architectures and competencies to compete in this world side by side with core-less players like Ant Financial. Does your current core system offer a competitive advantage against these non-bank financial institutions?

But what about challenger banks? The challenger banks we see are mostly still operating under the assumption they'll have a super-modern, real-time core with a kick-ass front end to differentiate. But some neo-banks, like Stirling and Revolut, are now starting to construct alternatives to these models, like marketplace banking. My own challenger bank,

Moven, doesn't have a core system—we just have a big middleware layer.

It all comes back to first principles. If you were building a bank's architecture from scratch today based on everything we know now, would you build it based on a traditional core system designed in 1960, but updated for real-time operation? Not if you understand banking 4.0 is about experiences surfaced through technology, and not the digitisation of branch-based banking products. Blockchain will be a necessary, core-building part of the architecture required for 21st century real-time banking experiences. Old-style core banking systems will not.

Endnotes

1 Distributed ledger technology.

2 Source: IDC Data (that's over 3,000 smartphones sold every minute, 1.7 billion annually).

3 Ethereum was actually the first organisation to issue an initial coin offering.

4 Source: *Business Insider*—"What does a tech startup do after raising $232 million selling digital coins to investors? Set up a VC fund".

5 "$200 million in 60 minutes. Filecoin ICO Rockets to Record amid Tech Issues", CoinDesk.com—https://www.coindesk.com/200-million-60-minutes-filecoin-ico-rockets-record-amid-tech-issues/.

6 Source: CNBC, August 2017—https://www.cnbc.com/2017/08/09/initial-coin-offerings-surpass-early-stage-venture-capital-funding.html.

7 See https://www.sec.gov/oiea/investor-alerts-and-bulletins/ib_coinofferings.

8 See CNBC—https://www.cnbc.com/2017/07/21/ripples-xrp-digital-currency-rose-3977-percent-in-the-first-half-of-2017.html.

9 Source: *Business Insider* article—"Bitcoin could go to $1 million", Henry Blodget, 8 November 2013.

10 Assuming Satoshi is actually a man, or a person. Some believe Satoshi is a creation of NSA. I have heard that Satoshi is actually four separate individuals who collaborated on the first white paper, one of whom is no longer alive.

11 Nobel Laureates Robert Shiller and Joseph Stiglitz both predicted big crashes in Bitcoin; see https://www.ccn.com/nobel-laureate-economist-predicts-bitcoin-crash-wont-go-to-zero-it-will-just-come-down/.

12 Available on Amazon and wherever good books are sold.

13 See Independent.co.uk—"UK crops left to rot after drop in EU farm workers in Britain after Brexit referendum", 5 February 2018.

14 See USDA Report—"The Potential Impact of Changes in Immigration Policy on U.S. Agriculture and the Market for Hired Farm Labor".

15 See Quartz.com—"Just five tech companies account for a quarter of the US stock market's blockbuster year", 30 October 2017.

16 Source: EDF/Fortune—"Renewable Energy Is Creating Jobs 12 Times Faster Than the Rest of the Economy".

17 Source: TFR commodities review 2016—www.tfreview.com.

18 Source: Compare http://www.corporateinformation.com/Top-100.aspx?topcase=b https://coinmarketcap.com/.

19 See https://www-01.ibm.com/common/ssi/cgi-bin/ ssialias?htmlfid=GBP03467USEN.

Part 03

Why FinTech companies are proving banks aren't necessary

6 FinTech and TechFin: Friend or Foe?

As […] technologies develop and season, they're going to create a totally different way of doing banking and financial services. Now we will see the possibility—not necessarily the probability—of what we call a "Kodak moment", where increasingly banks become irrelevant to their customers.
—Antony Jenkins, Former CEO of Barclays, founder of FinTech startup 10x Future Technologies

If you go to Google and type in FinTech, among the top automated search terms that appear are "FinTech killing banks", "FinTech disrupting banks", "will FinTech replace banks". If you follow through on such searches you'll find pages and pages of news stories from the major financial news outlets, along with blogs, press releases and so forth proclaiming that, yes, FinTech will kill banks. But then you'll equally find a plethora of articles showing that it's all much ado about nothing and banks are not only up to the challenge, but will outlive the "fad" of FinTech. Some will argue this is a zero-sum game, that it will all work out with FinTechs and banks living in some sort of technological harmony once the dust settles. The truth is somewhat more complex.

Will FinTech (or TechFin) kill banks? Most certainly some banks, but not all. Will banks (or regulators for that matter) kill some FinTechs? Absolutely, but again, the FinTechs that succeed will become an established part of the future of financial services and, as Antony Jenkins forecasted above, FinTechs and TechFins are materially changing what financial services itself means.

Investment levels show that the FinTech "fad" is far from over: it's either still getting started or we're right in the thick of it. Strong investment of US$8.7 billion in Q4/17 propelled global FinTech funding to over the $31 billion mark for 2017, sustaining the same high level of investment seen in 2016[1]. This brings the total global investment in the FinTech sector over the past three years to US$122 billion[2]. The number of VC transactions exceeded 1,000 for the fourth consecutive year in 2017. This is part of a wider trend of increased VC investment in technology firms; in fact, 2017 marked the highest spend in venture capital since the dot-com boom. A total of $84 billion was invested in over 8,000 technology companies and startups last year[3], with FinTech taking more than a third of that investment. Rather than this being a bubble like the dot-com boom, there are now numerous FinTech startups that are large, high-value brands with established and profitable customer bases. Many of these startups are at least as big as their equivalent competitors who are listed, public companies. Like Uber, many of these companies have elected to remain privately owned for now.

Ultimately this means that whether or not you truly believe FinTechs will kill banks is largely irrelevant. The investment flooding into emerging technology players is already changing financial services demonstrably, and these startups are changing financial services at a much faster rate than banks are able to respond to. As these new entrants continue to get greater and greater access to funding, this makes future disruption even more likely[4].

Let's make the argument even simpler. If Ant Financial and Alibaba, LuFax, Simple, Square, TransferWise, Betterment, Stripe, Venmo, Xero, SoFi, Credit Karma, Coinbase and others didn't exist, would banks be investing in technology at the same rate that they are today? Or would the status quo have continued to reinforce a slower rate of change? Ultimately the new benchmarks in economic performance, leveraging of social media and network effect, customer acquisition across digital channels, cross-sell and upsell strategies tied to behavioural models, and so forth, are inexorably linked to key FinTech players who have change the game and moved the goalposts.

For example: if you were Jack Ma starting up in financial services, would you begin by building bank branches or appointing agents and advisors to build your business? Or would you use first principles thinking to outline more aggressive growth methods in the digital age? I'll let Jack Ma answer that question:

> I made a bet [with the CEO of Walmart]: in 10 years we'll be bigger than Walmart, based on the sales. Because if you want to have 10,000 new customers, you have to build a new warehouse and this and that. For me?...Two servers.
>
> —Jack Ma, Founder of Alibaba,
> speaking at the 2015 World Economic Forum

Figure 1: Jack Ma speaking at the 2015 World Economic Forum (Image credit: WEF).

Jack Ma has been very clear that as the founder of the largest FinTech startup in the world, there's no advantage in the digital age to building physical infrastructure to grow a brand. If you want to grow fast—it has to be digitally enabled.

"For me? Two servers"

The future of financial services is clearly about *financial services experiences embedded in technologies that are ubiquitous*. Technologies that allow rapid scaling. Technologies that solve the big problems of financial inclusion, fraud and identity theft, friction, and so forth. FinTechs are consistently first to market with experiences on the technology platforms that account for the vast majority of daily access to financial services. In China, Alipay and WeChat were first to market, and dominated. In the US PayPal, Venmo and Square pre-dated the likes of Zelle by years. The first banks to launch digital onboarding were neo or challenger banks. As a result, when these players get scale, they end up forcing incumbents to mimic the experience that customers now know is possible[5].

Every FinTech in the world has the same basic mission. Kill not the banks, agents, brokers and insurers of the world, but *kill the friction associated with financial services* today. They do that willingly and it is at the very core of their mission. For banks, they often have to battle legacy system constraints, compliance-based apathy and resistance, lack of executive support, and the fear of cannibalisation of their existing "channels" before they can even start transformative projects. What this means is that FinTech's are consistently more efficient at deploying investment capital for the purpose of removing friction when compared with incumbents.

Thus, it is inevitable that the fastest-growing financial services organisations we see around the world today are not banks, but the FinTech, technology and challenger bank startups. Does this mean we won't need banks in the future? You don't have to channel Bill Gates today to know that in much of the world people are using FinTech's every day to do stuff that only banks used to do. In fact, in 20 markets surveyed by EY last year, consumer adoption of FinTech was on average 33 percent, with China as high as 69 percent of the internet-enabled population.

I'm not arguing that every bank will disappear. However, the standards by which banks are held to is no longer their own—it's more than likely that the day-to-day banking experiences you enjoy in 2025 will have been most heavily influenced by technology startups than by incumbent banks who have innovated. FinTechs and TechFins are shaping the landscape that is to come. Not regulators, not banks.

Norman Chan, the head of the Hong Kong Monetary Authority, cited this exact problem when announcing a seven point plan for Hong Kong to compete globally on a regulatory basis. In his speech given at the annual

HK Institute of Bankers conference, Chan said incumbent banks have been unable to innovate quickly enough, so for Hong Kong to maintain its leadership as an International Financial Centre the HKMA has turned to FinTechs. Let that sink in—Hong Kong is pegging their future as a leading financial centre on encouraging innovation from FinTechs, not relying on incumbent institutions. The lack of innovation by incumbent players has now become a market threat.

> Digital only banks have seen greater take up outside Hong Kong. For example, UK regulators have encouraged the development of challenger banks as a way of bolstering competition in the sector. Meanwhile, incumbent banks in Hong Kong have been much slower to close physical branches than rivals because of the high profitability of individual branches in Hong Kong, and the comparatively slow take up of digital services by customers...
>
> —Norman TL Chan, HKMA Chief Executive, 25 January 2018

When you look at the most disruptive innovations in the world over the last 250 years, from the steam engine to the telephone and computer, what we see is clear evidence that first principles design thinking creates the fastest innovations, the biggest leaps, the most disruptive market changes. Those shifts very, very rarely come from incumbents innovating themselves incrementally over long periods of time. It's why Antony Jenkins called it a "Kodak" moment for banks. The fact that Kodak invented the tech behind digital cameras, but still couldn't adapt to the digital age and thus imploded, is a relevant analogy.

This doesn't have to end in tears for banks. Firstly, money behaviour is pretty sticky so changes in customer behaviour admittedly occur more slowly in financial services than, say, music purchases or digitisation of video, but financial behaviour isn't so sticky that it can't be circumvented as the EY study cited earlier demonstrates. In many instances, the big disruptions we're seeing in financial services are the result of network effect[6]. Money needs to move—we pay merchants, we pay bills, we send money to our friends, we pay our rent—if those people are on a particular network we share in common then our behaviour shifts, along with our money. Payments represent up to 80 percent of our daily interactions with financial institutions, so if you change the way you pay, that opens up risk for credit access, savings, merchant acceptance and many other areas that flow on from that shift.

In China, where there are less legacy payments behaviour around plastic and cheques (for example), the shift has be able to occur much faster, because network effect has less resistance. If you're one of those bankers that insists that Brits and Yanks will still be using cheques in 30 years to pay for stuff, then you are in effect arguing that your economy is going to willingly fall behind China, India, Kenya and most of Europe in terms of day-to-day money movement, and probably as a financial centre of excellence. It's why I can never agree with the argument I hear from bankers that "regulators won't let it happen". That's ludicrous. Look at Shanghai, Hong Kong, Singapore, and London regulators—to name a few. They all are sandboxing, going open banking, enabling rules for ICOs and working with FinTechs, because they realise the future of financial services is being built today. If these countries and cities want to remain as leading financial centres, stopping FinTech advances would slow innovation considerably. Why on earth would a regular protect legacy behaviour in this fast-paced environment that is transforming financial services? They would do so at their market's peril.

Let's talk about where these new players are impacting specifically.

Where the new players are dominating

Startups have the advantage of being free of legacy technology systems and tough regulation, both of which limit the digital developments of established financial services firms. As a result, startup companies can more efficiently create mobile-focused services or products that threaten existing financial companies.

—"FinTech startups put banks under pressure"

—*Financial Times,*

12 September 2016

Already there are strong signals emerging that indicate FinTechs and TechFins are starting to rewrite the underlying economics of financial services. It's not just in building or deploying tech either, but operating expenses, acquisition costs, scalability, etc. Just like during the dot-com explosion, however, there are players capturing real revenue, players that are getting scale fast, and players that just won't make it out of the starting blocks.

It could be reasoned that there will be enough of these new players that are successful in getting traction that market expectations around certain metrics, KPIs and economics will inevitably shift. In that environment, incumbents may find themselves competing with one hand tied behind their back—a legacy organisation, technical and legal structure that simply is no longer economically viable in market terms.

Think about the core elements of the day-to-day retail banking business, such as customer onboarding and distribution—what Jack Ma was alluding to in that earlier quote. It goes without saying that no FinTech neo-bank is launching branches today[7], but think about the reasons why challenger banks haven't led with a branch-based distribution strategy:

- Compared with successful digital acquisition strategies, branches are simply too costly and too slow for the scale these businesses need, in the timeframe and with the available funding they have; most challenger banks have 12–18 months to prove their case and hence raise more funding to continue to grow.
- The cost of deploying a high impact physical location in a FinTech-rich city would likely be more than the entire development cost of a FinTech's basic app or technology, and branch activity is declining demonstrably.
- Every FinTech is trying to compete in real time for customers, thus they must eliminate the need for a "wet" signature or face-to-face interaction, because the need for such would slow down revenue and growth detrimentally.
- Investors simply don't fund branch networks for FinTechs because they're also all about rapid scale.

- Acquisition costs per customer in-branch are five to ten times
  the acquisition costs via digital.

Remember what Jack Ma said: "two servers".

We're starting to see significant differences in customer experience, establishing clear new standards as a result of challenger bank innovations. Whether we're talking neo-banks in the US, N26 across the EU region or the numerous challenger banks in the UK, digital customer onboarding is now a significant differentiator. When it comes to account switching in the UK, data shows that the length of time taken to open an account is a significant barrier to switching behaviour[8]. So, you'd think onboarding improvements would be a massive priority, let alone for reduced costs of acquisition. For incumbents, apparently not.

Of the challenger banks in the UK, all of them offer account opening within minutes of downloading the app or going to the website. Starling and Monzo offer one-step 100 percent digital account application and opening, and others offer two-step identity verification processes. Of the major banks in the UK, only RBS has made progress towards a 100 percent digital account opening process[9]. Let that sink in—every challenger bank in the UK offers digital account opening, but only one incumbent bank can claim the same. In the US only 18 percent of banks and credit unions offer an account opening process via smartphone[10], and of those only 24 percent allow customers to fully complete the process via mobile. For those of you doing the math, that's less than five percent of US banks and credit unions that in 2017 offered 100 percent digital account opening via mobile. Less than five percent! Moven, Simple, Bank Mobile and GoBank have all had these capabilities for many years.

WAYS TO OPEN NEW CHECKING ACCOUNTS

Q: How can consumers open new checking accounts at your financial institution? (Mark all that apply.) (n=230)

In branch — 98%
Website/online — 66%
Mobile specific app — 18%

Source: DBR Research © June 2017 Digital Banking Report

MOBILE APPLICATION PROCESS

Q: If you allow opening of checking accounts with a MOBILE APPLICATION, can the entire process (ID verification, terms/conditions, funding) be completed on this channel (mobile)? (n=181)

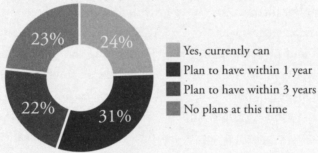

24% — Yes, currently can
31% — Plan to have within 1 year
22% — Plan to have within 3 years
23% — No plans at this time

Source: DBR Research © June 2017 Digital Banking Report

Figure 2: Digital Banking Report data showing digital onboarding capability US-wide.

In 2017 EY surveyed more than 22,000 digitally active customers and found 43.4 percent of them chose to use a FinTech due to ease of use/access. Clearly a primary driver of the growth in FinTech is simple account opening experiences and ease of use. Given the data is clear, the lack of efforts by incumbents to rectify account opening friction is a good proxy for the whole FinTech versus banks argument.

If you want to compete with FinTechs now and in the future, there's something you absolutely must do—*you need to get rid of the requirement to sign an application form with a wet signature.* Full stop.

Challenger or neo-banks also outperform incumbents on several other core metrics. According to KPMG[11], the average return on equity for challenger banks in the UK market is between 9.5 percent for larger challengers and 17 percent for smaller challengers, as opposed to larger banks at 4.6 percent. Key factors behind the better performance is due to lower legacy IT costs, as well as a simplified product portfolio providing a CTI (cost-to-income) ratio just below 50 percent for the smaller challengers, compared to 80 percent CTI ratio for their incumbent counterparts.

When you extrapolate these issues across multiple neo or challenger banks launching in a market like London, the medium-term effect will be to fundamentally change the way the market views retail banking economics. At some point (probably within the next five years), stock market analysts will start looking at retail bank branch networks and viewing all but the best-performing branches as inefficient mechanisms for retail bank operations, whether for acquisition or servicing. Compared with successful challenger banks, they'll be viewed simply as outmoded, high cost legacy infrastructure.

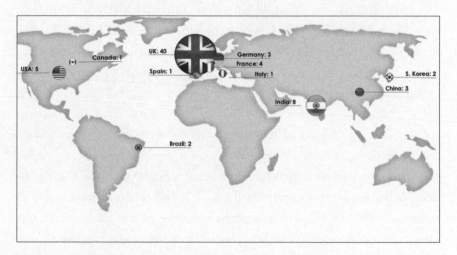

Figure 3: Challenger banks by country (Source: Burnmark as at December 2016).

When it starts to hit the stock price, when every earnings call becomes about how fast you can divest yourself of your legacy branch networks, reduce costs, speed of acquisition and what percentage of your acquisition is 100 percent digital, then simply put, the pressure will be on retail banks to look more and more like a challenger bank. At least from an origination perspective. The same is going to be true of wealth management, insurance, payments, you name it.

Research by PwC last year showed that 95 percent of banks believe that part of their business is at risk of being lost to stand-alone FinTech companies. This is no longer just academic.

Now I know the first defence that many incumbents will offer—*market share*. The argument will be that until FinTechs take real market share off incumbents, this is largely a moot point. But is it? Is the aim immediate dominance in a sector? Was Amazon dominant in retail sales in 1995 when their internet service launched? What about in 2005, 10 years later? Was Apple dominant in music sales when the iPod launched in 2001? Were those initiatives a failure in the early years because they didn't dominate their industry within just a few short years? The data clearly doesn't support that argument.

In the US market, regulators have chosen to drag their feet on FinTech licensing for banks[12], but there is already a well-established credit market that has been largely based on non-face-to-face distribution. Direct mail, outbound call centre sales, brokered lending—all have all been common models over the last 20 years or so. Thus, pure-play FinTechs in the lending space don't have the regulatory hurdles that FDIC licensed checking account operators have, and thus the market share changes have been more pronounced.

This shift is likely to get even more acute for incumbents as the likes of SoFi, CommonBond, Prosper, Lending Club and others venture out into more complex distribution partnerships to enable greater reach. Check out the data from TransUnion showing the shifts in unsecured, personal loan portfolios in the US market over the last few years. From just 2012 to 2015, FinTechs went from just three percent of market share to over 30 percent.

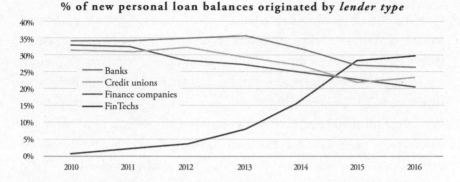

Figure 4: FinTech's impact on the US lending space (Source: TransUnion).

I don't know how you'd argue that this is just a coincidence or a non-issue for incumbents. But if you need further proof of why this represents a structural change, just look at the side-by-side operational cost structures of a FinTech lender like Lending Club compared with a traditional lender in the space:

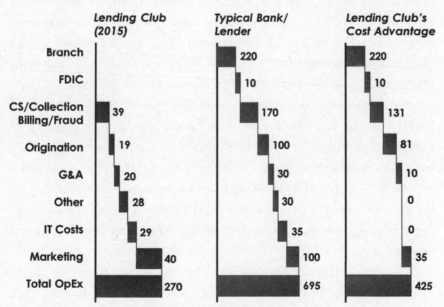

Figure 5: Lending Club based on data from Federal Reserve Bank of St. Louis and Foundation Capital (Source: Let's Talk Payments).

The data shows Lending Club's business has a 400-basis point cost advantage over a typical bank competitor. When it comes to origination there's an 80 percent reduction in average cost, and close to 80 percent advantage when it comes to collections and fraud. In fact, the only costs where Lending Club exceeded the average incumbent was in marketing. You might think Lending Club's IT costs would be more than a traditional bank, given that is their core platform, but no—there, too, they have a 20 percent cost advantage over incumbents. That's hardly insignificant. This is one of the reasons banks are increasingly working *with* FinTechs. The fact is that maintaining legacy architecture is super-expensive compared with working with a new technology stack.

These changes are not limited to the lending segment and challenger banks. For example, a recent report by EY showed that use of FinTech players for money transfer and payment services rose from 18 percent in 2015 to 50 percent in 2017, with 65 percent of consumers anticipating they would use such services at some point in future[13]. McKinsey reported in 2017 that one UK-based international money transfer service provides P2P international transactions at just 10 percent of the cost of the average bank in the UK[14]. PwC and Accenture research shows that between 28 and 30 percent of existing banking and payments businesses are at risk from FinTech disruption by 2020 alone. That's two years away, folks.

Accenture went even further in their research[15] of the impact of FinTech on the industry. According to Accenture, there are only one of two possible outcomes for incumbents based on the macro changes we are seeing as a result of investment and traction around FinTech companies:

Scenario 1: **Digitally disrupted**—as banks lose their profitability to the more effective FinTech companies in the digital age, they will continue to offer a product-based sales approach rather than to improve the customer experience.

Scenario 2: **Digitally reimagined**—banks will increasingly integrate innovations at the business model level. Their focus will shift from asset monopolies to improving a customer's life by embedding financial services experiences.

FinTechs are lean, agile and innovative

Startups rely on leading-edge technology, don't have to worry about any legacy architecture, and are only partially subject to the regulatory constraints that apply to conventional banks. They require fewer but highly specialised staff, and hardly any physical infrastructure. Their dynamism attracts digital talent. FinTechs disrupt the sales of banking products by fulfilling customer expectations using agile processes and greater customer orientation and accelerating their speed of innovation. They establish a "new normal" for mobile and online user journeys using unique, intuitive features, with regular new releases. They disintermediate client relationships from banks by providing aggregator services, putting banks in the position of pure providers of infrastructure and commodity products in extreme cases. As well as offering old products in a new guise, FinTechs develop completely new services, such as cross-border, peer-to-peer (P2P) payments, micro-lending or robo-investment platforms where almost all processes are based on algorithms and barely any human intervention is required. This makes some established offerings obsolete and diminishes the profit pools of banks.

FinTech—Challenges and Opportunities
McKinsey Report, May 2016

Partner, acquire or mimic?

> Innovation is simply not in the DNA of most bankers. They've been trained throughout their whole career to identify and avoid risks, and innovation is about taking small risks and failing fast and cheaply and learning from those mistakes to get to the right answer quickly.
>
> —JP Nicols, FinTech Forge

Since 2012, the top 10 US banks by assets have participated in 72 rounds totalling $3.6 billion of investment in 56 different FinTech startups alone. All 10 of those banks have blockchain and AI investments.

Research shows that FinTechs are consistently between 25 and 70 percent cheaper to market, or operating at a significantly lower cost base than incumbents[16]. FinTechs are faster and first-to-market at delivering the big innovations, which are the likely foundation of the future of banking from an experience and technologies standpoint.

If you're a bank, then, statistics indicate you have two choices. Deliver it internally at a slower and more expensive rate than a technology player, or partner with a FinTech to do the same, but faster and cheaper. And yet, the vast majority of banks today are not yet partnering with FinTechs. Regardless, McKinsey research shows that only eight percent of incumbents believe that they don't need to respond to these industry-wide changes. That means most banks already know they must respond—the question remaining is how?

First principles thinking is a key element in this landscape.

It would be illustrative to revisit the SpaceX example in their quest to deliver cheaper launch costs for rockets and spacecraft. Recall that the recent Falcon Heavy (FH) launch bought the cost of delivering 64 tons into orbit down to just $90 million—a 90 percent cost reduction from the days of the Space Shuttle, and reusability will bring that down further. The nearest government competitor to this is the long-awaited SLS, or Space Launch System, being developed by NASA and its contractors. But the SLS, which will only be able to carry 70 tons into orbit (just 10 percent more payload than the FH) and has an estimated cost of $1 billion per launch, is already three years overdue. The projected costs of the SLS are greater than 10 times the FH launch cost, for just a 10 percent increase in capacity. In other words, for the cost of one launch of the SLS platform that pushes 70 tons into orbit, SpaceX could have delivered more than 700 tons into orbit for the same spend. That's illustrative of the sort of comparisons we're seeing in incumbent-based digitisation efforts versus those in FinTech. Sure, you can build it yourself, but economically it simply makes no sense. If you can get the same result for one-tenth of the price in one-third of the time, why are you screwing around trying to copy what a FinTech has already built?

Bank Strengths	FinTech Strengths	Fintech Differentiation
Broad existing customer base	New ideas/thinking	Experiences tailored to specific consumer groups
Broad product set	Agile implementation	Greater flexibility in service approaches
Low cost of capital	Cutting-edge analytics and data management	New business models that change economics
Regulatory protections (deposit guarantee, etc)	Online customer acquisition	Inclusion and serving underserved customers
Revenue source (for FinTech)	Online/Mobile UX optimised design	Shift away from products to differentiated technology experiences

Table 1: The benefits of collaboration between banks and FinTechs.

FinTechs *bend space and time* for incumbents when it comes to technical capability.

To be fair, FinTechs need incumbents, too. They need the scale and revenue that partnerships with banks provide. Their growth is dependent on these sorts of partnerships to deploy their technologies. It sounds like a marriage made in heaven, but only if you recognise the key strengths and weaknesses of both parties.

In the end, banks actually have four choices in how to respond to the structural changes financial services is witnessing as a result of the explosion in FinTech-led innovation:

1. Do nothing (slow decline into obsolescence, ultimately very expensive)
2. Partner with a FinTech (cheapest and fastest)
3. Acquire a FinTech (potentially fast, but still expensive and culturally challenging)
4. Copy or mimic FinTech innovations (slow and very expensive)

What are the benefits of copying a FinTech instead of working with one? It's hard to define specifically beyond retaining budget internally, avoiding culture clash and owning the IP. It's unlikely those benefits justify the sort of costs and delays that would otherwise come from partnership with a more agile technology partner.

In almost all cases incumbent banks can only really iterate on what a FinTech has already done. Look at Greenhouse from Wells Fargo, Finn from Chase or Liv from Emirates NBD. What are these if they aren't clones of Moven, Monzo, Digit and Acorns? Imitation is the sincerest form of flattery, but when it comes to banking, technology development is also the most expensive form of flattery.

Hackathons, accelerators and incubators—shall we dance?

It is quite common for larger banks to start their own incubators or accelerators, offering up mentoring, legal, marketing, or technology support to startups to attract them. Such programs can also be accompanied with direct equity investments in participants. For instance, Wells Fargo invests between $50,000 and $500,000 in each participant in its accelerator program, which was launched back in 2014. Wells uses the program as an extended audition to consider purchasing the startups' products. Barclays runs an accelerator program that it recently expanded to New York, London, Tel Aviv and Cape Town—with investment of up to $120,000.

JPMorgan Chase partnered with the Centre for Financial Services Innovation[17] to create the Financial Solutions Lab, with a $30 million investment over five years. The advisory council for FinLab includes Kosta Peric from the Bill and Melinda Gates Foundation, Arjuna Costa from Omidyar Network, Susan Erlich from Simple, Arjan Schutte from Core Innovation Capital, and others.

On the down side, these kinds of programs are extremely costly to run. Banks should have extensive experience in dealing with startups through other kinds of collaboration before shelling out for such a program. Additionally, banks need to have very specific objectives when they start an accelerator to ensure they get their money's worth. Barclays have already invested the resources to develop 43 different financial blockchain applications in its internal labs, so it makes sense to strategically supplement that work through its accelerator program.

Some of these partnerships are now mature enough for tactical benefits to be measured. A recent survey from global law firm Mayer Brown[18] showed three key areas where incumbents say their partnerships with FinTechs are paying off:

- **Cost savings:** 87 percent of respondents said they were able to cut costs to some extent by working with FinTech providers. Most likely, these savings are coming from incumbents spending less on the development of new experiences, as well as the efficiencies FinTechs bring to legacy processes, their agile operating structures and the use of the latest tech.
- **Brand refreshes:** 83 percent of respondents said collaborations with FinTechs offered opportunities for incumbents to refresh their branding. Speed to market and cheaper development efforts allow incumbents to reposition themselves as better serving a particular market, or simply as cutting edge.
- **Increased revenue:** 54 percent of respondents said partnerships had resulted in boosted revenue.

Ultimately, however, if your organisation structure is not geared towards working with startups, these accelerators and hackathons don't get you big bang for your buck. If you have anyone in the bank telling you that you could run a hackathon and take the best ideas and implement them yourselves in the bank, then give up now. This might work once, but after that your bank would quickly become labelled within the informal network of FinTech professionals globally as an innovation bystander and tyre-kicker, and not as a team player. The only way these programs work is if you are really serious about engaging with FinTechs for longer-term partnerships.

The problem for banks is that even with an incubator or accelerator program, your access to FinTechs is extremely limited compared with stand-alone accelerators. The success of a stand-alone accelerator like Y Combinator is in part because it has funded more than 500 startups since 2005. By comparison, the innovation labs at some of the biggest banks house no more than a handful of startups at any given time. Some accelerators I've seen only accept one or two percent of the applications they receive. This is hardly a guarantee of diverse and comprehensive innovation through FinTech partnerships.

The other key problem we are seeing develop is that leaders of accelerator and innovation programs are increasingly being aggressively targeted by competitors who want to start their own initiatives. When a leader of an accelerator or innovation team leaves, in many cases the executive team that they hired beneath them dissolves or moves on too. It appears that innovation programs within banks often hinge on a key individual. When that individual moves, it sets back the team's progress considerably. Innovation needs to be an organisation-wide activity. That's possible when you are running a FinTech; it's almost impossible at an incumbent bank.

Killing FinTech partnerships— the barriers to cooperation

> We have a chance to rebuild the system. Financial transactions are just numbers; it's just information. You shouldn't need 100,000 people and prime Manhattan real estate and giant data centers full of mainframe computers from the 1970s to give you the ability to do an online payment.
>
> —Marc Andreessen, Andreessen Horowitz, October 2014

Looking at all of the above data, there are a ton of compelling reasons for cooperation between FinTechs and incumbents, but partnerships between banks and FinTechs are still in their nascent stage. The good news is, it is changing. In 2012 more than 50 percent of banks surveyed by Statista felt that FinTechs were largely irrelevant, but by 2017 that number had changed, with 93 percent of banks intending to partner with FinTechs. But what are the keys to success and the barriers to collaboration?

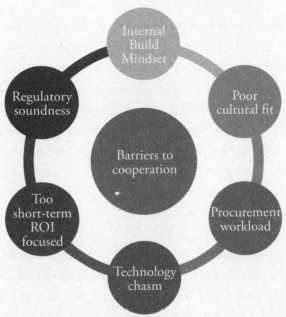

Figure 6: Some of the barriers to successful FinTech-bank partnerships.

Internal build mindset

I think we've covered this often enough already, but needless to say this will become harder and harder to justify over the coming years. I can tell you personally that at Moven we've engaged with a number of banks that spent literally years picking our brains about our tech. In the time these incumbents spent trying to learn as much as they could about our technology, they could have implemented the technology much faster and cheaper by working with us.

Licensing technology rather than building technology internally also gives the bank the ability to reject a path in the medium term without committing too many internal resources to it.

Poor cultural fit

For the next few years this will remain a potential area of conflict. A startup moves fast, doesn't worry too much about regulation until there's an event that threatens the business, and has a culture of risk acceptance that would curl the toes of most chief risk officers. A bank needs to be careful that their compliance, legal and risk teams don't kill off the advantages, enthusiasm and drive of a FinTech partner in a collaboration effort. While being risk adverse has been at the core of banking, the ability to transform your organisation digitally will increasingly depend on agility. Banks should seek to learn from the culture of FinTechs they work with and get the support of key internal stakeholders to give FinTech partners plenty of latitude when it comes to solutions architecture and delivery. Too often new initiatives coming into a bank are perceived culturally as a threat because of the change it forces, and the bank reacts like an immune system attacking a virus.

Procurement workload

It's likely that when you first meet a FinTech the procurement and legal teams will drive contracting. In that case bank procurement departments will tend to favour contracts that have previously been drawn up internally in the bank, because new contracts will need much longer approval times. The drawback is that in many cases an IT contract with service level agreements for technology partners (like Oracle, IBM or Temenos) will be massive overkill for a small startup working with you on integrating, say, voice AI technology. Internet security compliance and audit requirements, joint IP ownership claw back rights for project failures—or, in the case of termination, 80 pages of legalese—and so forth are all going to be massively problematic for a small VC-backed FinTech who is just out of beta with their technology and has no in-house legal team.

A 30–40 person FinTech operation shouldn't be spending months or tens of thousands on legal paperwork so some internal stakeholder at an incumbent bank gets to cover their derrière. That is an insanely bad use of FinTech resources. Simpler contracts and more checkpoints are critical.

Also keep in mind that in many cases when a FinTech comes to you with their technology stack, it will likely be in the cloud. What that means is that cyber security, uptime performance, data storage and residency, will all be the domain of the cloud partner. Ensure that you don't simply pass on legal work to a FinTech requiring them to act as an intermediary with, say, Amazon Web Services on your behalf.

Technology chasm

Of course, there's going to be a technology gap—that's why you are collaborating with the FinTech in the first place. Make sure that there are clear expectations about how this gap will be filled. Does the FinTech have an API-ready solution? Are you required to build to their API, or will the FinTech have to modify or extend their API to integrate with the bank's existing IT stack? Is work needed to prepare for the partnership just so your internal bank team can meet the data provisioning and formats requirements of the FinTech? We had a major bank out of Europe opt out of a strategic investment in Moven because their team said our technology stack was too different from their own—instead it could have been an opportunity to observe and learn.

FinTechs often have more up-to-date technology knowledge around the core components they're using. Bank IT departments are not used to being behind their IT service providers on technology—normally, it is more of a licensing process than a technology learning curve. Expect that in a collaboration your internal team may be learning from the FinTech, and the learning curve may be steep. Finding a CTO or internal project manager that isn't precious about the technology stack the bank has already built is going to be a challenge—especially when it comes to stuff like the cloud, blockchain and AI, where banks are clearly playing catch up.

Both teams need to strongly focus on outcomes.

Too short-term ROI focused

One of the cultural reasons FinTechs and banks clash is that a FinTech has likely grown up with venture capital funding designed to give the startup some time to develop and test their product in market. Profitability is not a strong consideration, even for mature FinTechs like Ant Financial—the focus is predominantly on growth. For bank technology projects, however, ROI (return on investment) horizons tend to be fairly short—maybe even a 18–24 month payback. This is going to be a source of contention.

In the medium term, much of the capabilities FinTechs are deploying right now don't have a clear path to profitability, but are essential to being able to provide differentiated financial services experiences on the technology layer. Short-term ROI focus to underwrite an internal business case could very well derail collaboration efforts before they start. This doesn't mean banks have to just write off large investments in new technologies. It does mean, however, that ROI might need to be measured by different key metrics that are softer than the typical IT project. These metrics might include brand equity from association with the FinTech, acquisition of new skills on an emerging platform, out-of-the-box thinking capabilities, or the ability to experiment with a new technology to establish feasibility.

Regulatory soundness

A FinTech comes to you and has a cloud-based AI service that will allow you to do contextual recommendations and cross-sell offers via voice and mobile, with real-time fulfilment for onboarding. What do you do? Technically this ticks all the right innovation boxes, but depending on which country you are in, and which central bank regulator you are licensed by, this FinTech may be in breach of a range of current regulations. You may not be able to deploy in the cloud, data residency might be an issue, and the regulator may still require a wet signature for a customer accepting a credit offer from your bank. This needs to be factored into the partnership.

However, regulatory compliance may not be the flashing stop sign it used to be for banks. Increasingly, FinTechs are getting adept at working with central banks and regulators to prototype new technology approaches that circumvent current regulations. Regulators are even setting up regulatory sandboxes to test these new offerings, or issuing waivers to existing regs.

Make sure that before you kill the partnership with the FinTech, or assume you can't proceed, that you at least give the regulator the option of allowing you to prototype this new technology in the field and see how customers respond to it. Maybe ask the regulator to allow you to release the technology on a limited basis to 10,000 customers initially to assess the risk to those customers.

This does require a different compliance approach from the incumbent. In the past the compliance team acted as gatekeepers, preventing the bank from doing projects like this because they would put the bank in breach. But FinTechs don't work like that. FinTechs will knock on the front door of a regulator, explain that other countries already allow them to implement their technology in their markets and that the technology has resulted in higher levels of customer satisfaction and lower incidents of fraud, and that this might be a justification for allowing a trial of that technology in your home market. This approach is part of the culture shift that incumbents are increasingly having to grapple with. The answer is no longer, "No, the regulator won't allow that." It's not "Let's talk to the regulator."

If you can't beat them, join them

Clearly the atmosphere is changing when it comes to bank collaboration with FinTechs. A few years ago, both FinTechs and banks were talking about the competitive landscape and "who was going to win" the fight. Today, there are ever more announcements of collaborative efforts. Certainly when it comes to technologies like the blockchain, partnerships are the norm, not the exception.

The smarter incumbents are now recognising that a "not made here" philosophy is unlikely to serve them well in the fast-moving and diverse ecosystem of FinTech innovation. Instead, they are shopping around for partnerships with the most innovative FinTechs. Events like Money 20/20, Finovate, Fintech Stage and Next Money are increasingly becoming platforms for this type of speed dating service between FinTechs and incumbent banks. But once a potential courtship is deemed possible, that's when the real work begins.

Banks must do a lot of work just to make collaboration efforts viable. It starts with a culture change in the bank, but it includes the fact that even the budgeting process and allocation of funds is going through a sea change. In 2016 banks invested around $5 billion in FinTech deals and collaboration, but $50 billion internally on their own systems and innovation projects[19]. If you want to be a digital-first organisation, that ratio is definitely going to have to change.

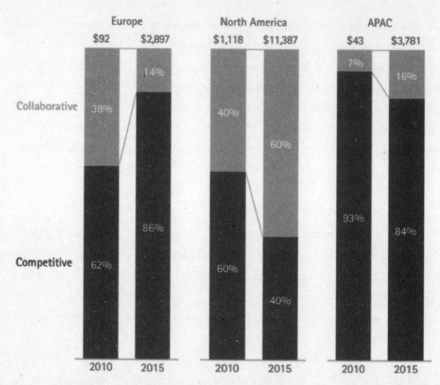

Figure 7: Collaborative versus competitive FinTech investments by region ($M) (Source: Accenture analysis of CB Insights data).

Lastly, strategy is going to be key. If you're a bank making $1 billion a year in net margins, when is the right time to start cannibalising your branch business in favour of a digital-first onboarding process? Organisationally, what is the impact of that? Partnering with a FinTech is going to deliver you capabilities that are quite possibly in direct opposition to your current lines of business in respect to distribution and fulfilment. And yet, if you don't act, you know there is another bank and a dozen FinTechs already deploying that technology in the market. Damned if you do, damned if you don't.

The reality is that whatever your strategy, it's pretty clear that agile, creative thinking is going to be essential in staying ahead of the digital curve when it comes to the evolution of financial services. In that case, your best bet is to work with the disruptive end of the market, rather than try to compete. Your best bet is to experiment with new technologies using a skilled, fresh set of eyes, rather than to try to reinvent the wheel internally when you know it will simply cost you more money and more time than through a partnership.

Yes, the time is now for collaboration and partnership between these two worlds. The benefits certainly outweigh the risks.

Endnotes

1   Source: KPMG Pulse of FinTech Report (2018).

2   Source: *Market Insider, Business Insider.*

3   Source: Bloomberg/Mercury News—"Venture capital hits $84 billion, highest since dot com boom", 11 January 2018.

4   I recognise as a FinTech founder that I may be biased in my view of where FinTech fits in the future of financial services.

5   I'm talking to you Zelle®, HSBC PayMe®, etc.

6   Think Metcalf's law, Gilder's law and technology adoption diffusion rolled into one inexorable wave of consumer adoption of new technologies, social media and messaging platforms.

7   Sorry, the UK's Metro Bank doesn't really count.

8   Source: British Bankers Association survey 2016.

9   Source: Mitek Scorecard—UK bank accounts: a survey of true digital capabilities in customer on-boarding (December 2017).

10 Source: The Digital Banking Report, 10 July 2017.

11 Source: KPMG Report: "A new landscape—challenger banking annual results" (2016).

12 At the time of writing, the OCC FinTech charter lies legally tied up in Trump administration and various state banking commission challenges.

13 Source: EY's FinTech Adoption Index 2017.

14 Source: McKinsey—"FinTech: Challenges and Opportunities", 2016.

15 See "The Future of FinTech and Banking: Digitally Disrupted or Reimagined?" Report from Accenture.

16 Source: Various—McKinsey, EY, The Financial Brand, Celent, Forrester Research.

17 Full disclosure—I sit on the board of CFSI.

18 Source: Mayer Brown—"The ABC of FinTech Survey", November 2016; a survey of 70 financial institutions in the UK.

19 "IT Spending in Banking, A Global Perspective", Celent, February 2015; "Digital Disruption: How FinTech is Forcing Banking to a Tipping Point", Citi, March 2016.

FEATURE
Why Banks Should Care about FinTech
By Spiros Margaris

We are still in the early stages of how the FinTech industry will impact the financial sector, regardless of any hype that might suggest otherwise. FinTech startups and tech giants will change the banking industry in ways that we could never have imagined, especially when we look back in just 10 years' time. A FinTech tsunami is heading towards the financial industry's shore, so banks should diligently prepare for the vast and disruptive changes to come. Most banks have historically been resistant to this message, but it is happening regardless. The reality is that most incumbents that aren't in the top 100 global banks are already years behind the average FinTech in their specific domain.

We've all heard the frog parable that basically says that a frog that is put in a pot of boiling water will jump right out of it. However, if the frog is placed in the pot with a comfortable water temperature and then the water is heated up slowly to boil, it will not realise the danger of likely death until it is too late. Although science does not corroborate the so-called "frog experiment", it serves as an excellent metaphor for the risk that organisations face by not adapting to the new environment created by technology-led banking experiences.

Future scenario-planning is a core skill for incumbent banks in particular. They should ask themselves: are the changes we're seeing in the experience layer and core building blocks of financial services led by FinTechs the boiling water in this metaphor? Or are there incumbents smart enough to realise the danger and act accordingly—in this case, adapting to the new standards in day-to-day banking created by FinTech startups?

The broader evidence suggests that while we have seen some banks taking steps towards capitalising on what the FinTech startups or technology leaders have to offer, such as cutting-edge technology implementation, innovative solutions and an excellent user experience, not enough are taking the threat seriously. The typical posture of the industry at large has been to see FinTechs as competitive threats. That is a pity, because I believe the FinTech industry can significantly assist incumbents in addressing their legacy systems limitations and, more importantly, their legacy thinking.

One positive effect coming from the FinTech wave is that it is certainly now easier for those inside a bank organisation who want technology to be as cutting edge as possible to get attention from senior management. Slowly but surely, the injection of innovations from the FinTech space has given way to top bank management feeling the urgency to stay competitive. These examples are becoming more common daily: such as Wells Fargo's Greenhouse, Chase's Finn and Emirates NBD's Liv apps in response to the likes of Moven and Monzo; or HSBC's PayMe P2P app and EasyPay in Hong Kong as a response to WeChat and Alipay's dominance there. There is also Schwab, Fidelity and Vanguard's own robo-advisor efforts in response to Betterment, Wealthfront and Personal Capital. In most cases, though, incumbents still lag three-to-four years behind the innovations created by leading FinTechs; and even after they launch, these same FinTechs remain ahead in terms of design innovations, features and thinking. The water is still boiling.

It makes sense, then, that partnerships between banks and FinTechs should be far more common today than they are. Some incumbents have experimented with the opportunities FinTech partnerships can offer them, but statistically this is true only for a handful of banks globally. Is this a question of trying to figure out how to work with each other as partners, given both bring different strengths and advantages to such a partnership?

FinTech companies usually have a faster and cheaper innovation process and are extremely customer-focused, qualities that are out of reach of probably all banks today. On the other side, the advantages banks bring to a possible partnership, such as revenue (for the FinTech), customers (scale) and brand are also extremely compelling. That is why I believe we are about to see a wave of collaboration between FinTechs and banks that will accelerate industry change. For those banks still resistant to such opportunities, they are going to find themselves falling further behind the changes in the industry.

One of the primary reasons the banking industry is being forced to adapt to this new world is plainly that customers are increasingly comparing offerings by banks to what FinTech startups or tech giants have to offer. It starts with simple things like: why can't I open my account through your app instead of a branch? Why does your app look so dated compared with these challenger banks? And why hasn't your internet banking design changed in a decade? It is clearly reminiscent of how Apple set the standard for design, user experience and innovation for all their competitors by focusing on delighting the customer. In the same way, FinTech startups have successfully redefined what the customer demands from a bank. FinTechs have set the bar for the user interface much higher than incumbent banks.

The solution is patently obvious. The smartest banks will increasingly see that FinTech startups should serve as virtual innovation hubs, which they can take advantage of by partnering with or acquiring some of them. Accelerator, incubation, innovation and hackathon initiatives by banks simply do not provide the desired effect of becoming more innovative, often because the culture of the bank does not allow innovative ideas to be adopted at the same rate as with a FinTech. However, these programs can be used to gain insight into FinTech offerings, and better judge the right FinTechs to partner with or acquire.

Due to their operational complexity, compliance constraints, legacy systems and thinking and just the organisation's sheer size, incumbents are by nature slow to adapt. Another reason for banks moving slowly might be the assumption that their older customers with money do not care about the difference, for instance, between a cutting-edge banking experience and the current state of the bank's technology. That would be a flawed and dangerous assumption, because we clearly see older people use cutting-edge technology like iPads or smartphones in their daily life. Regardless of age, demand for cutting-edge banking technology, reduced friction in financial services and best-in-class user experience will be a bar set by the success of FinTech players.

When you are delivering hundreds of millions of dollars or more in net margin each year, it is understandable why banks are hesitant to cannibalise their business model by more aggressively applying FinTech operationally, and that they would rather see it done slowly by the startups and act as a so-called *fast follower* when it succeeds. Statistically this lag is resulting in gradual (and sometimes dramatic) shifts in market share[1]. Thus, the better decision may be for the banks to cannibalise their own business, staying in control of the process and their destiny. In contrast to the startups, banks have the brand, customers and money to feed new business units, and therefore to increase the likelihood of success.

However, at the same time, banks need to address and manage the fundamental disadvantages they carry of lack of execution speed and focus. Ultimately, it still comes back to the fact that if you want fast, cheap innovation within your bank, you should be looking to change the culture internally to leverage more effectively off technology partnerships.

Whether your bank ends up as the frog in this scenario is to a large extent in the hands of its leadership. For many incumbents the frog metaphor will play out in the worst way possible because they failed to see an industry being reshaped by emerging players, imagining that there was enough momentum in their old business model to ride it out. Their smarter competitors will jump out of the hot water to aggressively pursue partnerships with the FinTech agitators and technology innovators, recognising the boiling water as one of the greatest opportunities the financial industry has experienced in the last 700 years. Do you want to be the frog or the boiling water? Be the water, my friend…

Endnotes

1   For example, in China mobile payments and micro-loans.

Fast startup versus slow corporate? The word "corporate" itself is now often used as an adjective to describe a type or mode of company that, as a FinTech startup, you don't want to emulate. CEOs of startups often say: "We don't want to go all corporate".

So what do we understand by the word corporate? For many people, when they hear the word corporate it implies: slow moving, bureaucratic, potentially out of date. Not words that we associate with the dynamic FinTech companies that we read about in the press. However, there are two thoughts on this that may give us a clue into what is driving the optical differential in growth, and they both stem from one word: "legacy".

Legacy, the gift or transfer of value from the past to the present time, the notion that value is being created and built upon.

Legacy, the term used to describe outdated systems and processes that are no longer current and competitive.

So when we are considering a large corporate, we do have to view it with both definitions in mind. They have, by their very nature, demonstrated an ability to create a scaled, profitable business that has endured for decades, serving multi-generational customers, returning money to shareholders and with a capacity to invest for the future. The legacy of value.

With this we also typically see an organisation that has its foundations in technology, culture and organisational design that is from a different time. It has an iterative approach to product, technology and organisational systems—which makes it very difficult to transform across all of these dimensions.

When we look at the growth of FinTechs, what we see is often the development of a business from a first principles basis, and this is true across all business functions, and in all of the inherent organisational processes within the business. It has the ability to create an organisation to fit the current times, the current challenges and to develop current solutions. In all elements of the business, whether that is the design of the product or service, there is no requirement to keep in mind the management of the existing business or customers. They are not constrained by the maintenance of existing revenue streams and the management and migration of existing customers. They are the notional blank sheet of paper. But hasn't this always been the case for startups?

And the answer is, yes, it has been—but with a difference. We now live in a time where technology has fundamentally, seismically shifted two of the biggest barriers to entries, or to put it another way, "moats around the incumbent's castle". This is the ability to create product, and the ability to distribute it.

This technologically-driven and -enabled innovation capability, coupled with an organisation that is using first principles design processes, without a legacy of customers (and even employees) that it needs to consider, has an enormous advantage: speed. Products are envisaged, prototyped, tested, amended, refined, and launched in timescales that may be faster than a large corporate. So is it all down to the technology? Well, it is in part; but there appears to be another, potentially even more impactful, difference between the fastest-growing FinTechs and the incumbent corporates: culture.

In creating an organisation from scratch, there is an ability to develop a culture that itself is designed to operate at a pace, shape and even a method that mirrors the technological design capabilities of our times. Leveraging agile collaboration tools such as Slack/Trello, in an environment where diaries are managed months in advance and involve complex steering committee and matrix alignment critical for all decisions, is an anachronism. This is why so many large corporates that are trying to transform their innovation capabilities are struggling—the legacy of the culture plays a very large role.

So we know that we have the ingredients for fast-paced growth in a first-principles based, technologically-driven startup. With the right leadership, culture and persistence they have an ability to develop product at pace that is not constrained by the existing norms of operating a scaled business. The ability to leverage technology to take these products to market is the key difference over the last 10 years. A FinTech app can be downloaded directly to one of millions of individual consumers in a matter of seconds from a device that fits in your pocket. Imagine how inconceivable it would have been 20 years ago for a company like Instagram, which had at the time 13 employees, to take a product to 30 million people? The distribution model of mobile download has a symbiotic relationship with social media-sharing capabilities on the very same platform. The marketplace has been levelled at least, and in the early stages may be even tilted in the direction of the startup.

But a word of caution. Firstly, our image is distorted, the unicorns are getting a disproportionate share of voice. This of course makes sense—the storytelling of the company from the garage becoming a global mega-brand is highly compelling. And conversely, the story of yet another startup failing to achieve a funding round is not.

Secondly, we are seeing a regulatory environment that is struggling to accommodate for, support and govern a range of rapidly emerging payment and financial services companies. As the FinTech startups hit true scale they are entering a phase where the incumbents are able to play to their own strengths. So the transition from a high-growth, even-scaled FinTech to a company that has served the test of time is a tricky one. The giant financial services corporates have mainly been able to weather the storm of economic downturn, and create a true legacy across generations.

And that leads us to maybe the final conclusion, and one that we see both the challenging entrants and the legacy incumbents embracing: partnership. Allowing the FinTechs to leverage their natural capabilities in terms of pace, early stage growth, and innovation; but then integrating this into the operating models of the incumbents.

7 The Role of AI in Banking

A robot may not injure a human being or,
through inaction, allow a human being to come to harm.
—"Handbook of Robotics, 56th Edition, 2058",
Isaac Asimov (1942)

In 1942, science-fiction author Isaac Asimov introduced the world to his three laws of robotics[1]. An incredibly prescient visionary, Asimov started the world thinking about the potential challenges sentient or cognitive technology might present humanity. The number one principle for robotics may end up being: *create more value than the human you displaced*—the primary threat from AI's may well be technological unemployment as opposed to robot overlords taking over the planet and enslaving humanity. While likely neither malevolent or benevolent, AI still has the potential to do large-scale damage structurally where employment and equality are concerned.

When you look for the organisations making big bets on artificial intelligence today[2], the lists always include technology majors, but as yet we don't see many banks investing anywhere near the scale of Microsoft, Google, Apple, Alibaba, Baidu and others. Industrial players like Boeing and Tesla are by necessity making big bets on AI, so it is entirely reasonable to expect that we should see a similar scale of investments coming through financial services, healthcare, etc. However, when we look at AI in financial services right now, the lion's share of progress appears to be coming from players like Ant Financial and smaller FinTech's who are able to specialise in these emerging technologies. Ant Financial themselves is reportedly investing more than $15 billion over the next three years in AI and quantum computing[3]. On their current valuation that's about 10 percent of their total market cap.

There are a handful of banks taking steps in the right direction. JPMorgan Chase spent 16 percent of their budget on technology in 2016, $9.6 billion in total and up from $1.2 billion in 2012, but they have not disclosed how much of that specifically goes into AI research and development. Goldman Sachs Strats division (quantitive strategy/technology) now makes up around 30 percent of GS' headcount, and they've recently been seen aggressively recruiting AI specialists in machine learning (ML), artificial intelligence (AI), program management and digital product design. BofA, BBVA, Deutsche and HSBC are talking about their strategic spend in AI, while TD acquired the AI startup Layer 6 in January of 2018, driven by Rizwan Khalfan, their chief digital and payments officer.

> The ability to anticipate the needs and preferences of individual customers doesn't exist in banking today, but will be a requirement going forward...There's such little talent and expertise in the AI space, and for us to be able to partner with organisations like Layer 6, who are considered both best-in-class from a research and a pragmatic perspective, is really the secret sauce.
>
> —Rizwan Khalfan, TD Bank Group

Rizwan points us directly at the core problem for the industry at large. AI is an entirely new skill set and banks don't have any real expertise in the space and, frankly, are a long way from having world-class capabilities that could compete with the tech majors. Given AI is not a core capability, and banks are starting behind the eight ball on both budget and talent, it's pretty clear that strategic partnerships, acquisitions and such will be essential.

The advantage of tech majors is that they have both the capital and technology pedigree to be able to focus on AI. FinTech's are already built from the ground up around technology, they have talent that is more easily adapted to AI R&D and they don't have process, policy or legacy that could slow them down. All this adds up to the likelihood of banks slipping further behind on AI over time. Thus, it is likely that when AI starts to operationally impact financial services, incumbents will have far less control over the outcome than, say, the impact of regulatory change or customer behaviour might have on AI.

When discussing AI in banking or financial services, it's important to define what exactly we're talking about. Many bankers make the mistake of thinking of AI as something that is a long way off, and when it comes it won't be focused on banking. These types of algorithms, which allow for leaps in cognitive understanding for machines, have only been possible with the application of massive data processing and computing power in recent years.

Talking about AI in general today is like people talking about Tokyo like it's synonymous with Asia. It belies a misunderstanding about different types of AI, and how and where AI will likely impact banking. For example, we're not going to need a bipedal android with artificial general intelligence to eliminate a plethora of banking jobs. Even today, with nascent developments in AI, we already have the foundations for material changes in the way we staff financial services over the coming decade.

In the 2000s, UBS moved their trading floor out to its headquarters in Stamford, Connecticut. The trading floor housed more than 5,000 traders holding pride of place in their 700,000 square-foot building. Today the trading floor stands empty, abandoned as a result of automation of the trading arm of UBS' business. In quantifying the rate of change, Goldman has found that today one computer engineer can replace four or five traders. Today one-third of Goldman's staff are already computer engineers as they speed up automation internally.

Goldman and UBS use complex algorithms that mimic what a human trader used to do—simple machine intelligence with human equivalent decision-making capability for a specific task. One good example of this is the project that UBS and Deloitte created in 2016—a simple, automated program for dealing with their clients' post-trade allocation requests. The system does an automated review of emails sent by clients detailing how they want to allocate large block trades across funds, then processes and executes the required transfers. This takes the automated system seconds to execute, reducing from the hour or so it would have taken a human investment banker previously. We simply programmed an algorithm to replicate what a human trader used to do.

The shifts in capability here really centre around the principle that we are no longer coding a set of rules in an IF-THEN-THAT type syntax into computer code. We build algorithms, databases and learning engines that can observe behaviour, and learn to act accordingly. We are building computers that learn. All we need to do at that point is feed in the data— of which we have plenty. Just ask Facebook.

AI will essentially evolve through three distinct phases[4]:

- **Algos and Machine Intelligence**—Rudimentary machine intelligence or algorithm-based cognition that replaces some elements of human thinking, decision-making or processing for specific tasks. Neural networks or algorithms that can make human-equivalent decisions for very specific functions, and perform better than humans on a benchmark basis. This does not prohibit the intelligence from having machine learning or cognition capabilities so that it can learn new tasks or process new information outside of its initial programming. In fact, many machine intelligences already have this capability. Examples include: Google self-driving car, high-frequency trading (HFT) algorithms, facial recognition software, insurance assessor apps using image recognition, and credit risk assessment algorithms (eg sesame credit).

- **Artificial General Intelligence**—A human-equivalent machine intelligence and learning system that not only passes the Turing test and responds as a human would, but can also mimic human decision-making. It will likely also process non-logic or informational cues such as emotion, tone of voice, facial expression and nuances that currently a living intelligence could (can your dog tell if you are angry or sad?). Essentially, such an AI would be capable of successfully performing any intellectual task that a human being could. Examples include: Sophia (Hanson Robotics) and Singularity.io[5].

- **Hyperintelligence** (Strong AI)—A machine intelligence or collection of strong machine intelligences (what do you call a group of AIs?) that have surpassed human intelligence on an individual or collective basis to the extent that they can understand and process concepts that humans cannot understand.

We don't need to wait another 10, 15 or 30 years to see this happen, and the Turing test is fairly meaningless as a measure of the ability of machine intelligence to disrupt a bank in terms of its day-to-day operations.

The range of impact of artificial intelligence is going to be broad. IBM's developerWorks team has an excellent primer on the advancements that have been made in artificial intelligence over the years, and how these are classified by the industry[6]. Terminology like cognitive computing, machine intelligence and artificial intelligence are not interchangeable, but do relate to the broader developments in AI that we're seeing evolve today.

To simplify the chart on the next page, essentially there are two broad areas where AI will impact financial services. These are the interaction/conversational AI layer between the customer and the institution, and internally from a process perspective—anywhere we currently have a human checklist, a transaction or activity against compliance, risk or credit assessment rules, wherever we take instructions and apply those to an application, buy or sell order, or wherever we have a legal or contractual relationship to execute against. Any process a human can learn within a bank that doesn't require strong dependency on social cues, an algorithm will be able to learn and replace that human in short order.

AI will massively affect marketing; it will radically change customer service expectations; it will dominate our ability to engage customers on a behavioural basis; it will replace huge swathes of process-driven jobs; and will revolutionise the way we view and operationalise risk in the organisation today. In fact, just taking that last element, it is entirely possible that risk management in financial services will become the exclusive domain of AI within the next 10 years. But this is not going to happen from within an AI department in the bank, not even from the IT department. This is a systemic attack on the core of what we consider the operational engine of modern financial services today.

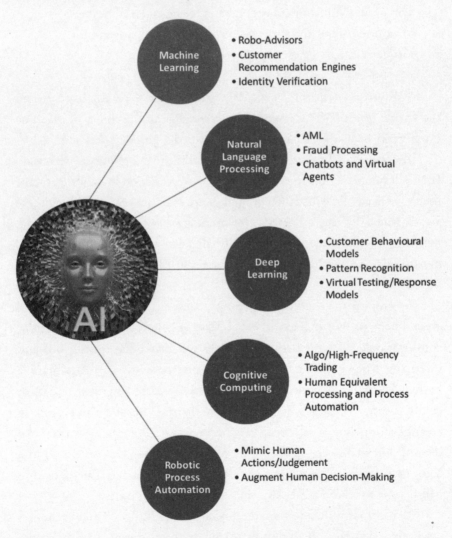

Figure 1: Various AI disciplines as applied to financial services.

This may sound like hype, but the worst case is that banks have three to five years before they have to start firing staff because of AI's impact; and the best case is 7–10 years. In January 2017, a McKinsey & Company study found that about 30 percent of tasks in 60 percent of occupations could be computerised; while last year, the Bank of England's chief economist said that 80 million US jobs and 15 million UK jobs might be taken over by robots[7].

Of course, not all jobs are created equally. In 2013, a highly-cited study by Oxford University academics, called "The Future of Employment"[8], examined 702 common occupations and found that some finance jobs— bank tellers, loan officers, tax preparers and insurance claim assessors—are more at risk than others, including economists, financial analysts, financial modellers and statisticians.

Deep learning: How computers mimic the human brain

Central to the revolution in artificial intelligence is not computers that are programmed, but computers that learn. But how do computers learn?

It all comes back to processing inputs (data) and mimicking neurons or the brain. In *The Economist* of 6 May 2017, data was characterised as the new oil of the emerging digital economy. Well, if data is the crude oil equivalent, databases, blockchains and data warehouses are the drilling rigs, and deep learning is the refinery that turns that oil into other useful products. Deep learning is at the heart of the emerging AI boom.

Deep learning neural networks have been architected to use the same basic learning principles that occur in the human brain. The human brain consists of special cells called neurons, which are composed of several parts, including brain fibres known as dendrites. As you learn, these brain fibres grow. The fibres connect your brain cells to one another at contact points called synapses. The larger your brain fibres grow, and the more brain cells they connect, the more information can be stored in your brain. When you reinforce learning over time or practice skills you've learned, the dendrites in your brain grow stronger, forming a fatty tissue layer and doubling connections between key neurons or memories.

In deep learning networks, we've created artificial neurons called *perceptrons*. These artificial neurons are the brain child of Frank Rosenblatt of the Cornell Aeronautical Laboratory, who designed these way back in 1957. Initially designed for image recognition, the first perceptrons were hard-wired logic circuits, and not the software-based code they are today.

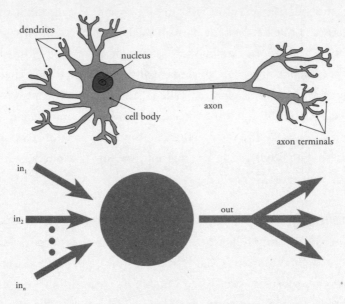

Figure 2: Deep learning neural networks use artificial neurons called perceptrons (Image credit: Christoph Berger).

In true computing terms the perceptron works with inputs applied to an algorithm as a binary classifier as it learns. For example, if the algorithm is being used to learn to distinguish between a cat and a dog, the algorithm applies varies vectors (inputs) against a bias to create a linear decision boundary. Simply stated, the algorithm filters inputs to produce a one or a zero output, but over time the algorithm can adapt its bias (shifting the linear boundary) as it learns to produce more and more accurate results. The capability to correctly identity the difference between an image of a cat and a dog gets better and more precise over time.

Historically, if we talked about how humans differentiate from technology, it was always about our ability as humans to recognise patterns, think creatively, understand abstract concepts, etc. By teaching machines to learn, it's clear that our ability to recognise patterns or to reason on things is no longer the clear advantage it once was.

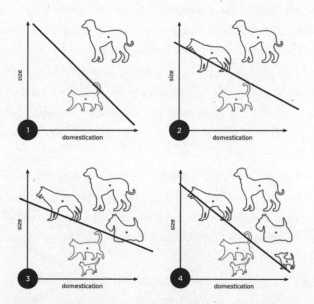

Figure 3: Perceptron updating its linear boundary as more vectors are added (Image credit: Wikipedia).

There are a variety of techniques used in deep learning, such as single versus multi-layer perceptrons, backpropagation networks, alternate step-functions and linear vectoring, but you don't need to be an AI expert to understand that AI is already starting to impact broad swathes of society.

We are already losing out to machines

In the European Union, United Kingdom, United States, United Arab Emirates, Singapore, Hong Kong, Australia and many other countries today, if you enter a port with a biometric capable passport, you'll have the option to go through an e-gate or similar. It might be a fairly obvious statement, but the reason for this is simple—computers today do a much better job at recognising a face or verifying your identity than a human customs officer ever could. Research shows that facial recognition software is 15–20 times more accurate at identifying a customer than a typical face-to-face interaction[9]. A fact that would indicate face-to-face bank account opening is no longer safe, incidentally. Statistically based on software comparators, it is probably the single riskiest thing a bank could do in this day and age.

China has developed a national identity database that can identify any one of the 1.4 billion Chinese citizens via software in two to three seconds[10]. While many in the West might scream about the civil rights issues associated with such policies, the fact is we've been seeing this sort of tech fictionalised in movies and so forth for decades now. Most modern policing organisations already have this capability, and the technology is maturing for a very simple reason. Governments can trust this tech to work better than human eyeballs.

How many of us would want our borders compromised by inferior technology today? Wouldn't we all want the best chance of catching a criminal or identity thief? In these scenarios, it's pretty straightforward to prove that algorithms, biometrics and identity databases can consistently outperform human workers.

In airports the applications are straightforward. Airlines like JetBlue and Finnair are trialling facial recognition systems to bypass checking your boarding pass at the gate. Before long you may be able to enter the airport, board your flight and pass through customs at the other end just by using your face. The golden age of travel may return simply thanks to biometric tech powered by an algorithm.

So what are we to make of the insistence by those banks and regulators that to open a bank account you must have a human physically present themselves in a branch? In the light of broader trends in identity verification, a requirement for a human bank officer to facilitate account opening is an anachronism. Very soon, based on both cost and performance, humans won't be competitive when it comes to the front line on the basis of identity verification alone. If your business is built on in-branch customer acquisition, you will find that AI capabilities in general are a big threat to your primary acquisition approach.

Some of the broad areas where artificial neural networks are already outperforming humans include:
- Image and pattern recognition
- Board and video games
- Voice generation and recognition

- Art and style imitation
- Prediction
- Website design/modification

Between 2009 and 2016, machine intelligent HFT algorithms accounted for 49–73 percent of all US equity trading volume, and 38 percent in the EU in 2016. On 6 May 2010, the Dow Jones plunged to its largest intraday points loss, only to recover that loss within minutes. After a five-month investigation, the US Securities and Exchange Commission (SEC) and the Commodities Future Trading Commission (CFTC) issued a joint report that concluded that HFT had contributed significantly to the volatility of the so-called "flash" crash. A large futures exchange, CME Group, said in its own investigation that HFT algorithms probably stabilised the market and reduced the impact of the crash.

For an industry that has developed trading into a fine art over the last 100 years, HFT algorithms represent a significant departure from the trading rooms of Goldman Sachs, UBS and Credit Suisse. The algorithms themselves have departed significantly from typical human behaviour. Very different behaviour and decision-making have been observed when analysing HFT trading patterns. What has led to this shift?

Perhaps it is the fact that HFT has neither the biases that human traders might have (for instance, staying in an asset class position longer than advised because the individual trader or asset manager likes the stock or the industry) nor the same ethical basis for making a decision. While some might argue that Wall Street isn't exactly a bastion of ethics, the fact is, an HFT algorithm simply doesn't have an ethical angle for decision-making (unless those skills have been programmed in). Those deep-learning algorithms have created different linear boundaries from humans doing the same job.

While HFT has been pioneered by the big trading companies, and has certainly helped them, what impact are algorithms having on investment portfolios and wealth management?

Robo-advisors, robo-everything

As with the other trends we've seen in the Bank 4.0 world, the first movers in the robo-advisor space were the FinTech startups. Betterment launched in 2010, and for CEO Jon Stein, "one of the most satisfying results of the work we started seven years ago is seeing the entire industry change". That change is a tacit acceptance that human advice is a marginal value add, and when it comes to portfolio performance over the medium term, robo-advisors may offer an opportunity for rebalancing and optimisation consistent with your return expectations that humans won't efficiently be able to match.

I've met Jon numerous times, interviewed him on my radio show, and I like the fact that he's largely a quiet achiever. You don't hear a lot from Jon in the media for months at a time, and he lets the results of Betterment speak for themselves. I am also a big fan of Betterment's startup story, as the first robo-advisory firm, because it demonstrates his tenacity.

Jon Stein and his roommate, Sean Owen (a Google software engineer), started building Betterment's platform back in 2007. Stein taught himself to code in order to build the early prototypes behind the platform. However, starting a business in a highly regulated industry that would require licensing and other compliance-related competencies required more than technical competency. Before starting Betterment, Stein had attended weekly poker games with Eli Broverman (circa 2003–2004). While Eli had come out of those poker games better off than himself (according to Stein), it was a relationship that allowed Stein to tap Broverman, a securities attorney, for help with the startup in the early stages. In 2007, while Stein was still studying at Colombia University's Business School, he and Eli met up for lunch at a Dominican restaurant on the Upper West Side and sketched out a plan to move forward with the ugly regulatory stuff that would otherwise have held Betterment back.

By 2008, the small team, including Jon's girlfriend (his wife today) doing graphic design, were working on funding and the launch platform. The licensing and business formation followed in 2009, and then in 2010 they launched at TechCrunch, with Chris Sacca (of Shark Tank fame), levelling some pretty tough criticism their way: "I worry that it's too simple.

People don't always trust it. People expect a little bewilderment that gives it credibility. This starts to feel a little like a toy."

Today that toy manages more than $10 billion in AuM (assets under management), and Betterment's growth is estimated at around 106 percent annually, although it appears to be slowing as they get larger (it was around 300 percent just three years ago). Stein says he is aiming for $1 trillion in AuM, so they have big aspirations and more growth to go. To reach that goal, however, there will need to be a substantial shift in behaviours around investing.

Today, we're at a pivot point for personal investing. In the past the assumption was you'd need both *advice* and *financial literacy* in order to be able to successfully invest as an individual. That's a problem today as the data shows that financial literacy amongst millennials is actually significantly worse than that of their forebears[11]. A survey back in 2015 conducted by Bank of America U.S. Trust found that just 47 percent of multimillionaires aged 18–34 use a financial advisor[12]. For those millennials that aren't multimillionaires, the statistics are even worse.

Assuming that millennials will be both literate enough to invest and seek out human advisors in the future is a big assumption. The emergence of automated investing tools like Stash, Digit and Acorns, and the development of robo-advisory tools, seems more likely to fill this gap in skills and behaviour.

When doing research for this chapter, I tried to find portfolio return comparisons between human advisors and robo-funds. From a moderate-risk portfolio perspective, when I used to work with private bankers and wealth advisors back in the day, we'd look for 10–12 percent annual returns as a safe assumption on a longer-term investment horizon. Typically, this would be a mix of equity and income producing bonds.

Robo-advisors today are performing right in that range of expected returns. Barron's conducted a survey of robo-advisors over the 2016 calendar year and found annual returns for the better-performing robos were in the 11–12 percent range[13]. That's also consistent with the average annualised return of the S&P500 Index, which was 11.69 percent from 1973 to 2016[14]. BI Intelligence forecasts that robo-advisors will manage around \$1 trillion of AuM by 2020, and around \$4.6 trillion by 2022[15]. As a trend, by 2030 we would expect robo to dominate the mass market investment industry.

On a portfolio performance basis then, the difference between a robo-advisor and a human-based asset management firm are negligible. Certainly, if you are willing to take greater risks with your portfolio, or you are investing larger amounts in more diversified pools or structured products, then you may find that a human team can perform with higher results. However, the firms and advisors that produce those results typically require a minimum investment that is out of reach of 99 percent of the population. Thus, it seems entirely reasonable that robo-advice will come to be seen as one of the greatest tools for large-scale affluent wealth management since the creation of "premier" banking. Accessible, automated portfolio management without the friction.

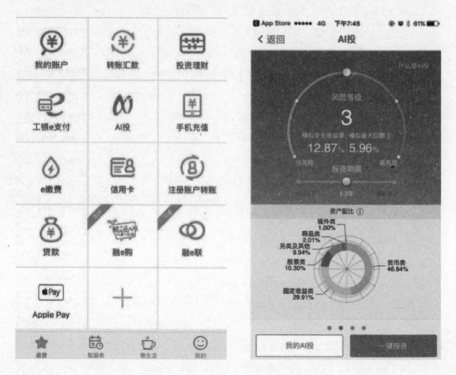

Figure 4: ICBC's Rong-e line of products, including AI投 or robo-investment.

Seeing this trend emerge, ICBC in China has made a big bet on AI and robo-advice. Their robo-advisor tool doesn't require a traditional risk profile questionnaire to get started. It learns from your investment style along the way and teaches you how to invest in your optimal range for your level or risk tolerance and your return expectations.

ICBC's AI投, or AI invest, represents what is certain to become a baseline capability for wealth management capabilities moving forward. It also will fundamentally change the legal and compliance requirements we have around "risk" for basic investment or wealth management. For the last three years, every time I've done an annual "risk" review with my bank in Hong Kong, HSBC, they've used a telephone to record our conversation so there is an audible record of me accepting the risk conditions. Each time I go through my annual review (which generally takes about an hour), at least 75 percent of the time is spent on compliance-related activities. They do all of this for regulatory and legal reasons.

With AI managing risk tolerance and optimising your portfolio for your required investment horizon and return expectations, the whole regulatory process required by the FSA, SEC, etc involving signing a piece of paper or a telephone system legally recording my formal response to a risk tolerance questionnaire will be quickly undermined. Human advisors will just look slow, clunky and bound by friction. Robo-advising will quickly become the benchmark on experience, and then on asset management performance. Regulators will be forced to adapt too.

For those of you still sceptical about robo-advice generally, it would be helpful to step back and see where AI-based advice fits from a technology perspective, rather than simply trying to articulate it as humans versus machines.

A bank account that is smarter than your bank

If you can imagine technology like Siri, Google Home or Alexa maturing in the next five years and being able to order you not just socks[16], but a pizza, and book Uber rides, flights, restaurant reservations and doctor's appointments. Once commerce is integrated into our tech so seamlessly, the next obvious area to tackle is day-to-day money interactions and financial advice.

If you think this sounds like a science fiction story, you are in for a big shock. Remember that back during the dot-com boom (or bubble), the majority of non-tech press was extremely sceptical about the effect e-commerce would have on retail businesses. Today online shopping dominates choice, with many categories of retail showing 50 percent or more of sales are either influenced by or initiated via the web or mobile[17]. For Christmas 2017, it was projected that almost 40 percent of all sales were done online[18], and Amazon owned the largest percentage of that. That shift in consumer behaviour has been devastating for retailers, with 7,000 stores closing in the US alone in 2017 (which is a 300 percent increase from 2016). In the UK it is expected that more than 5,000 stores will close in 2017, but that is actually down on previous years.

In markets like China, mobile commerce now dominates day-to-day retail activity for a wide range of segments, and today 75 percent of all e-commerce is mobile-led in China[19]. In parallel with a growing middle class, this mobile bias is creating slower growth in retail stores than we would have expected, given China's economic growth. The big growth is certainly centred around online portals more than physical retail, and the erosion in physical retail is plainly apparent[20].

In the near future you'll be making these everyday purchases increasingly via voice on a smart assistant built into your home and smartphone. Voice assistants are already being used to make purchases by 40 percent of millennials, with that number expected to exceed 50 percent by 2020[21].

So why is this trend towards mobile and voice commerce so important for banks to take note? If you live in a developed economy or an urban centre like Tokyo, New York or London, there's a fairly good chance that if you were ordering a take-out dinner for delivery, that you'd be using an app. If I asked you to check your balance, chances are you'd likely use the same approach. Today more than 50 percent of customers in most developed economies use their mobile for checking their balance versus any other bank channel. Twenty years ago it was dominated by ATM or phone banking. In 10 years it will be dominated by voice-based or agency-based commerce engines[22].

Consumer: "Alexa, what's my account balance?"

Consumer: "Siri, has my salary hit my account yet?"

Consumer: "Google, how long will it take me to get to the office if I leave in two hours?"

% of people using a smart speaker regularly to…

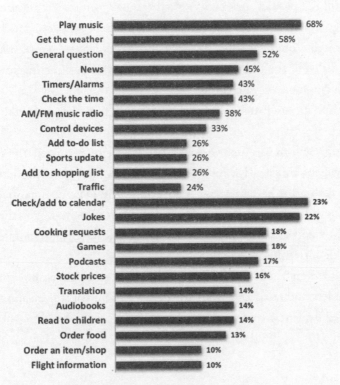

Figure 5: How people use smart speakers on a daily basis (Source: NPR and Edison Research).

Now, you would be wrong to dismiss this as simply another channel in the bank arsenal, because this is the start of actually redefining your day-to-day relationship with technology, not just your bank account. Voice has the potential to become the underpinning of day-to-day advice for you and your money, but increasingly it will be just the way you access a range of basic technology capabilities. ComScore says 50 percent of search will be voice-based by 2020, and commerce is obviously going the same way. But search leads to conversational commerce, which is more than just asking a question—it's a dialogue.

Increasingly we'll be asking our bank, via Google, Siri or Alexa, whether we can afford to go out for dinner; or, at my current rate of savings, when I can afford a deposit on a house or to buy that replacement vehicle I've been looking at; or what I need to do to pay down my credit card debt faster (if you still use plastic). Ask and ye shall receive. Voice will combine natural language, search and AI to provide answers to these questions much faster than through a branch or web channel. Primarily because voice will emphasise the utility of the bank to solve these problems, not directing you to a product to download via a channel.

The growth in capabilities behind smart assistants like Alexa is frankly unbelievable.

At current growth rates, Amazon Alexa will have approximately three million skills by September 2018, and 10 million by the end of 2018. That growth is obviously unsustainable, but it illustrates the massive potential of the technology in terms of capabilities and it does closely mirror the growth in apps on app stores over the last decade (albeit faster than mobile app store growth currently).

The capabilities go far beyond skills, they also speak to the capabilities of machines to understand us when we talk to them, or to have a conversation that is human equivalent.

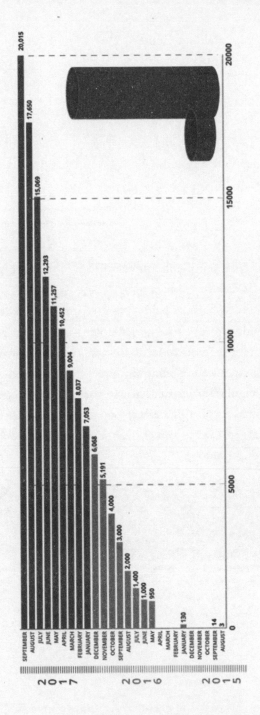

Figure 6: The growth of Amazon Alexa skills (Credit: Voicebot.ai).

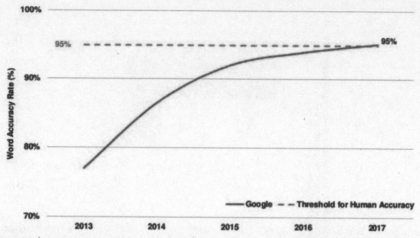

Figure 7: Google's voice recognition accuracy compared to humans' (Credit: Google).

This all adds up to one undeniable trend. The capabilities of conversational commerce on smart assistants is growing at such a rate that its impact on the way we use computing technology is greater today than the internet's potential for impact back in the year 2000. The frictionless, conversational nature of this technology will absolutely force service providers to adapt to a world where their services will have to be delivered via a voice-based technology.

Personal
•At home
•Social interaction/ integration
•Agent— Fun
•Education
•Health/Medical
•Fitness
•Music
•Entertainment
•Education
•News
•Social media
•Dating

Professional
•Agent—Personal assistant
•Agent—Professional
•News
•Research
•Social media

Shopping/ Commerce
•Agent—Commerce
•Recommendation

Services
•Travel

IoT/Technology
•Robot interface
•IoT management
•Smart home management

Figure 8: Various categories of personal AI impact emerging over the next 5–10 years.

The seamless nature of voice will force us to create compelling, frictionless experiences where advice and utility meld together. The movements toward "open banking" will give Google, Apple and Amazon amazing abilities to incorporate this data into voice assistants. You won't even need a bank app—these will likely become native services within the next 10 years.

Alexa: "You can't afford to buy a new car right now, but if you sign up for Uber today, Uber will cover half of the next two years' lease payments. You just need to agree to drive for Uber at least four hours a week. Is this something that interests you?"

Siri: "You are paying too much using a credit card today, I have other options for financing that could save you $230 per month that I could automatically link to your Apple Pay wallet. Would you like to see them?"

Voice will lead to customers learning to trust their AI assistant to recommend a day-to-day financial solution to them, rather than them going to look for it themselves. It will be like we trust Wikipedia or Google search today. We might still get an "offer" via voice, but given context and behaviour, voice interfaces might lead us in a new direction in terms of thinking about our finances that don't fit with our current banking relationship or the products the bank currently offers. For example, if your bank doesn't offer voice-based credit lines, then an offer for a new credit card might simply lose out to a bank who can do that via voice, on the basis of context alone.

Siri: "That's been taken care of. We've extended you a $730 line of credit to pay off your son's school fees for the quarter. The line of credit will be paid off monthly from your account, unless you tell me to pay it out. I can also suggest when you have enough funds to make an additional payment. Would you like me to do that?"

Frankly, if a bank doesn't start thinking about the digital bank account, accessible through voice and mobile, as their primary channel for day-to-day access and advice to their customers, then they will be caught off guard in the same way banks were when both internet and mobile apps first appeared. This time, however, the risks are much greater, because the shift from product to experiences will dramatically erode the ability to simply retrofit voice onto the existing channel middleware or bank core systems architecture.

What will you need to make voice and conversational AI work? Data. To start with...

The larger problem for banks is that Alibaba/Taobao, Tencent, Apple, Amazon, Baidu, Google, and other platforms incorporating payment gateways will often know more about their customers than the banks do. If a Beijing car dealer uses a bank debit card for a business trip to Shanghai, the bank knows what airline he or she flew, as well as the hotel and restaurants patronised. If he uses a mobile super-wallet like Alipay or Tencent WeChat, the bank knows nothing about that trip and the bank is data poor.

> "If the customer 'interface' is happening elsewhere, the bank has zero visibility over transactions," said James Lloyd, Asia-Pacific FinTech Leader at EY. "That's not a good situation to find yourself in."
> —*Wall Street Journal*, "The Cashless Society Has Arrived—Only It's in China", January 2018

Voice as the customer interface will result in increasing pools of financial-related behavioural, merchant and location data that sit outside the bank ecosystem within voice or aggregated technology platforms (mobile, augmented reality glasses, etc). For banks to be able to respond to your needs, they'll need the data that captures real-time behaviour—but Alexa, Google and Siri may not share what led up to an API request for a credit facility, they may just share the request.

Today we have three overarching pieces to the voice stack. We have the core VoiceOS and services layer, which is what handles natural language processing, search, weather, time and basic enquiries, along with installed skill activation. We also have the skills or apps that sit on top of the Alexa platform. Lastly, we have APIs that give access to smart sensors, home automation and other extensions of the platform.

So, first and foremost, banks are going to have to get comfortable with working in the cloud. They can have a private cloud connected to voice services like Alexa and Siri, but they'll get much faster capabilities on Amazon's own architecture, which is built for purpose. The reality is that Amazon's cloud is, in almost all instances, going to be faster and more secure than a bank's internal, on premise architecture[23].

Secondly, bank's need a data pool that can be queried across the voice layer. For this data pool they will need to have cross-silo data integration, what we used to call a 360-degree view of the customer. But this is more about anticipating natural language queries and customer behaviour where a voice event might be triggered.

Thirdly, banks will need broad data-based and technology-based partnerships that lead to better integration of their financial services capability into real-world, real-time scenarios where they can add value easily.

Finally, banks will need voice-based and behavioural-based design teams that are intimately familiar with how people use tech like voice day to day and where technology fits into their life. This is a completely new skill set for banks. This is not mystery shopping one of your investment products or trying to come up with demographic-based or psychographic-based credit card offers. This is behavioural gamification, economics and psychology as a design competency. In the voice world you are an experiential solutions provider. You are not pushing an offer for an existing bank product down a new channel—if you are, you will fail!

The only way voice works for banks as a business tool is if they accept that Alexa is an extension of their voice to the customer—but it only works in a conversational manner. Pitch me a product that I don't immediately need, and you will lose access to the channel, because I'll block you faster than a bad Tinder date. The key skill will be anticipating the customer's needs and responding in a frictionless manner, whether via voice, mobile, in an augmented reality head-up display (smart glasses circa 2022–2025) or similar.

Where automation will strike first

> In our bank we have people doing work like robots. Tomorrow we will have robots behaving like people. It doesn't matter if we as a bank will participate in these changes or not, it is going to happen... The sad truth for the banking industry is, we won't need as many people as today.
>
> —John Cryan, CEO of Deutsche Bank, September 2017

Consumer trends are clearly driving adoption of technologies like voice-based smart assistants, but from an overall perspective we can see that there will be multiple market forces pressuring financial institutions to adopt artificial intelligence.

Organisational Area	AI Competency/ Classification	Adoption Drivers
Regulatory Compliance	Machine/Deep Learning	Regulatory, Cost
Technology Improvement	Various	Supply-side Pressure/ Savings
Infrastructure Advancements	Cognitive, Machine Learning	Competitive (FinTech), Economics
Marketing/Sentiment/ Brand	NLP, Machine Learning	Competitive, Responsiveness
Onboarding/ Acquisition	NLP, Machine Learning	Economics
Trading Signals	Machine Learning	Economics
AML/KYC/Fraud Protection	Machine Learning	Regulatory, Economics
Credit Scoring/Risk Assessment	Machine/Deep Learning	Competitive, Behavioural
Pricing/Underwriting	Machine Learning	Economics, Profitability
Portfolio Management	Machine Learning	Performance, Productivity, Consistency
Optimising Back-office	Cognitive, Deep Learning	Economics, Demand-side
Procurement	Machine Learning, Cognitive	Productivity, Economics

Algorithmic Trading	Machine Learning	Competitive
Data Analysis/ Personalisation	Data Modelling, Deep Learning	Competitive, Supply-side

Table 1: AI competencies and drivers in banking.

Whether on the supply-side, demand-side, competitive, legal or economic, there will be consistent pressure over the next decade to invest in artificial intelligence for profitability and best-practice operations. Broadly speaking, the top four benefits driving AI adoption will be:

1. Identifying new business opportunities
2. Automating repetitive tasks
3. Improving workforce productivity, and
4. Competing with peers

The impact will be broad in scope, but is centred initially around IT, finance/accounting, customer experience/engagement and fulfilment.

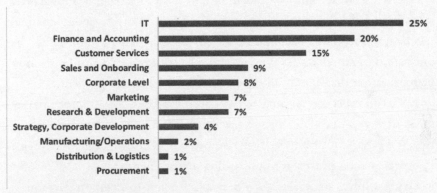

Figure 9: Where AI will have an impact on competitiveness in financial services by 2020 (Source: consultancy.uk).

As regulatory and consumer-facing technology pressures have come to bear on financial services over the last 20 years, we've seen a very purposeful shift to technology as a core competency. Artificial intelligence accelerates this trend of reliance on technology for profitability over the corporate levers of asset management, marginal interest rates and so forth. As we'll see in the next chapter, as we move away from universal banking models we'll discover that banks that had operational advantages based on quasi-governmental or regulatory protections are heavily exposed in an arena where delivery of banking services is technology-dominated.

As these technologies come into play, the requirement to reduce fixed costs and improve agility in service delivery will be acute. Essentially, we'll see banks increasingly having to compete with the likes of Ant Financial and neo-challenger banks whose economics are vastly different because they've already automated out humans for acquisition and delivery. By 2025, stock markets will be consistently asking the question of banks that have retained branch networks (or insurers/wealth managers with front-line representatives), if the economics of that real estate can be justified when other digital competitors are scaling faster, have better cross-sell and upsell ratios, and have higher margins due to their lower fixed costs. Defending existing distribution systems will become more difficult as AI impacts the way we think about the core operations of a bank or institution.

The reason AI will hit acquisition and customer relationships harder than back-office solutions in the near term is not just about channel mechanics like voice. It comes down to the fact that technology in the onboarding and relationship arena actually creates a magnitude of other benefits rather than just a full-time equivalent (FTE) replacement.

We can expect an automated onboarding process, for example, to pay for itself in year one of deployment, where FTEs have been released. In year two, it means we're already getting economic benefits from the investment. However, a robo-process for onboarding a customer can work 24/7/365[24] without holidays or weekends, where time taken to open an account is typically less than one-third of that of a human-involved process; it has much greater volume tolerance and scalability, and frankly will be less error prone. There's immediate FTE benefits to be sure, but the improvements in client servicing and risk are hard to argue against.

The only remaining argument becomes: *what if our customers like talking to a human?*

Redefining the role of humans in banking

For decades as IVR systems were deployed you'd hear people say, "I just want to talk to a human!" When we outsource call centre operations to offshore centres like India, you'd hear anecdotal criticism of the fact that the customer service representative answering didn't have a local accent or local knowledge. Thus, for many years having a real, local human answer your phone when you called was considered a competitive differentiator. The principle here was both service- and advice-related—you could expect better service than a clunky IVR that you had to navigate through, and because they would have local knowledge that would lead to better advice.

In fact, broadly speaking, information asymmetry has been the foundation of financial advisory, insurance sales and most front-line customer service roles in financial services. In contract theory and economics, information asymmetry deals with the study of decisions in transactions where one party has more or better information than the other. Thus, when you wanted a mortgage to buy a property, you wanted to invest in the market, or you wanted advice on even the best credit card for you to apply for, there was a human in a bank that knew more about those products or services than you could know. Having said that, in pure informational terms, this asymmetry was often heavily biased towards products offered by the bank.

In the last 30–40 years the advice we received from a bank branch wasn't, in fact, advice on how to buy a home or how to invest your money, as much as it was which product the bank could offer you to buy a home, or which investment product or asset class you should put your money into. If you wanted true advice independent of bank products, you would have to go to a broker, but even then brokers received commission on introductions, so their advice wasn't unbiased. You could engage the services of a money coach or similar and then you'd get unbiased advice on money management, but that came with a direct cost. The bigger problem for humans in the financial services advisory space, however, is that the information asymmetry that justified their existence is now coming to an end due to the advent of AI.

As discussed earlier, autonomous vehicles are increasingly being integrated onto our roads. Today, humans remain competitive with autonomous vehicles due to our ability to analyse and make decisions regarding driving conditions, obstacles and road markings, but our advantages are quickly being eroded.

More data, faster processing and cognition times, means better advice for the end consumer.

It won't be long before the improvements in both sensors and cars' "brains", or processing, means that they consistently outperform humans when it comes to driving. At this point, we'll see reduction in road deaths, decreases in insurance premiums for autonomous driving vehicles and even changes in road usage biased toward non-human drivers. It won't be long before autonomous vehicles can process more information, more quickly to make a decision, than a human—classic information asymmetry.

Getting back to financial services though, the same will apply. As algorithms, AI customer interfaces like smart assistants gather tons of data—they will soon have much more data than an analyst or customer service representative could ever hope to absorb. With machine learning techniques and increasing error correction capability, these algorithms and AIs will quickly be able to improve the application of this data in giving customers advice in real time that fits with their life. Whether portfolio management or investment advice, day-to-day money coaching, or help navigating credit options, algorithms will simply have information asymmetry over the human agents. They'll have better, more perfect data that can be applied in real time compared to a human service professional. At this point, the roll of humans at the front-end "advice" portion of financial services will be facing the same long-term threats as truck drivers will face from self-driving, autonomous vehicles. Not to mention that the advice an AI gives us will be much more consistent from customer to customer, and won't rely on the individual knowledge (and lack of bias) of the financial advisor.

Designing these systems, these machine-based interactions, understanding customer behaviour and creating new experiences based on emerging technology are going to be critical creative skills for the financial institutions of the future. These will remain human areas of differentiation over the next couple of decades at least. AI today and in the short term remains a collection of capabilities that humans used to do—driving a car, assessing risk, reviewing an identity document against a human, reading an email and executing a trade, etc. The leap from watching behaviour or observing an issue and redesigning a system or product or solving a design/process error is going to be beyond machines for a few years yet. AI will certainly impact elements of design also, but the overall interface between customers and the bank will be dominated by human creativity, and will be a massive area of change as banks transition from products to experiences. Your hiring practices shift focus out of the back office and related processes, and into design for the front office.

If you believe that, just because you are in a position of leadership in a bank, this doesn't concern you, the challenges will still be based on how well you work with AI.

How to lead when your employees are Algos

Since the industrial revolution, we've been designing education systems and management architectures built on manufacturing processes and production lines. Command-and-control, top-down, hierarchical organisation charts are the types of terminologies that have been common in describing traditional management approaches in large organisations. Over the last 30–40 years we've been focused on efficiency gains within this environment, so we've concentrated on process optimisation and metrics. Key performance indicators (KPIs), cost account systems, process re-engineering and so forth were all about making the operational heart of the organisation as efficient as possible, and managers rose to the top of that structure when they were good at enforcing processes and eking out small efficiency gains over time. But when your processes are commanded by artificial intelligence much of the architecture of traditional management becomes superfluous. If you want efficiency gains you tweak the algorithm or manage the data inputs, you don't do 360-degree performance reviews.

Harvard Business Review recently did some solid research[25] on this and showed that over the last 50 years personality traits such as curiosity, extraversion, and emotional stability have become more and more critical, twice as important as intelligence or IQ. The ability of banks and financial institutions to stay on top of technology change is already doubtful.

> The notion that there is some kind of intersection between banking and technology is a misconception. Through a process almost of osmosis, they have come to be one and the same thing...We've reached a point where the tech is developing much faster than people's capacity to work out what to do with it.
> —Cathy Bessant, Chief Operations and Technology Officer,
> Bank of America

What are the management skills that you'll need in the AI age to survive? HBR mapped out four key skills in agile leadership that are very different from those we used to hire for in banking:

- **Humility**—Willingness to learn and to know when you don't know what you need to move forward, reaching outside the organisation for input, trusting others to do their job, and understanding that a data scientist or ML expert might be able to make a critical contribution you can't match. Humility isn't something that managers of the Gordon Gekko era are used to, neither are the leaders of banks with big balance sheets. Lack of humility leads you to commit to outmoded strategies like branch-based engagement, plastic cards, paper cheques and insurance agents long after they've become irrelevant to your future.
- **Adaptability**—Recently, Siam Commercial Bank announced a severance program for staff and managers who could not adapt to the changes the bank was planning around digital[26]. In an AI organisation the ability to change rapidly, undermining ideas, positions or egos held by key stakeholders will be key. Managers will need to focus on learning rather than trying to be "right". Do you have tech advisors on your board? Do you keep a map of competitors' initiatives and key technologies in the space in terms of adoption?

- **Vision**—Vision comes to the fore in AI-powered banks because you have to fight legacy more than in most industries. Strong visionaries like Piyush at DBS, Torres and Gonzalez at BBVA, Thompson at Atom, Vichit and Arthid at Siam Commercial, Harte who lead CBA's transformation amongst others, are examples of strong personalities and visionaries dragging their organisations through a continuous process of innovation. Their language is different and they don't take no for an answer, and they continually learn. But think Musk, Bezos, Jack Ma for even better visionaries—their visions aren't short term, they think in timeframes of 50 years or more and are driven to use their organisations as platforms for long-term change. Bank CEOs bringing 30 years of retail banking experience to the team have no place in this world.
- **Engagement**—Keeping teams engaged in an era of constant change where your job could be taken by an AI at any time isn't easy. There's also a great deal of noise, so being able to filter the noise and listen for the critical signals that focus resources around outcomes is critical. Leaders in the AI age use digital all the time to engage their teams.

Does this mean that leadership will be radically different for banks in the near term? Yes and no. I quoted Cathy Bessant from Bank of America earlier, where she made the point that banking and technology are synonymous now. If a bank is not led by technologists with deep technology experience, then there will be resistance to the effects of artificial intelligence and technology more generally, and this will negatively impact your ability to build mission-critical future capabilities.

In the Bank 4.0 world, smart people skills will be eclipsed by smart machines and soft skills like those listed above will be increasingly critical. Strong leaders are those with vision that can adapt to rapid change constantly and don't fear change, don't stay invested in what they know or what they've built in the past, and can get others to embrace their vision. But most of all, the bank leaders of today need to know that the bank won't stay a leader if they try to keep it all in-house. In a world where technology constantly separates the winners and losers, banks won't be able to build it themselves fast enough and will need to be partnering constantly with those players on the leading edge of new emerging platforms.

Endnotes

1   See https://en.wikipedia.org/wiki/Three_Laws_of_Robotics.

2   "10 companies making big bets on AI"—US News, 19 July 2016—https://money. usnews.com/investing/slideshows/artificial-intelligence-stocks-10-companies-betting-on-ai.

3   Source: SCMP.

4   For a more extensive discussion on the impact of AI on society and jobs, please read my book *Augmented: Life in the Smart Lane.*

5   It should be noted that neither of these are currently AGI-capable, but are foundational elements for such potential AIs.

6   See https://www.ibm.com/developerworks/library/cc-beginner-guide-machine-learning-ai-cognitive/index.html.

7   See http://www.bankofengland.co.uk/publications/Pages/speeches/2015/864.aspx.

8   Source: http://www.oxfordmartin.ox.ac.uk/downloads/academic/The_Future_of_Employment.pdf.

9   Research shows that Australian Customs and Border Patrol Officers doing face-to-face verification missed one in seven fake IDs—http://theconversation.com/passport-staff-miss-one-in-seven-fake-id-checks-30606.

10 Source: *China Daily* (see also *Washington Post*, 7 January 2018—"China's watchful eye").

11 Source: PWC Report—"Millennials & Financial Literacy—The Struggle with Personal Finance".

12 Source: InvestmentNews—"Wealthy millennials decline financial advisers' services" (May 2015).

13 Schwab's Intelligent Portfolios robo was the top performer, by a narrow margin. Its portfolio gained 11.94 percent, edging out Betterment (11.68 percent), E*Trade (11.60 percent), SigFig (11.41 percent) and Vanguard PAS (10.92 percent).

14 Source: S&P500. However, it should be noted that inflation-adjusted returns are closer to 7 percent on an annualised basis.

15 Source: Business Insider Intelligence—"The Evolution of Robo Advising Report" (2017).

16 Check out the ad where actor Alec Baldwin orders socks on Alexa for reference purposes.

17 See https://www.bigcommerce.com/blog/ecommerce-trends/.

18 Source: NetElixir.

19 Source: eMarketer—https://www.emarketer.com/Article/New-eMarketer-Forecast-Sees-Mobile-Driving-Retail-Ecommerce-China/1016105.

20 See "The Accelerating Disruption of China's Economy", *Fortune*, 26 June 2017 (Paul Liu, Xuemei Bennink Bai, Jason Jia, and Eva Wang).

21 Source: https://www.forbes.com/sites/tompopomaronis/2017/12/15/e-commerce-in-2018-heres-what-the-experts-are-predicting/.

22 Agency-based refers to delegating a purchase to your voice assistant or personal AI.

23 See "Cloud are more secure than traditional IT systems—and here's why", TechTarget, January 2014.

24 Or 24/365, if you're a stickler for that sort of thing.

25 See "As AI Makes More Decisions, the Nature of Leadership Will Change", *Harvard Business Review*, January 2018.

26 Source: *Bangkok Post*—"SCB proposes severance for non-adapters"—https://www.bangkokpost.com/business/news/1405254/scb.

8 The Universal Experience

We were wrong about Universal Banking. Few cost efficiencies
come from merging many functions in a single bank.
—John Reed, former Chairman and CEO of Citibank

Your financial life is supposed to follow a fairly predictable pattern, at least in the developed world. You start off in school with a basic student deposit account, you might even visit the bank on a school field trip or excursion. Then you graduate high school and take on a part-time job. If you go off to university or college, you might take on a student loan (if you live in those primitive countries that make education a capitalist exercise) and if you don't, you'll likely start your first full-time job (or maybe a couple of part-time jobs). You take out a car loan to get your first car. Then you're thinking about getting married, getting your first home, and a few years after that you've got credit cards, life insurance, income protection, a second mortgage for an investment property—and you're starting to think about retirement.

This is the dream customer profile of the Universal Banker. Get them while they're young, and then every single banking product you ever need will be provided by the bank you grew up with in your home town. You'll constantly be cross-sold and upsold to, and because you "trust" the bank that gave you your first bank account, you'll simply use them as a one-stop shop for every banking product you'll ever need. They were there when you opened your first account, and hopefully by the time your kids need a bank you'll march them into a branch to keep the bank in the family.

Except, it just doesn't work like that anymore. The average consumer in the US, UK and Australia has a relationship with between four and seven different financial institutions[1], for the average business it's at least two, and sometimes upward of five or six, different institutions. More than half of investors have multiple brokerage and investment accounts also. The fact is, historically we simply don't maintain this idealistic single-bank loyalty, like a 50-year marriage, with our money. We are in open banking relationships all the time.

The expectations of the post-millennial consumer

Generation Y (millennials) is the first digitally native generation born into a world of technology. They grew up in a world where if you needed to know in which city Abraham Lincoln was born, who built the pyramids (aliens?) or when the next solar eclipse might occur, instead of picking up an *Encyclopedia Britannica* at the local library, you'd simply ask "the Google". More than that, as they started working and became consumers, they had access to a world of instant gratification and e-commerce that was unimaginable to their forebears. They could order pizza online, book movie tickets, airline tickets, hotels and, more importantly, they could find out what their peers thought of various restaurants, service providers and the like. Network effect and social media amplified this trend with the latest, coolest service, getting faster and faster traction as they shared with their friends their latest discovery.

Just like it would be counter-intuitive for a millennial to reach for an encyclopedia, to call up Domino's on a landline to order a pizza, or go to a travel agent's office to book a flight, it is also increasingly counter-intuitive for these consumers to "go to the bank". Research shows that millennials on a day-to-day basis are almost myopically focused on digital. They would never think of using phone banking to check their balance, they can't work out cheques and they wonder why anyone would ever send you one in the post. They live in a world where they expect banking to work in a frictionless, real-time manner.

Insist on getting a millennial into a branch to open up a new credit card facility, and it's statistically likely that you'll simply never hear from them again—they've already selected an alternative they've found online. If they are a post-financial crisis millennial, they're going to be paranoid about taking on unnecessary credit anyway. More on that in a moment.

Having said that, depending on which market you are in, strong digital usage by millennials does translate across the board to overall better engagement with your bank as a brand, including the occasional branch visit. Research by Jim Marous and the "Digital Banking Report"[2] shows that US millennials are accessing their bank via mobile 8.5 times per month on average, compared with just 3.1 times per month for non-millennials. They're also four times more likely to connect with the bank via email than non-millennials (4.6 times per month versus 0.9 times). Online account opening is the norm and preferred by millennials (61 percent), whereas on average about one-third of non-millennials prefer to open an account online (28 percent), versus face to face. For investment accounts, online is even more prevalent. They still occasionally visit a branch, but for the average millennial that's less than one visit a year today, and most of the time that's because the bank couldn't get it done any other way.

Interestingly, the research showed that 10 percent of millennials are now using a digital-only bank as their primary relationship, and 15 percent of high-net worth individuals are also using pure-play digital offerings.

Indeed, the US Federal Reserve released a study in 2016 showing mobile was the primary channel of choice for millennials 67 percent of the time. In the United Kingdom, mobile banking use increased 356 percent from 2012 to 2017[3], with millennials twice as likely to use mobile banking as their predecessors. UK challenger and specialist banks saw a 56 percent growth in gross lending in 2016, increasing their market share by 2.9 percent, according to the Council of Mortgage Lenders there. Virgin Money, an online-only bank, is now the eighth-largest lender in the country, above the Yorkshire Building Society and Clydesdale Bank, both long-established institutions.

It is pretty clear that if you are a bank targeting millennials, your primary interface day to day for nurturing that relationship is your mobile app, and you had better offer streamlined account opening online and via mobile, without the requirement for a face-to-face visit to the branch or a signature card. If you can't, you have definitely already lost business—whether you assert that you still have millennial customers using your branch today or not. Statistically, there is no other conclusion to reach. There are definitely millennials who came to your webpage, saw they'd have to visit a branch to open an account, and simply moved on when it came to deciding which bank they'd choose.

For post-millennials, the problem will be even more acute. Generation Z are growing up in a mobile, ubiquitous technology world. Not just internet access through a computer, but they will grow up with computers you talk to; supercomputers you carry in your pocket, gaming consoles, digital video cameras and the nexus of much of their social interactions; computers that recognise them by their face and voice; computers that predict their needs and behaviours, that monitor their health, and that are even a daily companion.

In the last 10 years, a typical response that I've observed might be something like "Hey, wait a second! We still have millennials walking into our branches. You're wrong. Once they need a mortgage or start investing, they're going to want to talk to a human!"

If a bank is thinking like this, they are falling back on the way they grew up banking, and are having trouble understanding a different frame of reference.

If you've grown up in a world where everyone goes to the branch to do banking, if you've done that your entire life, if you've built your business around that behaviour, you're unlikely to embrace a change or threat to the culture rapidly and easily[4]. This cultural bias, whether in society or in the workplace, is the natural effect of systems where behaviour is reinforced, and generally takes long periods of time to shift. I first have to seek to change your frame of reference, I have to get you into a mindset where you are willing to accept new behaviour, and you can identify with those exhibiting that behaviour, and then you may allow yourself to change your thinking patterns.

Today, it's increasingly rare to be paid in cash, unless you are waitressing in the US, or delivering food for Uber Eats or Seamless. Parents are paying their kids via Venmo because that's what their friends use, and they just ask their parents if they can pay them into their Venmo account. My 17-year-old daughter didn't want to think about a driving license after she was old enough to become a student learner driver; she initially thought she'd be fine with an Uber account the rest of her life, until she moved to a location without Uber. When it comes to paying an allowance into Venmo, Paytm or with WeChat, this is often due to network effect, where peer group behaviour creates a positive feedback loop that effects the community at home. "My friends all use Venmo, dad, can't you give me the money there?" Or in the case of my 14-year-old son, up until very recently he only wanted me to pay him in iTunes credits and PayPal so he could use it online.

Generational psychology cannot be underestimated as an influencer regarding banking institutions themselves. The market crash of 24 October 1929 caused a "run on the banks", and still, decades later, older customers cite the need to have access to a physical bank branch as a driver for their choice of bank "just in case". The global financial crisis of 2007–2008, the massive credit card debts of the 1990s, the looming student loan crisis in the US, the increasingly partisan and antagonistic nature of politics, reverberating echo chambers in social media, and so forth, is leading to a broad distrust of institutions like government and big banks for Generations Y and Z.

In the US less than a third of millennials own a credit card today (the lowest levels of their age group in the last 40 years since credit cards launched), while their predecessors used them at twice that rate[5]. This is based on survey data over the last seven years, so don't tell me it's an anomalous stat. As millennials get older they're clearly not as keen on taking on debt as previous generations were. Traditional credit card rewards programs aren't stimulating the use of credit either. The total rewards paid by the top six US card issuers doubled from $11 billion to $23 billion between 2010 and 2016, in a clear attempt to attract more young people to use credit cards[6], and yet millennials remain obstinately unmoved.

It is clear to economists who study payment patterns that millennials are gravitating toward payment methods that skirt both cash and credit. Why carry cash when you can whip out a debit card for the smallest transaction—a sandwich or a bottle of soda—or use an app like Venmo or an online payment service like PayPal? All of those typically draw funds directly from a bank account.

—"How Millennials Became Spooked by Credit Cards",
The New York Times/DealBook, 14 August 2017

This is part of a broader behavioural shift in payments. The reality is that if you're tapping your phone to pay, you're going to be less and less likely to prioritise a credit card over a debit card as a payment vehicle. The improved utility of mobile payments themselves is tending toward more focus on your balance in your spending account, and that is creating greater awareness for what you can afford. Millennials and Gen-Z, being more focused on the tech, are simply adjusting their behaviour faster than their forebears. Thus, we see a direct correlation between technology use and acceptance of these older paradigms, like credit cards and revolving debt. It turns out that a device that allowed you to "impulse purchase" in the moment because you only felt the impact when you got a statement at the end of the month, doesn't fit with today's real-time world.

Banking products and systems are very slow to change, even when faced with these behavioural shifts. However, if you look at the history, you can see banking evolution as a step-change in respect of access, behaviour and preferences.

In the evolution from community banking to universal banking, the objective was to create the same stickiness that used to come from geography, through choice and access. A bank that allowed you global access to its platform was only necessary as we started to travel the globe more. A bank that promoted credit cards, personal loans, mortgages, fixed deposits and so forth was only possible as the middle class grew. The underlying assumption was that you would have some form of *loyalty to your primary financial institution*. That you'd only ever really need one bank relationship—anything else was either overkill or disloyal to the bank that gave you your first passbook when you were 10 years old on that field trip.

In the 1980s and 1990s, being the primary financial institution was the goal of every major banking brand in the world, and universal banking was the way each bank thought they'd achieve this. However, if you weren't my primary financial institution, your goal was to try to capture as much of my business via specialising on specific products—a credit card, car loan or investment account perhaps. As the internet has grown, we've seen an explosion of choice from all sorts of mainstream and alternative financial services providers. The need to develop alternative acquisition approaches led banks to establish partnerships with car dealers to sell you a lease or car financing, to establish relationships with retail merchants to offer discounts or in-store financing deals, and with property developers to offer mortgages. As time went on, the likelihood of your bank being the sole or primary financial institution diminished as bank products and services were no longer limited to that single bank brand that inhabited your town.

Figure 1: The evolution of banking systems as it pertains to access and bank–customer relationships.

The emerging generation of customers, however, will have a much different expectation of the so-called "bank". If they have a problem or need a money solution or advice, they'll ask their technology layer for a solution. In the short term they'll use their mobile phone to search on questions like "how do I buy a car" or "how can I afford to buy a home".

In parallel they'll ask their peers and their parents. Some of that will result in reinforcing traditional banking behaviour, but as they become more independent and as bank utility becomes more ubiquitous, it will simply be a case of "ask and ye shall receive!" Even more importantly, in the medium term you won't have to ask, because by the time we're wearing augmented reality glasses, the tech will learn our behaviour, our needs, and start to actively anticipate solutions. If anything, we'll be looking for a *primary financial manager* on our technology layer rather than a primary financial institution[7].

The customers of tomorrow will expect that when it comes to money, payments, credit access, etc, that it just works. Zero friction will be the rule, not the exception. In this new world, if you ask me to sign a piece of paper or visit a building to get access to a service, a post-millennial consumer won't think you are crazy...they simply won't understand what you are talking about. The cognitive dissonance will be acute. It would be like asking them to check their encyclopedia for the latest price of Bitcoin.

Rebundling experiences

The first phase of FinTech was an unbundling of financial services. Whether in investment services, day-to-day banking, student loans, in-store credit, and pretty much every other area of retail banking you can think of, there has been a plethora of startups who have claimed they're going to eat the bank industries' lunch. Goldman Sachs' "Future of Finance" report says it's plausible that up to 20 percent of industry revenues could be captured by external entrants (translation: FinTechs and tech players).

However, unbundling and non-traditional competitors aren't exactly new. Banks like HSBC, Citigroup and others have carved off their securities division, mortgage business and credit card functions into separate operations for years.

The marketplace lenders, for example, are offering an alternative for small business owners who otherwise must wait three to four weeks or more to get a bank loan (if they can get one at all). By looking at different data points and evaluating a business' financials in a more systematic way, marketplace lenders can get the same thing done in hours or days. That efficiency does make a difference. Think about a restaurateur who needs to quickly replace a broken stove, or someone who needs to finance a couple of trucks to expand their business. It may not be the best deal for them, but speed counts.

—"The Great Rebundling of Financial Services", BankThink, October 2015[8]

In an October 2015 article on the rebundling of financial services, Brad Leimer and Marc Hochstein went on to describe a world where banks could use technology to bundle more efficient services based on FinTechs, to essentially rebuild a universal banking approach based on technology platforms. LendingClub loans for debt consolidation, a Betterment account for investment, Moven for financial wellness coaching, etc. Banks like Fidor in Germany and USAA even tried this type of approach, and Starling Bank's business model is based on it.

Marc and Brad were right about the tech rebundling of financial services. However, it's looking like the technology that will deliver financial services of the future won't do so at the bank level, it will do it increasingly at the personal experience level.

Behaviour increasingly will be centred around the technology platforms we use on a daily basis. Train your personal AI on Google and you'll be using an Android phone, Google Home and Google Smart Glasses. Train your personal AI on Apple and it'll be Siri, CarPlay, Home Pod and Apple TV. Amazon will be embedding Alexa in as many devices as possible, too. This is like the operating system and personal computer platform battles of the past—PC versus Mac. Eventually these smart assistant voice technologies might even become interoperable.

Today we have apps on our phones. We have an app for banking, an app for taxis, an app for booking movies, etc. But in the voice-based future we are accessing services or skills embedded in the platform. We don't load up an app on our Alexa speaker at home, we just tell Alexa to enable that skill. Unlike the world of mobile app stores we live in today, once we enable that skill we are able to access the underlying features of that service without opening an app. It is like that skill becomes part of our tailored operating system for that device.

This is where financial services bundling will start to be reframed. We might open a new account, or get access to a new credit facility, without ever knowing the bank that is behind that facility, or maybe only finding out after we've selected the features of the facility we accepted.

The other element that is critical here is recommendations and ratings. Today, banks have been able to avoid side-by-side comparison generally in favour of direct channel reinforcement for access. But when voice and AI become a critical part of bundled financial services experiences, that ability to answer the question, "What is the best loan for me in this situation?" would be vastly different to the way we shop for financial services today. Retail, restaurants, hotels and such have all had recommendation engines, social media and feedback systems that dramatically change their brand's credibility in the market. In banking, while there has been pressure applied via social media at the brand level, it's been harder to directly apply this to specific bank locations, products and services. The next layer of technologies will increasingly do just that.

Geolocation, context, behaviour, social feedback and sentiment, and identity indicators, are data points and technology platform capabilities that largely lie outside of the existing bank architectures. This is going to create a platform of new brokers and intermediaries that becomes essential in the delivery of financial services in the future.

The new brokers and intermediaries

Throughout this book we've talked about many of the new technologies and competencies that banks will need to build, but we've also talked about the fact that first principles thinking and new technology layers increasingly "own" or dominate customer access, data or experiences. To that end, I've tried to put together some illustrative examples of brokers and intermediaries that will over the next few years become increasingly essential to day-to-day banking interactions with customers and partners. These players are, in some instances, an evolution from existing players, like public cloud vendors (Amazon Web Services, AWS), telecoms operators and mobile phone app stores; but in other instances, they offer new capabilities that will be faster to integrate than for banks to build internally.

In many instances, such as voice-smart assistants, in the short term you might feel that having an AI teller built into your app or web front-end puts you in the running. However, in the longer term, the technology layers for smart assistants will be OS-based built into your smart devices, home and car, and be much more sophisticated in terms of natural language processing and platform capability than your chatbot. If you aren't working with these external platforms, it is increasingly likely that your homegrown capability won't even get utilised by your customers. Of course, building voice capabilities internally today isn't necessarily a bad thing, as it will get you ready from a data structures and API perspective for working with players like Amazon, Apple and others.

Let's look at some illustrative pools of capabilities being developed outside the institution today:

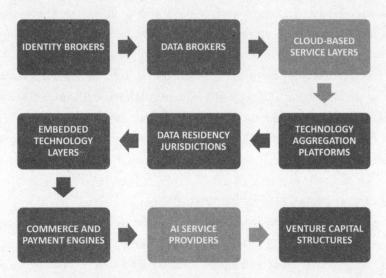

Figure 2: How capability is being developed.

Identity brokers

As already noted, in the mobile payments arena the world is increasingly dominated by IP-based players that aren't part of the bank-owned or grown payment networks that dominated the world of plastic. Facebook, Apple, Google, Alibaba, WeChat and others are all likely better at identifying individuals than banks are today. Governments like Canada are trialling known traveller digital identity systems on the blockchain that will one day replace passports[9]. As discussed in earlier chapters, rather than collecting KYC information from scratch, as banks do today, in the future they will use an identity marker like biometrics, behaviour or similar to check against databases like this to verify the customer's identity. As Dave Birch pointed out earlier, banks may become key players in this trusted identity architecture, but that still won't mean when you open a new account you'll have to supply all your identity information again.

Data brokers

You probably think that Google, Facebook and Apple have the most data on you, right[10]? Well, if you live in the US or Europe, those organisations are probably not even in the top 10 of companies that have data on you, or data that helps us understand who you are and what you do. A 2014 Federal Trade Commission (FTC) report[11] describes an industry that collects data from many sources without consumers knowing, that is multi-layered and intertwined, and that stores billions of data points covering nearly every US consumer. In the EU, while the General Data Protection Regulation (GDPR) regulates how companies use, protect and utilise EU citizens' data, this doesn't provide banks with an informational advantage over other organisations. In fact, with open banking regulations, increasingly non-bank technology providers will have greater access to your banking data.

But here's what data brokers know. Your data profile is going to be increasingly critical to organisations that are technology led. Ultimately, this means that if you are in the *banking experience business* you're going to have to be working with data brokers that help you understand when and where a customer is going to need the utility of your bank. The data you have in the bank is no longer enough to make that connection; and the data you do have is technically owned by the customer—and they will use it to access services outside your institution.

Cloud-based service layers

Today a great deal of the core architecture a challenger bank carries, like cyber security, identity verification, session management, app store and mobile-OS integration, are simply plug-in services sitting on top of Google, AWS or Microsoft Azure[12]. For many banks, private clouds are a sort of enhanced data warehouse. For challenger banks, we see the cloud as a veritable shopping cart of services we can bring to bear without having to build them ourselves. In addition, cloud services like AWS today regularly outperform banks' own internet security stack by a factor of five to ten. Amazon is getting pummelled by DDOS attacks, hacking, spoofs, and every type of security threat you could imagine, tens of thousands of times per day. Downtime of AWS-based apps is increasingly rare, as their systems become tougher and tougher.

In the cyber security world, this is often spoken of in terms of a type of immune system response. As you solve more and more attacks, your architecture becomes more resilient. In the case of AWS, they simply get more attacks than any bank in the world, so therefore they've had to make their systems stronger and smarter. I bet you 10 Bitcoin that if you put your bank head to head against AWS on cyber security, they'd beat you like The Rock at a WWE wrestling match[13].

The point is, for a challenger bank, the decision to go cloud is a no-brainer. It gives you a whole suite of services you can spin up fast, has military-grade security capabilities and you can turn on processors and storage space like a light bulb when you need to rapidly scale. You don't need to buy more hardware continuously.

Technology aggregators

Whether aggregation specifically in the financial services space, or aggregation of other services, increasingly technology-based aggregators will play a critical role as a new generation of gatekeepers. In China, Alipay and WeChat have effectively become payments aggregators and this has become a significant issue for banks in China, and increasingly around the world[14]. Smartphone operating systems and app stores are natural technology aggregators today, as are voice platforms like Alexa. In 2015, JPMorgan Chase, Bank of America (BofA) and Wells Fargo precipitated a battle between the big banks and popular personal financial management and aggregation services like Intuit/Mint, Geezeo, MX/Money Desktop, Yodlee and others. BofA, Wells and JPMorgan Chase argued the reasons for slowing data responses to requests from these sites were security related. However, since then customer demand for these services has only accelerated, resulting in more and more data sharing agreements between banks and aggregators.

The reality is that there is a first-mover advantage here, where banks with preferential data sharing agreements will get better leverage off aggregation platforms.

Data residency jurisdictions

Let's say you are starting a challenger bank in Vietnam or Panama and you want to use the cloud to do that. You go to Mastercard and Visa and get a BIN so you can issue cards. You go to the regulator and get a FinTech banking charter and you're ready to go. There's only one issue: Amazon doesn't have a local instance (availability zone, or AZ, in their lingo) in that country. So you'll have to use AWS servers in Singapore or Google cloud in Brazil. Technically this isn't an issue at all. Latency is fast enough that the lag between a transaction at the POS in Vietnam and posting it on the cloud server in Singapore happens essentially in real time.

The problem is that your customer data isn't stored in Vietnam. Now as Amazon adds AZs around the world this may become less of a problem, but Amazon sees their cloud business like they do their retail business. They use regional hubs combined with local distribution. There is no reason to expect they may ever have instances in Vietnam. Thus, you have Vietnamese customers with their data held offshore in Singapore. It is almost certain that the central bank in Vietnam won't be too hot on this idea.

Customer access layers

In 1990 every channel a customer used to get access to banking was bank-owned; today the majority of day-to-day banking access is through non-bank-owned and bank-controlled channels. This means as a bank you need a long-term strategy of specifically engaging with the vast array of technology platforms that have better access to your customers day to day than you do.

Figure 3: Illustration showing banking access today through non-bank-owned or bank-controlled channels.

AI service providers

Facebook, Apple, Google, IBM and Microsoft are all spending big time on AI research and development, which is resulting in technology companies leading R&D spend globally today. Since chief executive Sundar Pichai took over the top job at Google in 2015, Alphabet has spent $30 billion on AI and related infrastructure, which includes the data centres necessary for the computing power that makes Google Assistant function as well as its cloud computing division and AI-backed consumer hardware line-up. Clearly we won't see banks spending at this level on AI, but even if they did, they wouldn't have the broad reach that Google might have, for example. This means that if you want to plug your bank into an AI service layer that your customers are using daily, it won't be a bank-specific AI. Today, the entire US banking industry is spending approximately 1–2 percent on AI research and development when compared with the tech sector. The math is fairly straightforward.

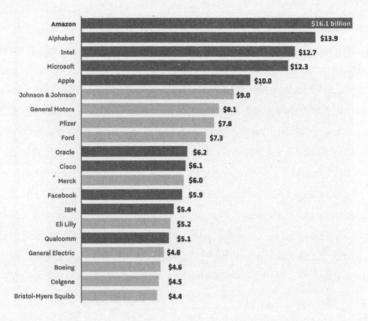

Amazon	$16.1 billion
Alphabet	$13.9
Intel	$12.7
Microsoft	$12.3
Apple	$10.0
Johnson & Johnson	$9.0
General Motors	$8.1
Pfizer	$7.8
Ford	$7.3
Oracle	$6.2
Cisco	$6.1
Merck	$6.0
Facebook	$5.9
IBM	$5.4
Eli Lilly	$5.2
Qualcomm	$5.1
General Electric	$4.8
Boeing	$4.6
Celgene	$4.5
Bristol-Myers Squibb	$4.4

Figure 4: Tech companies taking the lead in R&D spend (Source: Factset).

Venture capital structures

If you're going to be investing in FinTechs you can create your own VC capability, such as those that BBVA, Citi and Santander have done, but that requires some pretty deep pockets, likely north of $100 million to be really serious. If you're not a global banking player, this is going to be pretty difficult, but there are options. Increasingly, smaller banks are joining as limited partners or strategic investors in FinTech-themed VC funds, such as the fund created by SBI Group (previously known as Softbank Investments) or Anthemis Group. This puts them in a network of like-minded investors and gets them access on a priority basis to the individual FinTechs in the portfolio.

Ubiquitous banking

As the shift towards embedded banking becomes complete, the leading banks won't be those with big distribution networks, they'll be the banks with broad data capabilities that generate advantages in contextualisation of day-to-day banking. Increasingly that will take not only a purposeful shift toward redesigning the way the utility of the bank fits in the lives of customers, but also a massive commitment to partnerships with non-bank partners that have the access or data to make a real difference in a real-time bank offering.

As a bank, recognising that you can no longer be the primary financial institution by waiting for a customer to "come to the bank" will allow you to start thinking about how to design compelling interactions day to day that make your particular set of capabilities indispensable to your customers. Becoming the primary financial experience for your customers won't be through products, people or even channels—it's all through anticipating and delivering experiences, when and where the customer needs it the most. The era of ubiquitous banking is almost upon us, and that means that banking will be embedded in the lives of your customers, but not banking as we know it today.

Endnotes

1   Source: Various—AT Kearney, Forrester, Kitchenman.

2   Source: Digital Banking Report/The Financial Brand (March 2017).

3   Source: British Bankers Association.

4   Go back and read the last section of Chapter 7 on AI if you identify with this.

5   Source: BankRate.

6   Source: MagnifyMoney compilation of FDIC filings from the six largest credit card issuers (May 2017).

7   This is not a new concept—Ron Shevlin has spoken about this previously.

8   "The Great Rebundling of Financial Services", by Marc Hochstein and Bradley Leimer, BankThink, 13 October 2015.

9   Source: World Economic Forum Press Release—"Canada to Test Advancements in Biometrics and Blockchain to Welcome International Travellers", January 2018.

10 Certainly Mark Zuckerberg, anyway.

11 "Data Brokers: A Call for Transparency and Accountability"—Federal Trade Commission, 2014.

12 Yes, I know there are more cloud providers than this.

13 I know he's retired from WWE. I still wouldn't take him on…

14 Source: "Big banks on notice that they're losing ground to China's fintech giants", *South China Morning Post*, 9 August 2017.

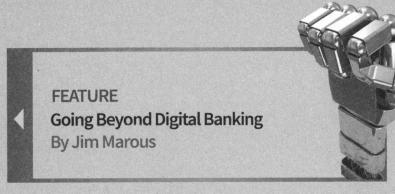

Going Beyond Digital Banking
By Jim Marous

The success of e-commerce, P2P payments, Uber and digital voice assistants all have a significant commonality—they provide an experience that simplifies daily life. With consumers using their smartphones and digital apps more than ever, winners in the future will be those organisations that can create embedded, contextual digital experiences that don't rely on physical channels.

The modern consumer doesn't have time to visit a bank branch (despite some saying they still want them around). They don't want to sit through a new account-opening process, meet with an investment advisor, write a paper cheque or pull out a debit or credit card. They want simplicity in their life that can be achieved through the application of advanced analytics (AI), digital delivery and real-time personalised recommendations.

Modest-sized FinTech firms and large tech giants continue to make retail banking inroads worldwide, providing services that leverage the best in digital technology to deliver a customer experience that removes cumbersome steps from both routine and more involved banking engagements. Relative financial newcomers like Alipay (China), WeChat (China), Rakuten (Japan), Atom (UK), Monzo (UK), Starling (UK), Moven (US), N26 (Germany) and Revolut (UK) have joined household names like PayPal, Amazon and Google to disrupt the banking ecosystem, leveraging modern infrastructures and innovative cultures.

> Many of the tech giants possess the ingredients of success: digital prowess, large customer bases, organisations well versed in improving the customer experience, and ample leeway to extend their corporate brands into banking.
>
> —Bain & Company, Evolving the Customer Experience in Banking

More concerning may be that some of these firms are generating a level of trust previously reserved only for traditional banks and credit unions. As a result, an increasing percentage of consumers are willing to use financial products offered from these non-traditional firms—especially where the experience is superior to that offered by legacy organisations.

Going beyond digital banking basics

At a time when some of the most complex interactions—such as starting a business, applying for an auto loan or home mortgage, sending money overseas and building an investment portfolio—have been digitised, it is more important than ever for traditional financial institutions to digitise entire engagements, especially the opening of basic banking accounts. This will take a complete revamping of most banking websites, mobile banking apps and back-office processes.

Migration to digital makes excellent financial sense. For example: routine transactions that require bank staff not only cost 20 times more than those done online or through mobile, but consumers also prefer to handle routine banking business digitally. For instance, while "self-serve" leaders in the Netherlands, Poland and Australia transact the vast proportion of their transactions without ever interacting with a human, 40 percent of US respondents still go to the branch teller at least once a quarter to make a deposit, compared with 21 percent using digital channels and 18 percent using ATMs. Even within geographic markets there is a significant gap between the leaders and laggards in the quest for digital optimisation.

For those who say that the migration to mobile banking and the use of some digital services appears to have levelled off, this is more a reflection on the inability of most financial organisations to improve their digital capabilities, rather than consumers not wanting something better. The bottom line for banks is the challenge that consumers expect even better experiences in mobile banking apps, digital payments, robo-advice, and voice banking. This only seeks to increase the likelihood of non-traditional competitors getting a foothold over the next few years.

Banks and credit unions must begin to explore emerging technologies that leverage consumer data, advanced analytics and new digital tools, such as voice-controlled digital assistants. Research shows that 25 percent of US respondents said they use voice assistants such as Siri, Alexa or Google Assistant on their smartphones or Alexa or Google Home at home. And, while only five to six percent of respondents currently use voice technology for their banking in the US, Australia and the UK, between 20 and 25 percent-plus are open to trying the technology for their banking in the future.

Banks that master the digital basics will be able to further secure customers' loyalty by quickly putting the new technologies to practical use in test-and-learn prototypes that can be improved in a few iterations and then broadly rolled out. In determining which new technologies should be rolled out, financial institutions must look at the options from a consumer benefit perspective, as opposed to simply as a way to reduce costs.

Amazon model provides a guide for banking

There is no denying the explosive growth and competitive impact of Amazon to the retail industry. For their retail business, the foundation of this success is Amazon Prime. Amazon's Prime membership program has 80 million members in the US according to recent estimates from Consumer Intelligence Research Partners (CIRP), up from 58 million at the end of Q1 2016. Today, that means that 64 percent of US households now have Amazon Prime memberships[1].

While most casual observers would think that the increased loyalty around Amazon Prime is about free shipping, it is really about changing consumer behaviour through reduced friction.

Reducing friction to radically alter behaviour is what was behind one-click ordering, Super Saver Shipping (encouraging customers to fill their shopping cart) and the entire family of Alexa devices (using voice commands to simplify ordering). Reducing friction and improving the consumer experience is also what is behind the recent decision to acquire Whole Foods.

Core to the Amazon strategy is the company's infamous Flywheel (pictured below). The Flywheel, dubbed "The Virtuous Cycle", was created before Amazon added business segments in addition to its retail marketplace, such as Amazon Web Services.

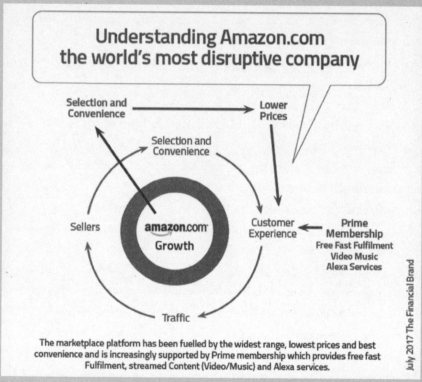

Figure I: Amazon's Flywheel (Source: The Financial Brand).

Looking at the original Flywheel, it is evident that all the pieces revolve around a continuous improvement of the customer experience. A strong customer experience will lead to more shoppers, which will in turn bring more sellers. More sellers will lower costs and prices through competition while bolstering selection for customers. Lower prices and more selection will bring in more customers—and the cycle repeats itself.

As the Flywheel increases momentum, there is a massive amount of customer insight being collected, analysed and acted upon for improved recommendations and behaviour modification. Instead of collecting data for great internal reports, Amazon applies all of the learning (in real time) to enhance the customer experience and increase loyalty.

Due to the breadth of the Flywheel effect across the business, they realise an additional advantage. They can make lots of small bets at the fringe of the Flywheel. Meanwhile, the core business continues to be healthy.

The bottom line is, Amazon Prime wins by making life easier for its customers. By providing a comprehensive selection of products, accessible with only a few digital clicks and taps, at competitive prices, the brand experience is reinforced. We are already seeing the same impact in banking. The largest banks (Chase, Bank of America, Wells Fargo) are gaining market share by reducing friction over digital channels.

Allowing for the end-to-end digital opening of new accounts using a laptop, tablet or phone removes friction from a previously arduous task. Providing voice access to balances, basic transactions and customer support sets a financial institution like Capital One, USAA and others apart from the competition. Using artificial intelligence (AI) and a customer's habits and financial activities to predict future behaviours and needs will be the foundation for future banking relationships.

Amazon is setting the bar for customer expectations beyond the retail industry. The banking industry can learn from Amazon Prime. Or it can allow Amazon and other large tech companies to leverage their exceptional customer experience layer to provide many of the banking services legacy organisations provide today.

Open banking: a digital "perfect storm"

The combined forces of advanced technology, high-speed internet, increasing penetration of smartphones and the increasing popularity and functionality of application program interfaces (APIs) has created a "perfect storm" for innovation beyond the app. The increasing affordability of each of these components has further strengthened the storm.

In an excellent report, "Open Banking: How to Flourish in an Uncertain Future", Deloitte states: "Technologies such as 'Infrastructure-as-a-Service' (IaaS), 'Platform-as-a-Service' (PaaS) and 'Software-as-a-Service' (SaaS) have allowed new tech-enabled entrants to enter the retail banking sector with lower IT overheads. They have also allowed them to respond more flexibly to changing market needs."

There is a growing consensus among industry observers that, while the initial transformation of the banking industry may be an expansion of traditional and non-traditional providers offering new alternatives to existing banking services, the ultimate transformation may be far greater. In the future, the banking ecosystem will expand far beyond just financial services, or financial services may become relegated to being just a small component of a broader non-banking ecosystem.

The banking model of the future will be some form of marketplace banking. "In marketplace banking, the traditional banking business model is transformed into a data-intensive, platform-based marketplace, where several financial services providers continually compete to offer customers tailored, good-value products", states Deloitte in the earlier quoted report. "As a result, traditional bank services are augmented by a variety of offerings through an ecosystem of providers."

A marketplace banking ecosystem would give consumers access to highly-personalised services that leverage customer data made available through open banking and APIs. As opposed to today's closed access budgeting tools, the new ecosystem would allow consumers to optimise all of their banking relationships—lowering costs and increasing returns.

Beyond traditional banking services, the new ecosystem would allow banks to become the "hub" for other, non-financial ancillary services provided by other banks or organisations in other industries. In this scenario, bank APIs would centralise an array of life-stage services, reducing friction and improving the customer experience.

Instead of disjointed components of a life-stage process—like a home or car purchase, starting a small business, or having a child—all involved players (banks, insurance, retail, governmental units, agents, etc) could be brought together in a holistic marketplace

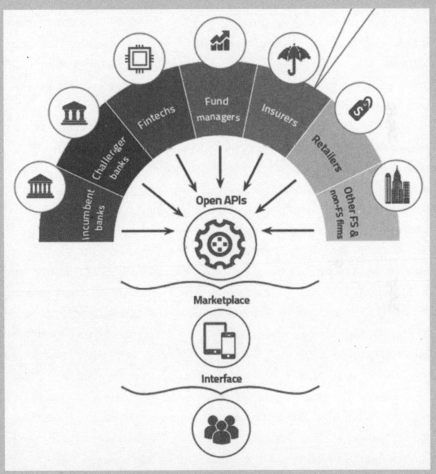

Figure 2: The future of marketplace banking (Source: The Financial Brand).

A good defence is a strong offence

The best way to prepare for the inevitable increase in competition that the continued expansion of banking services offered by Amazon, Google, PayPal, Facebook and an increasing number of startup banks will bring is to be proactive in the development of personalised digital solutions. This will most likely involve new partnerships inside and outside of traditional banking organisations, and a redefinition of what a banking ecosystem includes.

If banks don't reorient their approach and radically accelerate their rate of progress, loyalty will suffer, and they will watch small FinTech firms and large technology institutions poach more business. Meanwhile, their economics will erode as too many routine transactions continue to flow through expensive branch and call-centre networks.

As digital technologies and advanced analytics have provided exciting opportunities for financial institutions, only the largest organisations are truly positioning themselves for the digital future. While there are notable exceptions, the question is whether the majority of institutions are too small to succeed in a highly competitive digital banking ecosystem—where winners will be determined based on the ability to use data and insights to deliver exceptional digital experiences.

The most significant challenge for most smaller financial organisations in becoming a "digital bank" is to have the expertise and personnel to deploy digital and advanced data solutions. Not surprisingly, another challenge facing smaller organisations is the structure of data available to build digital solutions.

These challenges are not insurmountable, but they are significant. In most cases, smaller financial services organisations will not have the resources internally to address these challenges—especially considering alternative priorities in today's marketplace. Smaller banks and credit unions will most likely need to evaluate a build/buy/partner decision.

With available talent in short supply, this leaves most smaller (and many larger) organisations with a decision whether to buy or partner with a specialised solution provider to deploy digital banking solutions.

But more important for smaller institutions will be the need for top-level commitment to deploy resources to meet the increasingly demanding needs of the marketplace.

In the end, there is a great advantage in the customer insights that traditional financial institutions of all sizes possess. The key is to apply these insights in ways that directly and positively impact the digital experience, similar to how large tech firms currently improve shopping, social, search and payments.

Endnotes

1 Source: Forbes/Internet Retail—"Sixty-four percent of US households have Amazon Prime", June 2017.

The author traces the highlights of Emirates NBD's digital journey. Emirates NBD is one of the largest banking brands in the Middle East and a leader in digital innovation in the region. The bank won BAI's prestigious "Most Innovative Financial Services Organization of the Year" award for 2017.

With some of the highest smartphone penetration on the planet, emergence of a young millennial population and advent of FinTech disruptors, the UAE and the Middle East are witnessing the perfect storm on banking digitisation.

Starting with offering online banking and SMS banking in the 1990s, Emirates NBD was one of the first in the region to embrace digital. Our digital transformation program started in 2012 with the enunciation of a top management-led vision that set digital as a critical priority. For us, it was a digitise-or-die moment.

In 2013, Emirates NBD put together a strategy to execute a multi-year digital transformation. We started our journey with the setting up of a young multi-channel transformation team and drawing up a blueprint built around six pillars: improving service and sales through digital touch points, optimising branch and contact centre journeys, end-to-end process digitisation, enhancing data management and analytics, transforming technology platforms to become more agile and enhancing fraud.

Emirates NBD is fortunate to be based in Dubai, UAE, where the government has a proactive smart city strategy centred on digitisation and innovation. As part of the country's transition to becoming a knowledge-based economy, 2015 was declared the Year of Innovation and 2020 is the year the UAE aspires to send a mission to Mars.

We had a task ahead of us, to transform a generation of bankers, teaching them to think outside the box. We wanted our customers to know that we were listening to their demands for digitally disruptive products that suit a newer lifestyle. And we wanted startups to bring us their latest products so we could be the first to market, even during this rapid pace of change. The digital world being a great equaliser, ideas can come from anywhere, allowing us the possibility to crowd source innovation from various stakeholders, including staff, customers and vendors.

Walking the talk

We started our journey with fixing the basics and addressing prominent customer pain points, such as introducing electronic statements, enhancing our call centre IVR and launching a next-generation mobile banking solution.

One of our early winners was in the area of money transfers. The UAE is the third largest outward remittance market in the world, sending out US$44 billion in 2016. Remittances are an integral part of our expatriate customers' routines, a significant majority of the population today. We launched a DirectRemit service that makes possible 60-second money transfers at zero fees using mobile or online banking to a multitude of home markets. Today, DirectRemit volumes have grown almost 10-fold since launch and has garnered close to a five percent market share. Today improvements in that platform enable our customers to make on-the-go money transfers to friends and family, simply by using the beneficiaries' mobile numbers.

To encourage customers to save, we rolled out Shake n' Save, the first gamified savings account in the region, enabling customers to save when and where they want to, simply by shaking their mobile phone. Rising obesity levels in the region were bringing health and fitness into focus, so we provided customers with an incentive to become more active with the launch of the Fitness Account, the first savings account linked to the Apple Watch. The account earned interest based on the number of steps the customer walked or ran every day, encouraging them to be healthier, physically and financially.

In branch we developed in-house tablet apps that helped reduce queue times as well as improving our processing capabilities. Our CRM systems were enhanced to offer paperless signing up for new products: today, about half of our personal loans are originated without any paper documentation and two-thirds of all customer requests are fully straight through. A new mePay service was launched, enabling customers to transfer cash to anyone in the UAE through the ATM without the need of a bank account number, as well as allowing for cash withdrawals using one's mobile phone without the need for a card. Today, 92 percent of all our transactions happen outside the branch and our branch network is transforming into a sales and advisory space.

To drive continued digital transformation and become future-ready, Emirates NBD has announced an investment of circa US$300 million over the next three years to support digital innovation and multi-channel transformation of processes, products and services. This has been focused initially on integration with the UAE's smart government initiative (including blockchain) and reducing friction. Additionally, we've set up an incubator for FinTech startups in the region.

One of the outcomes of these developments is the creation of the Emirates NBD Future LabTM. Among other activities, Future Lab works with vendors and partners to conduct research on emerging technologies such as blockchain, artificial intelligence, augmented reality and the Internet of Things, while acting as an accelerator for creating viable products.

One of the successful outcomes of this lab is our futuristic branch at Emirates Towers, Dubai, part of the Dubai Future Foundation's prestigious Museum of the Future, where customers can get acquainted with futuristic beta-concepts of banking and payment solutions. Innovations include the Connected Car in partnership with Visa, integrating day-to-day payments seamlessly; the Future of Shopping with MasterCard, showcasing immersive virtual reality-based shopping experiences; and augmented reality-based home purchase in co-operation with SAP. The most popular exhibit is, however, Pepper, our humanoid robot that greets customers as they enter the branch, converses with them in English or Arabic and provides assistance on products and services.

In November 2016, Emirates NBD announced the set-up of the region's first intelligent, voice-based, chatbot-driven virtual assistant, EVA (or Emirates NBD Virtual Assistant). EVA allows customers calling our call centre to interact and receive assistance using conversational English or Arabic (a first in the world), offering a more intuitive and personalised experience than wading through an IVR maze.

We are also the banking partner for the FinTech Hive, the UAE's first FinTech accelerator program, which is run by the Dubai International Financial Centre and Accenture along the lines of similar initiatives in London, New York and Hong Kong. A recent study says that there could be over a 100 FinTech companies in the MENA region, with one-fourth of them in the UAE alone. Startup fever is reaching tipping point in the region, with over US$3 billion raised in 2016 by tech firms and inspired by the region's first unicorn, Careem, a ride-hailing service.

Social media to social banking

It may seem more straightforward now, but for traditional banks, making the transition from being formal entities that spoke to the customer from behind glass partitions to being "liked" and "followed" on social media was a difficult paradigm shift.

We partnered with Twitter to be the first bank in the region to offer customer support through our @EmiratesNBD twitter handle. Our extensive series of "how-to" videos on YouTube guides newer customers on day-to-day banking and which products are best suited to their needs. Our worthy.ae platform publishes independent content on financial literacy and wellbeing.

Emirates NBD also has been making significant strides in the area of social banking by making many of our branches disabled-friendly, piloting of an automated sign language to text translator, creation of digital donation platforms and distribution of Braille currency.

New vistas

With sustained investments behind digitisation, banks have now the opportunity to up the ante and become disruptors in their own right.

One such opportunity is e-commerce. With the UAE e-com industry on the cusp of big change—Amazon recently announced their entry into the market with the purchase of locally-grown market leader Souq.com—online shopping in the UAE is growing rapidly and set to double to US$10 billion by 2020.

As Brett mentioned earlier in the book, in mid-2017 we launched our own shopping portal, SkyShopper, that allows customers to shop and pay for a wide range of goods and services, ranging from flights, hotel bookings, electronics and fashion to entertainment and groceries, all under one digital roof. While it is early days, customer interest in the platform has been high and we see the service as being a strong catalyst in the growth of this industry, and long term in helping the transformation to a cashless society.

The emergence of a large millennial segment and their digital affinity prompted us in 2017 to launch Liv., the UAE's first digital lifestyle bank targeted at millenials. Liv., built from the ground up by a millennial team, provides customers with a unique digital banking experience built around lifestyle. The app is a friend and wing-man first and a bank later, helping customers manage their daily life and social engagements apart from a cool banking experience that includes instant account opening, free transfers, POS payments, bill-splits and the like. Liv. already accounts for one-fourth of our new accounts acquisition.

Our new FaceBanking™ video banking service allows customers to bank face to face from home or office, or carry out live chats with a banking advisor. The new service empowers customers to connect 24/7 with an advisor through our online or mobile banking platforms, and carry out enquiries and transactions, including signing up for a personal loan or credit card instantly.

Back in the 1960s when I grew up in a small town in India, the branch manager of the neighbourhood bank was an iconic figure. He knew everything about every family in town, and took lending decisions after a subjective assessment of factors, both financial and social. When my father wanted an education loan to send my elder brother to university, the bank manager sat him down to discuss my brother's choice of subjects, lament the state of education in the country, and after multiple cups of milky tea, signed off on the loan with a handshake and a hug.

Today, a loan can still happen over a cup of tea or dinner. But the difference is that you can do it from the comfort of your office or home, without even knowing the name of your bank manager. You go online, chat with an advisor—perhaps even a robot advisor—complete a digital form, upload a couple of documents, and the loan is credited by the time you finish your cuppa. It is high-tech but also high-touch. And that's what will continue to win the day for progressive banks like Emirates NBD if I have anything to do with it.

Suvo Sarkar is a retail banking professional with over 30 years of multi-functional experience with five leading financial institutions and in multiple geographies across Asia, the Middle East and Africa. Currently, he is the Senior Executive Vice President and Group Head of Retail Banking and Wealth Management of Emirates NBD, the biggest bank in Dubai. In 2018, Suvo was recognised as the "Retail Banker of the Year" at the Retail Banker International global awards. He can be reached on suvosarkar@EmiratesNBD.com.

Part04

Which banks survive, which don't

9 Adapt or Die

Neither RedBox nor Netflix are even
on the radar screen in terms of competition.
—Blockbuster CEO Jim Keyes, speaking to investors in 2008

Disruption is not new. When you look back over the last couple of centuries, you see time and again evidence that incumbents underestimated the impact of change on their industry. In the banking sector today, the huge potential changes we're facing are no longer just focused on front-end user experiences. We're seeing currency, capital markets, wealth management, bank licenses, labour force and economics all under attack from new emerging systems, paradigms and technologies.

I guess the question should be asked, though: when looking at the likes of Kodak, Blockbuster, Borders, Yellow Cabs, record labels and cable TV, when could we have known with certainty that they were going to be disrupted? What are the warning signs, and are there those same indicators for banks and financial institutions today?

The biggest question probably is: why is it, when faced with disruption, incumbents don't react faster? The threat of Amazon to the retail sector has been clear for over a decade, but despite their steady increase in capabilities and reach, incumbents who had plenty of time to plan a response have mostly been left reeling[1]. It's like a mixture of disbelief in the speed of the change combined with fear over being disrupted, which often creates a condition like a deer in the headlights of an oncoming vehicle. You know you need to move, but you still get hit anyway.

What are the indicators that banking and financial services, more specifically, are about to be disrupted?

1. Power is consolidated

One of the most typical elements of predicting when an industry is ripe for disruption is imbalance or dominance by a few leading players. When industry behaviour is consolidated amongst a cabal or oligopoly—a few small players that have consolidated vast market share—the likelihood of change is lower, as those incumbents feel they dominate their sector so completely that they are immune to competition. That sort of entrenched behaviour leads to greater incentive to preserve the status quo, especially when it comes to shareholder returns in the medium term.

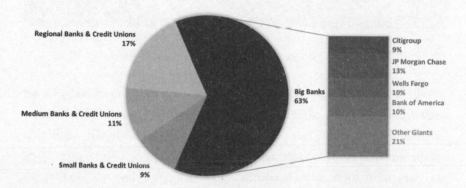

Figure 1: US bank share of assets by type (Source: 2015 Fed Data).

In the US, UK, EU and China banking sectors, this dominance by a few players tends to skew regulation in favour of these larger incumbents who wield enormous power politically. The "too-big-too-fail" movement during the global financial crisis is a simple indicator of the inflexibility of the industry in allowing disruption of these dominant players.

In the US in 1995, US majors held just 22 percent of market share by assets; today that's closer to 70 percent[2]. When consolidation leads to a few players driving the industry, this leads to less likelihood of an orderly transition to new technology states.

2. The industry is inflicted by outdated technology

When Netflix, Borders, Polaroid, Kodak and others went under, it was largely considered a failure of adaptation to emerging technologies. The biggest banks often have the most complex legacy systems, and that makes it difficult for them to implement new technology quickly. Creating a smartphone app seems pretty simple, until you realise you have to deal with your core banking back-end and a business model, which requires compliance based on customer signatures on a physical piece of paper.

Figure 2: Transforming a bank is like turning a massive freighter; startups are more like speedboats.

Responding to new, agile disruptors takes extremely flexible technology and organisational structures. The bigger the ship, the longer it takes to turn.

It's not just the 1960s era core banking systems coded on COBOL. It's the fact that at the very core, most banks still require manual processing and paperwork for account opening, accessing a line of credit or, in the case of cheques, even sending money from one person to another. While some incremental changes are taking place on top of this layer of legacy process and technology, the reality is that when disruptors look at this tech they see an opportunity for disruption. If you still require a signature, you are probably going to get your butt handed to you in this story.

Think about the technology failures at banks of late[3]. Transaction system failures of POS, ATM networks, internet and mobile banking hooked into antiquated back-end technologies that were never designed to cope with the load they're experiencing today. Swift network failures and hacks have also accounted for hundreds of millions in losses. Massive card and credit score database hacks and compromises. Bank-to-bank payments networks that still take three to five days to send your money from one bank to another. The requirement to see someone in a branch when your account is locked up because of some administrative mistake, or because you simply forgot your password. The requirement to submit 15–20 pages of documentation to open an account and prove your identity. Everywhere these historical processes and outdated legacy technologies make an appearance, we know there is some startup already in the process of attacking those outmoded operations.

3. Trust is still an issue

> I think the public trust in us might take a generation to re-establish itself.
> —Antonio Simoes, UK Chief Executive,
> HSBC Banking Corp, 2016

According to Gallop research[4] only one in four Americans trust their banks after the global financial crisis. In the UK it's even worse, with just 12 percent of UK respondents having a strong or very strong level of trust in banks. In the EU in general, trust in banks varied between 14 percent (Ireland) to 36–38 percent in the Nordic region. Obviously trust in banks hit a historical low in 2008 during the financial crisis and it has been slow to recover—primarily because banks have not really changed in the minds of customers since the crisis. This lack of trust appears now to have become somewhat embedded generationally in Gen-Zs' and Gen-Ys' attitudes, which significantly lowers the barriers to new competitors emerging and capturing market share.

The argument that a potential technology major[5] or FinTech "doesn't have a banking license" is certainly not a barrier in this environment, where trust in banks is a penalty rather than an asset. The argument that a banking license is some magical standard of trust could not be further from reality today.

I believe trust is essentially a function of utility. The more usable a banking service is and the more the brand demonstrates its effective utility, whether from a licensed institution or not, the more consumers will tend to trust the brand's capabilities.

How much do you trust banks?

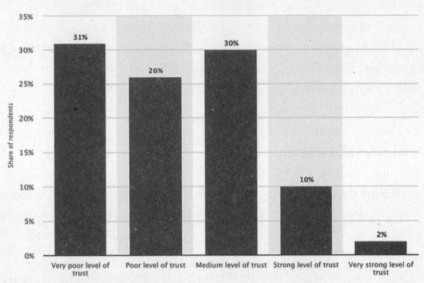

Figure 3: Trust in UK banks (Source: Statista 2018 data).

This explains why in China, companies like Alipay and Tencent WeChat are *actually trusted more* by the majority of consumers than traditional banks. In a survey conducted by E&Y and DBS in 2016, they found that this was a huge contributing factor to the rapid adoption of non-bank services in China[6]. As the interface between the consumer and the brand shifts more and more to daily technology interactions, the primary thing that needs to work is the technology and the utility associated with it. A bank's adherence to regulations to maintain its banking license has very little correlation with customer trust if its technology fails.

Let me illustrate it this way. Imagine you are a global, top 50 bank with billions in assets and locations around the world, and your in-house core system mainframe fails due to some random technology glitch and it takes you a week to get it sorted out. Let's say that fault repeats itself three or four times over the space of a few months. Consumer and small business stories start emerging about individuals having massive issues because they've not been able to pay their bills or employees due to your technology issues. How much is the fact you've got a banking license or you've had a branch in that town for 50 years going to matter in the consumer trust department?

The fact is that on newer technology stacks, with more agile cloud-based architectures and an entire business built with technologists at the core, newer players are statistically less likely to have technology-driven failures at the customer layer.

4. Despite negative customer sentiment, business practices aren't changing fast enough

Whether you buy into the metric or not, Net Promoter Scores offer an insight into how positive customers perceive the average bank. NPS scores range from –100 to 100. A score over 50 is generally the target, being considered very good to excellent from a customer's likelihood that they'll recommend or "promote" your business. When it comes to banking, NPS averages range from –17 through to 34 globally (depending on geography). But most large banks rank below 20. Amazon, Apple, and Google all perform consistently well above the best banks on NPS.

In recent years, more and more bank CEOs are talking about customer experience as a core competency or driver, but as yet the rubber has not hit the road. Startups like Transferwise, Monzo and Starling in the UK; Betterment, Venmo, Simple and Moven in the US; Revolut and N26 in Europe; and Alipay, LuFax and WeChat in China have all grown market share almost exclusively through customer referral and network effect, as opposed to traditional marketing approaches. This shows that these startups still have a basic customer experience differentiation that directly contributes to growth and competitive posture. In the recent British Banking Awards, Monzo and Starling won the awards for best bank based on their superior front-end experiences.

At the core of non-bank, shadow bank or alternative financial services adoption is fundamental changes in distribution mechanics, and it's the biggest concern for incumbents. If you are essentially limited to acquiring customers in-branch, or even if digital acquisition is still less than 30 percent of your revenue pipeline, this is a pretty fair indicator of risk.

> This new period we are entering is not so much about production anymore—how much is produced; it is about distribution—how people get a share in [and access to] what is produced. Everything from trade policies to government projects to commercial regulations will in the future be evaluated by distribution. Politics will change, free-market beliefs will change, social structures will change.
>
> —"Where is technology taking the economy?"
> McKinsey Quarterly, October 2017

If you examine it systemically, books, music, retail, taxis, airlines, hotels, etc have all moved to online distribution over the last 20 years. We are now talking about augmenting that with voice commerce and other embedded technologies. This is a fundamental, global shift in behaviour and distribution mechanics, away from reliance on physical points of sale. While banks like to imagine they will be the sole industry to buck this trend, the reality is book stores, record stores, retail outlets, and travel agents are simple forecasts of what will happen to branching. At this stage, there is zero evidence to support the assertion that banking is demonstrably different to other sectors in respect to engagement requirements, particularly with the shifts we're already seeing in relation to branch utilisation.

As we start to more effectively deploy internet access in the developing world, most of the two billion or more unbanked consumers will come into the financial system almost exclusively through digital. All this adds up to the fact that by the middle of the next decade more account holders globally will be digital first or digital only than banking via a branch (more about this below). Thus, by 2030 it is highly unlikely that a new Gen-Z customer will be thinking about walking down to the high street to visit their branch to open an account, especially when we've had another 10 years of focused development of frictionless onboarding for account opening.

We're talking about roughly the same period of time between when the iPhone launched and today. Within that timeframe we will see the disappearance of banks that are reliant on branches for account opening, unless they are some esoteric brand catering for a very small segment of hipster customers. How many of those can survive? In the United States, maybe 50 percent at most. How many of the thousands of community banks and credit unions in the US today rely on branch-based account opening to survive? At least 95 percent of them. Do the math.

Oh, and the regulator can't save you. Just ask the recording and movie industry, which spent hundreds of millions over more than a decade in an attempt to stop downloads.

5. Industry press and seasoned players can't stop talking about disruption

Here are a few recent headlines in the industry press:

- *CIO Magazine:* "The FinTech Effect and the disruption of financial services"
- World Economic Forum: "Big Tech, not FinTech, causing greatest disruption to banking"
- *Forbes*: "The race is on to disrupt traditional banking"
- *Business Insider*: "Banks face 'Kodak Moment' as FinTech disruption builds"
- *The Business Times*: "Disruption is the new norm for FinTech"
- *The New York Times*: "FinTech startup boom said to threaten bank jobs"
- *Financial Times*: "Bankers fear they will get Amazon-ed in tech disruption"

It's pretty clear that there is a significant shift in the dialogue in the space. When everyone is talking about disruption it's probably already happening.

6. Bank executives are responding

According to research from the Economist Intelligence Unit, more than 90 percent of bankers project that FinTech will have a significant impact on the future landscape of banking[7]. Almost a third expect that FinTech will win an equal share or even dominate the market. Sixty-five percent of CEOs see disruption as an opportunity for their business according to KPMG's 2017 Global CEO Outlook. In that same report, CEOs said agility in responding to disruption over the next three years will be more important than the last 50 years!

A Mergermarket survey of 2016 also revealed that regional and community banking executives in the US see future collaboration between the FinTech and banks as essential for survival, with 54 percent of bank respondents calling FinTechs a potential partner and 89 percent believing that partnerships between the two will be the norm over the next 10 years.

7. The way we bank is fundamentally changing

Fundamentally the biggest shift in banking is that "banking is no longer somewhere you go, it's something you do". If you're a millennial or Gen-Y, chances are you already do the majority of your banking online or via mobile. If you're under 30, chances are you visit your branch as little as possible by choice. PwC research last year identified that this trend has created a new, dominant class of behaviour they classified as omni-digital: that is, customers who use a range of digital channels for most of their banking activity.

While there are some demographic differences here, the overall trend is clear. Given that a large part of the operating expenses traditional retails banks face is the upkeep of their bricks-and-mortar distribution channels, this reduces investment by incumbents in digital out of both fear of cannibalising their existing business, and purely in budget terms. Challenger banks, which are all essentially branchless, might have smaller market shares today, but the savings they make by not maintaining expensive branch networks can translate directly into R&D on new services that will further cement their ability to capture market share.

In that same PWC survey mentioned earlier, only 25 percent of customers said they wouldn't bank with a bank that didn't have branches. That means that 75 percent of customers would bank with a "bank" that didn't have branches. It's clear that while branches will remain with us for many decades to come, they are no longer considered essential for access to banking.

Key survival techniques

> The average lifespan of a company listed in the S&P500 has decreased
> from 67 years in the 1920s, to less than 15 years today.
> —Richard Foster, Special Advisor to the President on
> Healthcare Innovation, Yale University

It's pretty obvious then, at least to anyone paying attention, that disruption is now reshaping the banking and financial services landscape, just as it has other industries. Disruption is hitting the banking sector differently for different types of banks, but there are signs of it everywhere. In the United States the number of community banks in 1984 was 17,401; in 2017 only 5,278[8]. Yet the largest banks in the US have grown their asset base considerably over the same period—$31 trillion of lending has moved to the so-called shadow banking system[9] (including FinTechs), and that's more than three times the credit banks provide in the US. European Central Bank data shows that the number of lenders in the EU is already in decline, having fallen from 8,237 in 2010 down to 7,110 in 2015, and further consolidation is expected[10]. India has announced it will reduce the number of PSBs (public sector banks) down to roughly half what it is today. The GCC region and China are also expecting significant consolidation. In China, Japan and Korea the pressure on smaller regional banks is acute as technology players get traction.

It might be stating the obvious, but the first thing that needs to change in response to how we handle this level of disruption is the way organisations and leaders think. Adapting to change is becoming a survival skill in this disruptive age, where technology changes are speeding up, not slowing down. Some organisations say they'll see where the disruption goes and then they'll be a fast-follower, copying the innovations of the FinTech leaders.

Figure 4: The problem with a follower strategy in an industry facing disruption (Image Credit: Marketoonist.com)

As Ron Shevlin pointed out in his excellent post "The Fast Follower Fallacy"[11], if you wait to follow when faced with industry disruption, you will inevitably lose market share. He says fast-follower is just another name for "late mover", especially at the speed first movers are adapting to change. There are a few reasons for this assertion, but the most critical one is that the lack of technology pedigree in incumbent players means by the time an innovation is showing significant traction, a follower is still two to three years behind the leader who introduced that innovation, with another two years of development time ahead of it just to catch up. That's probably half the time you have left to turn your ship. If you are facing two or three major disruption technologies in a relatively short timeframe, your future as an incumbent is now clearly in jeopardy.

So, what can you do to respond? One key answer is a relentless pursuit of great customer experiences at the core of your mission. This will drive the organisation to remove friction, try engaging the customer with new experiences, and force innovative workarounds that break current policy and process strangleholds.

Here's what Tiffani Bovi, former Gartner VP and now Salesforce.com's Global Customer Growth, Sales and Innovation evangelist, says: "Looking at it from sales and growth specifically, the biggest trend right now is how important customer experience is in developing and supporting a brand and improving sales performance. The customer decides when and how they want to interact with brands, and this impacts the way companies sell to their customers. Big macro trends, such as social, mobile, cloud, big data, and IoT help create different experiences, but *ultimately the customer is becoming far more disruptive than the technology itself* and shaping entirely new industries[12]."

IBM research in 2015 showed that 65 percent of banking executives thought they delivered excellent customer service, but only 35 percent of their customers agreed. This perception gap is likely to grow as challenger banks, TechFins and technology majors extend their user experience lead on technologies like mobile apps, voice-smart assistants, augmented reality glasses, and so forth.

But there are a few other tactical things you can do to start transforming your organisation's customer alignment, agility and adaptability.

1. **Put technology people on your board**

    For community and smaller banks in particular, having a board that came through the local community over the last 20–30 years was a strategy that worked when knowing the community was at the core of meeting their customer's needs. Today, meeting customer needs is much more down to technology delivery than it is understanding what the local retailers and farmers are concerned about, or whether the central bank is going to raise interest rates.

    The sort of technologists you need are those that are well networked on the newer technologies, have had their own startup in the space, or that have dealt with digital transformation at an organisation like your own. The objective here is to get a top-down view to inform the executive committee better. Identify which technologies you should be prioritising—and for smaller banks who rely solely on vendors to provide their platforms, which partnerships are going to be key to an agile experience. VCs that have large FinTech portfolios could be useful, as they may be able to get you introductions to prospective partners that could give you a technology edge.

Chris Skinner in his blog[13] recently highlighted this problem, where he pointed out that banks might say they are "becoming technology companies", but the reality is that their management structures belie those claims. Accenture analysed the background of around 2,000 executives from 100 of the top banks by assets globally to assess what technology experience they brought to the table[14]. The results were appallingly dismal:

- Only three percent of CEOs of leading banks have professional technology experience
- Only six percent of board directors have professional technology experience
- 40 percent of banks have no board members with any professional technology experience

2. **Hire lots of millennials and Gen-Zs (if you can)**

Millennials (those born between 1980 and 1995) recently became the largest segment of the US labour market at 34 percent, and the greatest share of the US population (24 percent). Gen-Z, born after 1996, is growing both in numbers (21 percent of US population) and consumer purchasing power. By contrast, key senior management decision-makers and corporate board members tend to be from those groups born before 1980 (Boomers: 22 percent; Gen-X: 21 percent). In China, 31 percent of the population is made up of millennials (九零後 or *jiǔ ling hòu*) and it is regularly noted that they're "more entrepreneurial, individualistic and open minded"[15] than their predecessors. In less than 10 years millennials will make up 75 percent of the global workforce. They need to be informing the future priorities of your bank.

You need millennials within your teams—but hiring them is tough, unless you have a culture that attracts them. ESG (environment, social and governance) values are becoming core imperatives for millennials as a group—for many of them addressing social issues, environment concerns, income inequality and finding their voice as a generation are critical. If you don't have a formal position on these issues in your company, expect to be asked about it during the hiring process. Think about the likelihood of attracting a millennial to start building a career in banking as a teller today. That's just crazy talk given the above perspective.

Passion projects are increasingly going to become important to the next generation. Most importantly you need a culture that says something positive. Financial inclusion, promoting renewables, promoting lower crime, greater equality—find a cause that your organisation can get behind. Profitability for shareholders isn't going to motivate these candidates. As one commentator put it: put the "why" in work.

3. **Get agile**

Easier said than done. How do you move like a speedboat when you are a supertanker? There are some large organisations who are agile today, but the most consistent places to find them are technology leaders that started as startups and became large players. The likes of Google, Uber, Facebook, etc have maintained agility despite being larger employers than most of the banks in the world.

I'm not talking "lean startup theorem" here. I honestly think that's a distraction within a bank; but I am definitely talking about the ability to change your organisation's process and policy rapidly.

There are five core characteristics of Agile banks:

Customer First Mission	Broad Revenue Generation Capability	Rapid Product and Distribution	Prototyping and Learning Centre	Opti-channel and Digital Omni-channel
Agile banks don't try to fit their existing product suite and processes to customers. They're constantly adapting and trying new approaches to engage.	Agile banks get most of their revenue, do most of their cross-sell and upsell via digital. They've re-architected the organisation to minimise fixed costs like branch networks, and focused on variable costs where performance-based budgeting drives outcomes.	Distrubution is extremely flexible. Channel decisions take days and weeks, not months to play in terms of launching new initiatives.	Test, Test, Launch, Fail, Retry. The risk adverse nature that leads to bulletproof testing of new initiatives is replaced by the concept of alpha and beta releases to customers. This is a huge one for traditional players and regulators to get over.	Phygital strategies, or optimising physical and digital channels to work in concert, is pretty key for future agility. Reliance on one channel for any core activity is a constraint Agile banks don't want—they watch customer behaviour and respond accordingly.

Table 1: The core characteristics of Agile banks.

Lack of agility can also negatively affect the capacity for banks to take on partnerships with FinTechs and technology firms that are more agile. If a startup is releasing versions of their new app every few weeks, and banks have three-to-six monthly product release cycles, the culture clash is going to be severe. In most cases the organisation is just not equipped to work faster, and thus the benefit of a partnership with an agile organisation could be largely lost, or worse—the partnership could fail.

I know we could write a great deal more on agile organisation structures, but that topic is so large you need to do some specific research if you're heading down that path. I will say that if you are going to do "transformation", at some point you'll have to tackle the organisational structure as we identified earlier in the book.

4. **Stop hiring bankers, attract differentiated talent**

    It is key that new skills are infused throughout the organisation. A focus on people who have worked in banking before, or "banking experience essential" on the job description, is only going to reinforce the traditional decision-making process and reduce your likelihood of survival. But hiring the programmers, designers, data scientists, and deep learning specialists that will bring a breath of fresh air into the organisation's thinking is tough when your culture is bankers or banking first, instead of customer experience and technology transformation focused. A recent article by a coder that had worked for mainstream financial institutions in the UK for nearly a decade is telling:

    > Banks will tell you they're tech companies. Don't believe them. Technologists are second class citizens in banks—if you work near the trading floor (I did), the traders are in charge. The politics in the technology team are immense and the career progression is limited. You won't be working on innovative new technologies. Most banks are cutting costs and this means you'll be focusing on maintaining the infrastructure.
    >
    > —"Banks are no place for coders",
    > eFinancialCareers, Richard Ling, March 2017

    How does a bank compete with the likes of Google, Facebook, Uber, and the tens of thousands of FinTechs also competing for talent? Peter Lawrey, Stack Overflow's most active community commentator and a high-frequency trading coder, made the observation in a 2015 interview that banks are having to pay 33–50 percent higher salaries just to attract talent[16]. In most cases, however, banks just don't compete. If you want the best technology people, you do need to present your organisation as a business that eats and breathes the potential for technology to change your destiny.

In a benchmarking study by Emolument.com in September 2017, it found that two-thirds of software developers working in banks believed their bosses *didn't care* about the working environment or them personally. For those we'd traditionally call bankers the survey showed the opposite statistic, with two-thirds saying they were *happy* with the way the organisation prioritised their needs. That reinforces the anecdotal evidence that within many banks digital or technology is still not considered "real banking".

In an effort to attract talent, the more innovative banks I've seen are "googlising" their offices. I visited Banco de Chile in 2017 and was told by COO Ignacio Vera that interviewing staff in their incubator offices had been "an essential element in turning around our ability to attract talent".

Figure 5: Banco de Chile's Lab Environment in Chile has been successful in attracting design and developer talent.

In 2014 Capital One acquired the design firm Adaptive Path[17]. They did this as part of a deliberate culture shift, where design became central to the future delivery capabilities of the bank. This is obviously a key strategy in attracting talent, getting rapid delivery capabilities and changing an organisation's culture. As acquired talent is injected into the organisation, they can often be seen internally as the new benchmark in respect of culture and approach. This can help, but only if your organisation is receptive.

Hundreds of banks over the years have started innovation departments only to see them wither on the vine when the head of innovation departed for a better gig, or closed them down because they didn't fit the culture of the bank. The issue here isn't that the innovation team doesn't fit the culture of the bank, it's that the immune system of the bank works hard to reject something new that threatens change. Change is perceived as risk, and risk is the last thing banks want to take on.

5. **Prioritise the most impactful digital journeys and get started**

   Transforming your entire business overnight is basically impossible, but you can start building experiences that circumvent traditional organisation structures, departments and technology. Experiences that demonstrate successful transformation.

   Bain and Company research showed millennials were placing calls to their banks at 1.7 times the rate of customers aged 65 plus. But that isn't because younger customers love talking on the phone[18]. The research showed that in more than half those instances they had tried using a digital channel first and had failed—whether due to usability issues or simply that the digital channel did not support what they were looking for. Well-designed customer journeys make good economic sense. Each digital interaction with a customer incurs a variable cost of about 10 cents, compared with more than $4 for an interaction with a human teller or call-centre agent. The incentive to get those customer journeys working properly is strong. But how do you prioritise the journeys that will lead your transformation efforts?

   A simple method I've used over the last decade or so with strong business case performance has been a weighted, business impact scoring methodology. You take the key elements of revenue generation, customer relationship impact, customer friction, organisation cost savings, and risk management and look for those customer journeys that tick the most boxes. The key is that journeys that positively affect the bottom line and improve engagement, reduce attrition and increase revenue per customer naturally flow to the top. Here's an example I prepared earlier for typical retail banking transformation:

Proposed Digital Customer Journey	Generates Revenue (Yes/No)	Deepens Relationship (Yes/No)	Reduces Customer Friction (Yes/No)	Cost Savings (1=low, 5=high)	Risk Weighting (1=low, 5=high)	Total Weighted Score
Digital Onboarding/ Account Opening	Yes	Yes	Yes	4	1	23
In-store Instant Credit Approval	Yes	Yes	Yes	2	3	19
Token-based Cardless ATM Withdrawal	No	No	Yes	1	1	10
Lost Card Reporting via App	No	No	Yes	3	1	12
Pre-approved Car Loan	Yes	Yes	Yes	3	3	20
Credit Card Usage Offer	Yes	No	No	2	1	11
Stock Trading App	Yes	No	Yes	1	4	12
Credit Card Payment	No	No	Yes	2	1	11
Personal Financial Management	Yes	Yes	Yes	1	1	20
Update Contact Information	No	No	Yes	5	1	14
Change Credit Limit	Yes	Yes	Yes	3	3	20
Home Buying Assistance	Yes	Yes	Yes	2	1	21
Handset Insurance	Yes	Yes	No	1	1	15

Table 2: Customer/Business impact scoring matrix.

The weighted formula used in this example is as follows:
$$=((IF(B="Yes",5,0))+(IF(C="Yes",5,0))$$
$$+(IF(D="Yes",5,0))+E)+(5-F)$$

Essentially, each column is given a weighting, and the journeys with the greatest impact to both customer and business profitability rise to the top. The formula could be adjusted, but the current formula provides a strong balance between business objectives and customer prioritisation. Many of a bank's traditional products and experiences simply don't rate well using this methodology and would not make the cut.

An example from Table 2 is a Credit Card Usage Offer—something that the cards guys would inevitably want stuck in the mobile app as a high priority. The problem is that it doesn't solve a customer problem, and it doesn't have a massively positive impact internally either. Whereas an instant In-Store Credit Approval performs much better, scoring almost twice as high on the potential score. In many regards you could view this as the same fundamental offer, but one is experiential and the other is product-focused.

This illustrates the point once again: if a bank is going to work on customer journeys, it shouldn't be to just adapt a product designed for brand distribution on to new digital channels, but should include the customer journeys or scenarios that will make the most impact. A poor example of this is Capital One's Alexa deployment, where they focused on paying the customer's credit card as one of the first-use cases they developed. Why were they trying to shove a plastic card into a voice experience? Everything about voice commerce suggests a plastic card with a 16 digit number is an anachronism. This is a missed opportunity.

What is the core utility a bank offers, and how best can that utility be presented through the technology layer in real time? That should be at the heart of great CX design in everyday banking.

> How do you take 19th century management and measurement practices and make them work in the world of today—the world of Steve Jobs and Mark Zuckerberg?
> —Jason Berns, Senior Director of Innovation—Under Armour

Research from Innovative Leader found that the vast majority of companies don't even have effective metrics to measure their successful transformation. The research did show that both activity metrics and impact metrics were critical in measuring the success of transformation efforts. Activity metrics being the inputs into transformation—the number of employees involved in innovation, number of ideas generated, number of new projects started, patents filed, etc. Impact metrics were the tangible results of innovation—revenue growth, new market share/entry, new product or service revenue.

Here are the top five measurements that came out of that survey of 200 leaders of innovation:

1. Revenue generated by new products
2. Projects in the pipeline
3. Stage-gate process (i.e., projects moving from proof of concept to implementation)
4. P&L or financial impact
5. Number of ideas generated per quarter

If you want to transform, you should be measuring how successful your team is at adapting.

Survival starts at the top

> We can't solve problems by using the same kind of thinking we used when we created them.
>
> —Attributed to Albert Einstein

If you've made the decision to survive the disruption of technology and FinTech, rather than accept the slow decline into obsolescence, then you must start by committing to changing the culture of the bank. You might want to be a technology company—but that adds up to a lot more than simply saying you are a technology company, swapping out the office furniture with bean bags, and slapping some pastel paints and whiteboards around the place. It requires a culture shift, starting at the top. It requires leaders that both want to transform the business and have the skills to make it happen.

Let's think about what the data is telling us.

The fastest growing financial institutions globally are either technology companies that acquire customers at scale quickly and cheaply via digital direct approaches, or those incumbents who are spending literally billions of dollars a year to innovate in a host of areas. FinTechs are gradually taking market share, and while they don't dominate the sector, their growth means they will absolutely be a part of the future that is coming, and others are likely to get consolidated out. It is not just happening in the acquisition arena either. Technologies like artificial intelligence, blockchain and cloud architectures are fundamentally changing the way we build financial institutions for the 21st century. When it comes down to it, technology is not at the heart of the modern financial institution. It's the heart, the brain, the legs, the vocal cords—heck, it is what we know as banking today.

If you don't have technology people on the board of your bank, and if your CEO has spent their entire career as a banker and doesn't know a GPU from a CPU, then call me a cynic, but I just don't think he's going to be the guy to lead you through the transformation required.

When I see the likes of HSBC promote a CEO who has practically zero technology experience and has spent his entire career in the bank[19], I'm going to bet they will probably fail to transform their business[20] before it is materially disrupted. HSBC's leadership is still built around a core of traditional thinking, and that is going to be the biggest hurdle to rapid organisational change. HSBC does have a Global Head of Digital for Retail Banking, Josh Bottomley, a really solid guy. But when you look at the leadership profiles on HSBC.com[21] he doesn't even make the cut, emphasising the disconnect between the skills needed to adapt versus the skills needed to just continue being a 20th century bank. Sure, the Group COO, Andy Maguire, has technology in his portfolio, but he isn't a dedicated technologist, and technology is certainly broader in impact than just operational aspects. The best the HSBC leadership team could offer on their "About Us" page with regard to a tactical technologist was a Head of Financial Crime Risk. That's hardly transformational, that's essentially a compliance role. They do have a technology advisory board that meets quarterly[22]—but again, how is that supposed to move the ship fast?

As an ex-HSBC-er, this distresses me immensely, but it is indicative of the core problem with broad corporate statements about digital transformation such as HSBC's "simpler, better and faster" technology mission statement. I'm not picking on HSBC specifically[23], I'm trying to illustrate the need to get real about change. You simply can't claim to be transformative, innovative, customer-first or "a technology company", unless you actually have leadership that gets the tech stuff. Leadership that can execute for the 21st century.

By contrast, if you go to BBVA.com's corporate leadership page, you'll see immediate messaging about digital and customer experience transformation (from the chairman); you'll see social media metrics around BBVA's reach; you'll find plenty of people with a strong technology pedigree in the leadership layer; and you'll see a history of acquisitions and partnerships that walk the talk. Go to Ant Financial and you'll see that the *entire* leadership team is based on years of strong technology experience and competency[24], starting with the executive chairman Peng Lei (Lucy Peng).

I regularly speak at events where a CEO of a community bank or credit union will come up to me afterwards and say, "Gosh, after hearing about all that, I'm so glad I'm retiring next year." I guess I don't need to point out that this is not actually a solution to the organisation's impending difficulties.

Yep, transformation is super-hard. The bigger the organisation, the harder it is going to be to turn that ship. But just saying you are digital isn't enough. Digital needs to be at the heart of your business, and the organisation chart doesn't lie.

In *Bank 2.0* I put it this way. I asked a simple question in the concluding chapter: "Does your Head of Branches have a more senior organisation role than the Head of Internet [or Digital]?" That question, which I asked almost a decade ago, is still at the very heart of your ability to adapt, but today the Head of Digital should be senior to the branch head. Why? Because if you are going to survive, you must recognise you are now competing against a new class of competitor and every FinTech CEO, every technology major CEO, is also the Head of Digital at their organisation. The answer in 2009 when I wrote *Bank 2.0* was in most cases "no". The answer today is still not much different.

Banking is no longer about banking competency. Banking will forever be a technological pursuit from this point forward. Revenue will be largely technology dependent within just a few years. Brand, reach and scale will be technology dependent. Customer engagement is already 95 percent technology delivery, based on daily behaviour. Your ability to attract great talent is about culture and your ability to leverage technology. Artificial intelligence at the heart of your future business won't be built by guys who started off as a teller in a branch.

You can't adapt to the incredible changes that are occurring in our industry by simply being great at banking. That's no longer enough. You need an unyielding focus on being embedded in your customer's life through the technology they have at hand, and by transforming your capability to deliver on that promise, when and where the customer needs you.

First principles thinking means the ability to start from scratch and approach the problem in a fundamentally different way. If you're iterating on the same basic banking model you've had for the last 30 years, you just won't get there fast enough.

Banking will be everywhere, but only through the technologies that allow it to be ubiquitous—not through real estate and humans. If you don't have the right leadership transforming your business, if you don't allow yourself to think differently about what banking is, your bank simply won't be there.

Endnotes

1. See "One statistic shows how much Amazon could dominate the future of retail", *Business Insider*, Kate Taylor, 1 November 2007; Amazon is driving half of the growth in retail—Sears, Macy's and ToysRUs are all victims of this shift.

2. Source: FDIC Data. See also "Banks are getting bigger, not smaller", *The Independent*, 12 March 2017.

3. Including Australian, UK, US and German majors.

4. Source: Gallop Poll "Confidence in Institutions" July 2017—http://news.gallup.com/poll/1597/confidence-institutions.aspx.

5. Amazon, Apple or Alibaba, for example.

6. Source: E&Y/DBS Survey 2016 "The rise of FinTech in China".

7. Source: "The disruption of banking", The Economist EIU.

8. Source: FDIC Statistics at a Glance (30 September 2017 figures)—Total no. of FDIC Insured Institutions 5,737 (92 percent of that total are community banks).

9. Source: American Bankers Association.

10 There is one bank for about every 50,000 citizens in the Eurozone, a similar level to the US, but far more fragmented than the UK's one per 170,000 people and Japan's almost one per 900,000 people.

11 Source: The Financial Brand.

12 Interview, March 2016, Salesforce.com—emphasis ours.

13 TheFinanser.com.

14 Source: "Bridging the Technology Gap in Financial Services Boardrooms", Accenture Strategy Report 2016.

15 See Goldman Sachs Report "The Asian Consumer: Chinese Millennials".

16 Source: JAXEnter, "Banks 'pay 33 percent to 50 percent more' in developer salaries", March 2015.

17 See Techcrunch, "Design Firm Adaptive Path Acquired by Capital One", 2 October 2014.

18 If you have teenage children, you'll know from experience how hard it is to get them talking on the phone.

19 See http://www.hsbc.com/about-hsbc/leadership/john-flint.

20 HSBC has stated for the last couple of years that they wish to be "simpler, better and faster".

21 See http://www.hsbc.com/about-hsbc/leadership.

22 Source: BankingTech.com, FinTech Futures "HSBC to capitalise on tech innovation with technology advisory board"; Tanya Andreasyan, 18 January 2017.

23 Well, I guess I am, to be honest.

24 See https://www.antfin.com/team.htm.

10 Conclusion: The Roadmap to Bank 4.0

> Disruption isn't about what happens to you,
> it's about how you respond to what happens to you.
> —Jay Samit, author of *Disrupt You*

When we talk about Bank 4.0 it is good to establish both a timeline and a definition for clarity:

BANK 1.0: Historical, traditional banking centred around the branch as the primary access point. Started with the Medici family in the 12th century.

BANK 2.0: The emergence of self-service banking, defined by the first attempts to provide access outside of bank working hours. Commenced with ATM machines and accelerated in 1995 with the commercial internet.

BANK 3.0: Banking when and where you needed it as redefined by the emergence of the smartphone in 2007, and accelerated with a shift to mobile payments, P2P and challenger banks built on top of mobile; channel agnostic.

BANK 4.0: Embedded, ubiquitous banking delivered in real time through the technology layer. Dominated by real time, contextual experiences, frictionless engagement and a smart, AI-based advice layer. Largely digital omni-channel with zero requirements for physical distribution.

If we try to represent this graphically, we would show the economics of banking (primarily distribution and delivery mechanics) on one axis versus friction (in customer experience) on the other.

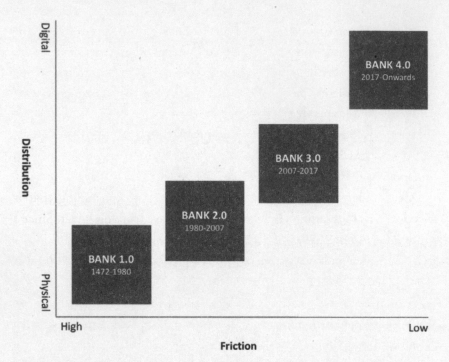

Figure 1: Embedded, ubiquitous banking must be fast, frictionless and real time.

To be clear, Banks 1.0, 2.0 and 3.0 all still exist today. There are banks that are still fundamentally Bank 1.0 in nature, operationally and in customer engagement. There are banks that still don't have a mobile app and limited online capability—they would fall into the Bank 2.0 category. The majority of banks still don't offer account opening on a mobile, and thus would barely qualify for Bank 3.0 status—sort of Bank 2.5. The number of banks that are truly omni-digital today, that are attempting to shift to Bank 4.0, number in the dozens globally, maybe. Most will never get there, including some of the challenger banks, for what it's worth.

The move to Bank 4.0 is punctuated by significant shifts in customer behaviour, the emergence of major non-bank competitors with scale that exceeds the reach of the biggest banks in the world, and an entirely different skill set necessary for success. Financial institutions that believe they can survive this onslaught by continuing to deliver basic banking through a branch off the back of a signature card are indeed at the greatest risk of disruption. If you are a bank and want to survive this transition over the next 10 years or so, you can only do so by redefining your organisation, rebuilding your core delivery capability, evolving your team, restructuring around a completely new organisation chart and by changing faster than you would have imagined possible. If you are a bank today you are potentially Kodak, Borders, Nokia, Motorola, Tower Records, Blockbuster, JC Penneys and Sears, Digital Equipment Corporation, Polaroid, Compaq, Borland and their ilk.

Technology-based disruption is not some anomalous thing that is selective in its focus, that might just choose to leave banking intact. Since I wrote *Bank 2.0* in 2009, we've already faced massive changes.

No challenger bank existed in 2009. FinTech investment in 2009 was less than US$2 billion globally, and in 2017 it exceeded US$31 billion (not counting ICOs). In 2009, peer-to-peer lending accounted for less than $1 billion globally; today it has 30 percent market share (unsecured lending) in the United States and is approaching US$1 trillion in total annual loan portfolios. In 2009, mobile payments were being debated and Apple was yet to decide their strategy; but up until October 2017 China alone did US$12 trillion in mobile payments across two non-bank networks, Tencent and Alipay. Blockchain existed as the underlying technology behind Bitcoin, but no bank was considering this technology operationally in 2009; in 2018 hundreds of banks are involved in blockchain initiatives globally. In 2009 only one bank in the world offered digital account opening (Jibun Bank, Japan); in 2017 there are hundreds of banks who offer mobile-based account opening, with challenger banks being in the majority as a class. In 2009, 5,000 Bitcoins would have cost you less than $30 to buy; in the closing moments of 2017 those Bitcoins were worth US$100 million. Since 2009, total bank branch numbers in developed economies have declined by 8–22 percent, with an average decline of 1.5–2 percent per year. Since 2009 financial inclusion has boomed in India, sub-Saharan Africa, and elsewhere around the globe, with more than one billion people getting access to a simple store of value; virtually none of those individuals have entered financial services through traditional branch access.

Little by little we are seeing fundamental changes across multiple lines of business in financial services. Access is being redefined. Economics are being rewritten. Regulation is being refamed. Day-to-day behaviour has shifted permanently away from in-branch engagement, and revenue is going the same way. The number of banks globally is shrinking as consolidation occurs, and at the same time the number of technology and FinTech players offering banking services is exploding. If these trends continue, it must result in a fundamentally different banking sector emerging from the other end. A permanent redefinition of what a bank account is, and what banking means for its customers.

To emphasise the potential of this disruptive behaviour, let me give you some of my predictions for the 2025–2030 period:

- By 2025, the largest deposit-taking organisations will be technology players, whether technology leaders like Alibaba, Amazon, Google, Tencent and Apple (potentially), or pure-play FinTech disruptors who have simply worked out how to scale deposits more efficiently.
- By 2025, almost three billion unbanked will have entered the financial services system over the preceding 15 years without ever having stepped foot in a branch.
- By 2025, *every day* more people will transact and interact with their money on a computer, smartphone, voice and augmented reality than those that visit the world's collective network of branches on an annual basis.
- By 2025, more money advice will be dispensed via artificial intelligence, algorithms and software than the entire collective network of human advisors in financial institutions today.
- By 2025, around a quarter of all daily e-commerce and mobile commerce will be voice or software agent driven, and those supporting voice will get a revenue bump of 25–30 percent compared to their non-voice-enabled counterparts.
- By 2025, the biggest retail banks in the world will almost all deliver the majority of their revenue via digital.
- By 2030, a dozen countries around the world will be mostly

cashless, including China's urban population, the Nordics, Singapore and Australia.

- By 2030, AI will have accounted for the loss of more than 30 percent of today's jobs in banking; and while some of those jobs will be replaced with deep learning specialists, data scientists and so forth, the new jobs won't come anywhere near replacing the numbers lost.

Technology first, banking second

The latest news is not only that Alipay is getting into the banking game, but Amazon is as well. At Money 20/20 in Singapore in 2018, Piyush Gupta observed that despite banks' confidence that they have brand and network advantages over tech giants, these new players have access to billions of customers already and their acquisition cost is effectively zero. There is no bank that can claim the same today. If you are going to be a technology player, you have to start with the basic assumption that your organisation must change.

The foundation of banking in the 1.0 era was simply being great at banking—good ROE, good credit risk policies, good distribution and network, etc. The foundation of banking in the 4.0 era is being great at technology—full stop. Being great at banking will actually be a penalty in the Bank 4.0 world, because that complacency could prevent you from changing quickly enough. In the Bank 4.0 era you can survive delivering banking services without any core banking skills (or core banking systems for that matter) beyond the distribution layer, as long as you have the appropriate investments in technology and design. Every time we've introduced a new technology layer into the operating environment of banking, we've little by little redefined banking itself.

When the first bank mainframe ERMA1 was introduced it led to the introduction of bank account numbers for the first time. When the ATM came, it led to us shifting from passbooks to plastic cards. When internet and mobile came we had to move off batch processing to real-time, straight-through processing capabilities. When social media came it led to IP-based, person-to-person payments systems that pressured

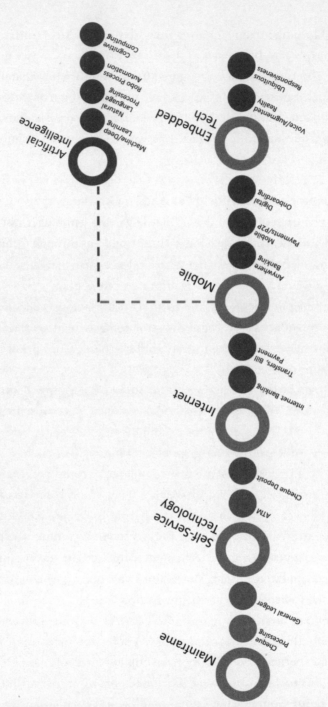

Figure 2: Technology leaps that have progressively accentuated disruption to the traditional process and policy model.

banks to change from two-to-three day processing times, to the expectation of real-time (or near real-time) capabilities. Every major new leap in technology led to permanent structural and operational changes around that new technology. There's no relationship, product, service or process within banking that hasn't been changed by technology over the last few decades, and now even regulation itself is being transformed by technology.

The key shift with Bank 4.0 is that the technology is no longer transforming elements of the bank, it is transforming the way we bank irretrievably from the past. Gupta at DBS says banking must become "invisible", simply embedded in the world around us through technology— we agree wholeheartedly.

> Francisco González, BBVA's executive chairman since 2000, believes that sooner or later the giants of the internet—Amazon, Facebook, Google—will be his main rivals. Because "the digital world doesn't allow many competitors", in 20 years the ranks of banks worldwide could be thinned from thousands to dozens, which will need scale to survive. Wariness of regulation may delay the e-behemoths, but not forever. "If you are not prepared for this precise moment, and you are not as efficient as they are, you are dead."
>
> —"BBVA reinvents itself as a digital business", *The Economist*, October 2017

When BBVA identifies an opportunity for a new service or experience, they try to respond like a FinTech would. After identifying an opportunity through their quarterly "demo days", three days later a team will have been formed to execute. Within four to six weeks a prototype has been deployed and tested on a small group of test customers: sometimes employees, sometimes willing end consumers. BBVA then aims to launch that new service or experience within a few months of the prototype or proof of concept. This sort of turnaround is unheard of at most banks, and still isn't fast enough for González and Torres at BBVA. They are looking to compete with Amazon, Facebook and Google, after all.

But remember at the core of this is a simple extrapolation of an overarching trend. Technology is increasingly about these things—instant gratification, ultimate personalisation, frictionless engagement and margins based on scale. The internet was the start and we took value chains and commerce processes and simplified them for the web. Mobile had smaller screens with restricted content delivery capabilities, so we need simpler applications, faster fulfilment. Voice simplifies this again—you're not going to read out your credit card number to Alexa before it lets you buy something on Amazon. Every step of the way we've been removing friction, and the economics of the leading businesses has been framed by digital delivery. It is why I keep emphasizing branch economics are being undermined by simple changes like digital onboarding, and the ability to scale digital banks much faster.

It is not that I hate branches—it is just that in the face of ever-simplifying digital delivery design paradigms, branches become increasingly inefficient at creating scale and margin.

Technology is inevitably leading us to a time where financial services must be frictionless. The heavy lifting of KYC, IDV, compliance and risk will all just become algorithms and data collection challenges—not processes, forms and legal rules that require interpretation. It will all be code. Thus, if your business is not encoded, it's slower. As Elon Musk said, the reason they put robots on the factory floor instead of humans is simple—humans require Tesla to slow down the production process to "human speed".

Bank 1.0 is human speed. Bank 4.0 is machine speed. Now: do you think you are ready as a bank to tackle this technology-first future?

The Bank 4.0 "digitisation" scorecard

If you want to know how close you are to becoming a Bank 4.0 player, use the questions below to score yourself:

1. **First principles is your mantra**—Your organisation doesn't work off conventional wisdom, doesn't iterate off the analogy of the existing banking business. Frankly, you're prepared to burn it all to the ground and start again, because you realise the way banking works today based on a system that is 700

years old isn't the way it's going to work 20 years from now. You are excited to reimagine banking from scratch. Any traditional operations are there to provide enough profit or working capital to transform into a Bank 4.0 future. You are willing to sacrifice quarterly returns to support a new innovation initiative, and you've convinced your board to get on board. If you've ever pulled budget from a new digital initiative so you can make your quarterly numbers, you aren't a digital bank. If you have ever heard someone in the executive team use the phrase "that's not how we do banking" or similar—you aren't a 4.0 bank.

2. **A digital CEO**—Either a technology geek who has risen through the ranks to be a CEO, or a CEO who has had a "come to Jesus/FinTech" moment and has told the entire bank their mission is to be digital, and can speak with authority on technologies like AI and voice. If your CEO hasn't given your business a mission to be a digital player, you won't transition to Bank 4.0. Digital is not a department, channel or separate competency, it is simply the job of the bank, and the CEO is the head of digital with a great team behind him or her that is fully committed. You can have some specialised competencies under this, but if you have a head of digital who reports to the executive team, then you aren't a digital bank; you are a traditional bank with some digital competency. Apple and Amazon don't have heads of digital—Tim Cook and Jeff Bezos are the heads of digital.

3. **Legacy technology and architecture isn't a constraint**—A real-time banking core or strong middleware with the ability to create any product instance or service experience from your digital platform in real time, and the ability to handle real-time settlements on payments across any platform, is a given. Keep in mind that Amazon, Ant Financial, Tencent and their ilk don't need a core system to do their version of banking, so you'll think the same way. Essentially, you are

building a set of technology platform capabilities to deliver experiences when and where your customer needs them—if the current technology doesn't allow you to do it, you'll just work around those constraints.

4. **Clouds aren't a coming storm**—You think of cloud like you do any other piece of technology or resources available: if it helps you execute more efficiently or gives you access to better capabilities, you'll embrace it. You don't need to have all your technology in-house or on-premises, because an internal firewall is simply no guarantee of the best technology or best security. If you don't currently have a significant experience delivered via the cloud, you aren't a digital bank.

5. **Experience design is a core competency**—You have a team that is constantly prototyping and revisiting every aspect of customer interaction, trying not to just optimise it but to revolutionise it. Building real-time experiences is the fastest growing budget line item in digital, save for maybe a core system replacement and real-time payments retooling; the ability to create experiences for customers rapidly, in days or weeks, is essential. If you don't have an in-house design team, you aren't a digital bank. If your CTO has never done a wireframe sketch on a whiteboard or piece of paper to explain where the business needs to go, you aren't a digital bank. If your traditional marketing budget exceeds digital direct, you are definitely not a digital bank. If a product department or head can override experience design, you're not a digital bank.

6. **Data science and machine learning are your new core**—The ability to leverage off your data, and the ability to capture more data and to crunch that through algorithms to identify new opportunities, new segments and new behaviours, has energised the business. The biggest question remains: how quickly you can operationalise this capability, not if, but when. If you don't have a Head of Data Science or a strong budget for AI, you aren't a digital bank. If you don't know

at least a handful of AI companies working in the space, you aren't a digital bank.

7. **Regulations are never an excuse**—To be a digital bank you will never use regulation as an excuse. Here's the test: in the last six months, you've gone to the regulator with a technology or experience pilot that doesn't fit into current regulations to get approval to proceed. If you haven't done this, you aren't a digital bank. If your compliance team is allowed to kill new experience initiatives, new real-time capabilities or attempts at reducing friction for the customer, you aren't a digital bank. Your compliance team thinks of themselves as consultants to help navigate the changing regulatory environment so you can get stuff done.

8. **You are partnering with, investing in, or acquiring FinTechs**—The smart digital banks know the bigger they get, the harder it is to innovate purely as a function of size. So the smarter banks are finding ways to learn faster through partnerships with very agile teams that are thinking differently about the problem. If you've run a "hackathon" but don't fund a FinTech startup, you aren't a digital bank. If you have a procurement team that deluges a small 20 person startup with 80 pages of legal agreements that were adapted from your last Oracle services agreement instead of streamlining this partnership, you aren't a digital bank.

9. **You don't have to build it yourself**—Often when it comes to new technology like mobile, voice or AI capability, you'll have bank technology teams spend millions of dollars just to have complete control over the process and keep it all in-house. Digital banks value speed of execution over owning the tech, and so are agnostic as to whether it is developed internally or just accessed via plugging in a partner's technology. Bank 4.0 players realise that FinTechs and their ilk are going to be faster and cheaper than building it internally nine out of 10 times, and their organisation is built to engage as such.

10. **Your bank is open**—Whether mandated via regulation or understanding that your bank is no longer an island, but a platform of services, is liberating in respect to the potential opportunities it presents. You already have thousands of APIs that allow access to data and core capabilities for external parties who want to incorporate your bank platform into their customer experiences. Whether it is someone like Uber opening bank accounts for new drivers, Amazon offering loans to small business merchants, or aggregators and platforms like Mint.

11. **You have technology competency on the board and throughout the executive team**—Mobile, voice and augmented reality will all be core competencies over the next 10 years, but the banking sector is significantly behind most other industries in terms of innovative approaches (not necessarily in adoption though), so having a non-bank technology person on the board to level board expectations is really key. If your executive team on the website doesn't include a couple of technology veterans, you aren't a digital bank.

12. **You are branch, revenue and relationship agnostic**—You are well past arguing that people love branches. You think you'll keep them if you can continue to justify a right-sized network (much smaller numbers and square footage) based on economics, but you are already channel and revenue agnostic. Whatever channel the customer uses, you will support. If you cannot sign up a customer for a bank account in-app, you are not a digital bank. If you still require a signature for any product or service you offer your customers, you are not a digital bank—no FinTech uses signatures to onboard customers, period. If you don't do more than 50 percent of your revenue in retail via digital, you are not a digital bank.

13. **Everyone's job is digital**—Everyone is passionate about building great experiences for customers and everyone believes that the best way to do that is digital, not "future branches"

or other such silliness. If you have a senior executive that has shot down a digital initiative in favour of the status quo, you are not a digital bank. If your annual digital budget doesn't exceed your real-estate budget, you are not a digital bank. If at least 30 percent of your staff don't know how to do some basic sort of coding, you are not a digital bank.

14. **Technology is not a channel**—In a Bank 4.0 world, mobile, voice, augmented reality and internet aren't channels, they are simply technologies embedded in a customer's life. The problem with talking about omni-channel, opti-channel or multi-channel approaches is they are all based on the core belief that branch banking is the core banking behaviour, and other channels are "add ons" to that core distribution channel. This thinking reinforces iterations off the branch model of banking. A Bank 4.0 CEO looks at the core utility of the bank and figures out the most seamless, frictionless way to get that capability to a customer when and where they need it. They're not taking branch products, application forms and processes and trying to retro-fit them for mobile or web. If you think you need a plastic card to do payments, you're not a digital bank. If you talk about your multi-channel capability, you're not a digital bank. If you talk about the benefits of seeing a human in-branch versus a digital engagement, you're not a digital bank.

Everyone wants to be a digital bank; the reality is very few are. At the heart of the Bank 4.0 shift is a fundamental change that erodes the value of current distribution channels and the products we put through those channels.

Experience not products

What's it going to take to survive? That's the billion dollar question, but it starts with the obvious: to compete against technology-first players you need to evolve into a technology-first state. But technology is not the end goal—compelling embedded banking experiences are. As a platform, your bank needs to be integrated into its customers' lives when and where they need it the most—this is where the technology is taking us. Understanding that technology means they'll never have to "come to the bank" ever again.

Capital One, BBVA, DBS, USAA and others have all said they want to be technology companies or leading digital banks; but if that's the case, getting from where they are today to becoming an organisation that is experience-led and technology-first will require a substantial organisational makeover. The resources required to win in this environment have almost nothing to do with traditional banking.

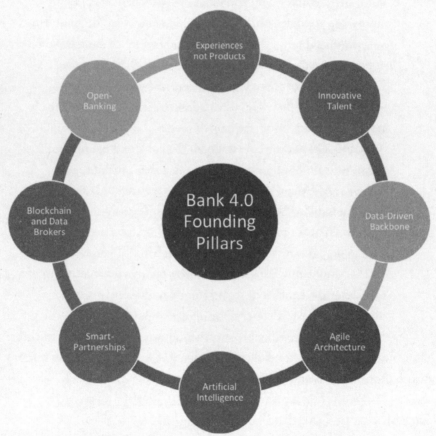

Figure 3: The foundation of a Bank 4.0-ready organisation.

Throughout the preceding chapters we've discussed many aspects of the Bank 4.0 revolution—the key elements for success are summarised here:

- **Experiences, not products**—The only way to win in the Bank 4.0 world is to rethink the entire product paradigm and deliver the utility of your bank platform embedded into people's lives. The principle here is simple: technologies like mobile, voice and augmented reality are all attacking friction—the ultimate frictionless engagement in banking doesn't look like a savings account pushed as an offer on a mobile phone, it's simply an experience that helps you save. The same applies to every other aspect of banking. If you are trying to get someone to pay their credit card via Alexa, you've missed the point entirely.

- **Stop hiring bankers**—We've said it before, and we'll say it again, you need to attract innovative talent that understands deep technologies like voice, machine learning, blockchain, cloud integration, biometrics and experience design. Banking experience is a legacy that you don't want in a first principles reimagining of day-to-day financial services.

- **Data is the new oil**—The "bank" of the future will be driven on data, but not the transactional data or credit reference data you have today; the future is about data that provides context for delivery of bank utility, in real time. Where, when, why, how? Data is the fuel to power artificial intelligence, advice and seamless engagement. Without an organisation-wide data strategy, you just have legacy silos that don't know your customers.

- **Legacy isn't an excuse**—Legacy core system architecture can never be an excuse for not executing a compelling experience with a customer. If your systems enforce a process that originated in the branch and has been gradually adapted to digital, then you won't get to Bank 4.0 status. You need to have a team that will aggressively adopt middleware, cloud and FinTech solutions to plug the gaps wherever they appear. Progressively over time you'll build a new stack that relies only on the core for general ledger-type operations, and more and more delivery capability will shift to middle and engagement layers. Agility is at the core of Bank 4.0 architecture.

- **AI, of course**—A central shift to where the bank fits in the world will be the reshaping of "advice". Today we rely on humans face to face to advise clients and customers, but in the future advice that translates to a real-time experience will be increasingly AI-driven. As machines learn about your behaviour, risk and the best tools to solve your problems, these will respond to changing conditions as they occur. AI will be at the core of a paradigm shift in banking advice, delivered contextually through the technology layer.

- **Don't try this at home**—Key to agility is recognising that if you try to replicate what a FinTech has already done you'll burn a couple of years—and 10 times more in costs—than if you simply licensed the technology that an external team has already developed. As more and more tech gets plugged in, banks and FinTechs will become very adept at deploying new capabilities very quickly through APIs and common cloud layers. Don't forget the core reason behind this is not just that these partnerships will be faster and cheaper than traditional in-house efforts, but that FinTechs will be more likely to use first principles thinking and to take an approach that is counter-intuitive for banks iterating on branch models.

- **Open the kimono, don't block the blockchain**—Despite the current furore over Facebook data sharing and Equifax data breaches, the reality is that the world runs increasingly on data. The objective here is not to stop data sharing, but to bring a system of auditability and permissions to sharing data effectively and securely. This is where open banking, data privacy regulations, blockchain and the role of the new data gatekeepers are critical in navigating the next few years. If you want to be able to ask Siri whether you can afford to go out for dinner tonight, or ask Alexa if you can afford that new flat-panel video wall that Marty McFly would be proud of—as a consumer you will need to give access to the data that drives that contextual advice, and you're going to want more than the hope that Apple and Amazon deal with that data appropriately. In this world where responsiveness to data is 80 percent of your customer relationships, if you aren't plugged in to a data cooperative that enables safe collaboration, then you are a data island that is increasingly irrelevant. Banks today are data islands. Tomorrow's Bank 4.0 won't even do identity collection as they do today; they'll simply verify your identity against a known profile available on a blockchain. Otherwise they'll be disadvantaged.

Look back through this list of core competencies and you'll see almost nothing that would be seen as typical *banking* capabilities. That's because I already assume as an incumbent bank you know how to do "bank"—but you have a massive leap to be able to compete with Amazon, Alipay and the top challenger banks like N26, Monzo, Tandem, WeBank, Simple, Moven and others. These organisations aren't investing in becoming banks like those of the Bank 1.0, 2.0 or 3.0 era—they're investing in technology that transforms what we call banking into something new. We can't expect this innovation to plateau over the next few years—if anything, innovation will heat up.

Remember that there are only two innovation paths available to financial services: *either iterate on the branch model of banking or revolutionise through first principles thinking.* The revolution in banking isn't happening via redesigning the branch or simply retrofitting products we used to sell in the branch to new channels like voice; it is happening in radically evolving engagement, distribution and relevance. Amazon and Alibaba have vastly superior data with which to understand the relationship of consumers to their money; their acquisition cost is much closer to zero than a bank will ever be; and despite assurances of the leading banks of their continued relevance as government-licensed institutions, the ability to connect with a customer in 2025 won't be based on a charter—it will be based on data.

Organisational impact

The organisational chart is changing too. Organisation of the bank will centre around four key competencies:

1. Customer experience or delivery execution
2. Business operations
3. Technology operations
4. Banking competency

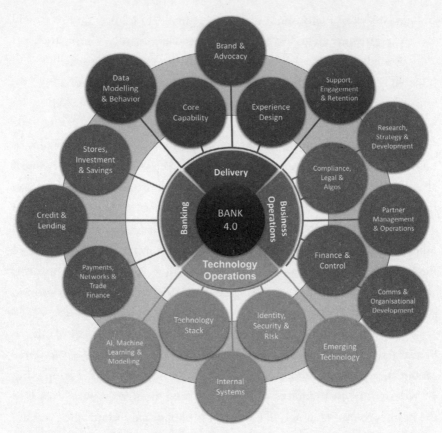

Figure 4: The Bank 4.0 organisation focuses on frictionless, agile delivery for revenue and relationships.

In the Bank 4.0 organisation, banking is not the defining characteristic of the organisation function, unusually enough. The only way the core utility of the bank gets delivered is through execution capability. Revenue and relationship are driven by the ability to reduce that core utility to the simplest, most frictionless experiences possible. Wet signatures, compliance processes, and product features have given way to code. Credit risk processes have given way to behavioural data. Channels have given way to triggers, context and behaviour, too.

The biggest impact to the organisation chart is clearly what is missing. Missing are the product departments that have long been the basis for budget battles and defining product structures. Mortgage, credit card and CASA facilities are all gone, the products associated with those departments transformed into experiences that are significantly more compelling and actionable, without adapting a paper application form from a branch into a digital application. If your organisation chart is dominated by product teams fighting for budget, how are you going to become experience first based? You can't. Remember some of the key illustrations in Chapter 4. Credit card use cases can be much more effectively instantiated through technology in real time, without plastic—for example, getting cash to buy groceries when you're in Whole Foods and realise your salary hasn't hit your account; or wanting to buy that new iPhone but you can't afford it without credit. The answer isn't applying for a card, it's applying for credit—an experience that by its nature will redefine the way we organise the business.

The credit card department gives way to teams that can surface the utility of credit contextually where it makes the most sense. Sure, you need credit access; but no, you don't need plastic, you don't need to apply months or weeks in advance—you just need the core credit capability surfaced through the technology layer.

Again, the ability to partner brings an agility that is absent in the vast majority of banks today: where new IT projects are numbered in years, not days; where procurement pushes vendors through legal hoops that would put Trump's legal team to shame; where legacy systems, legacy process and compliance roadblocks challenge the sanity and resolve of the most ardent innovators. An agile bank needs to move much faster than the organisation chart of a Bank 1.0–3.0 can handle.

The key message is that this is about competing with TechFin and FinTech players for revenue and relationships. Products don't create relationships or trust. Your ability to deliver does.

As customers we've just got used to the friction and hoops that banks put us through. As soon as Ant Financial, Tencent, Amazon and Apple started to show us a better way, the benchmark shifted. But the economics of banking fundamentally changed too, because Amazon and Alibaba can both acquire customers for dimes on the dollar, compared to the $200–350 per customer for a basic cheque account relationship in the US, for example.

The BATs, FAANGs, and GAFAs all have access to hundreds of millions of customers and banking is just another service they can deliver to their already willing customer base. In this banks are at a distinct disadvantage.

RegTech and rethinking macro-competiveness

Whether RegTech, "SupTech" (Supervisory Tech), data residency, AML monitoring, financial crime or simply compliance with the laws of the land, the regulation of financial services is set for a seismic realignment as customer behaviour evolves. Regulators are going to have to change even faster than banks to remain relevant. We can already see the battleground forming globally around things like FinTech charters, sandboxes, blockchain and crypto, etc. If you're in a market that is resisting these things, like in the US, you can expect two things to happen: firstly, Silicon Valley and Silicon Alley will continue to try to find workarounds that you'll have to constantly swat out; secondly, your global financial centres will start to look like that 1970s station wagon that Chevy Chase drove in *National Lampoon's Vacation*.

Let me make one prediction over the next 10 years: I predict that somewhere, a competent digital regulator will decide that there's no reason why customers of a bank need to be residents of a specific geography, they just need to be adequately identified. Once that happens, jurisdictions and financial centres will not just compete for venture capital dollars and talent, they'll start to attempt to be truly global centres for banking where a digital value store for a customer doesn't need to be tied to where you live. Following that, every progressive jurisdiction in the world will realise they need to compete for open-value store, payments and credit access. Estonia already started down this route with digital citizenship, but it'll be far easier to allow digital KYC that is borderless. It will start with data and investment—data residency will be the battlefield after venture capital investment in FinTech levels out.

At its core, however, the key "first principles" shift is that regulated markets will be based on regulation encoded not just in law, but in computer code. That requires a complete reskilling of regulatory bodies. It also means that the ability to respond to extremely agile FinTech platforms and players means hardcoding process and policies reduces competitiveness. This in turn means that regulators increasingly will shift to supervisory technology, rather than legal frameworks that are inflexible.

If the industry is going to be agile and adaptable, it starts with a flexible regulator.

Deploying capital for change

In all of this dynamic change, one thing will become increasingly clear: the ability to compete will hinge on efficient resource allocation. When you're an incumbent, you have to juggle servicing existing legacy customers who lag on the technology, keeping those old legacy systems running long enough to survive, and making your quarterly numbers so your stock price doesn't tank.

A FinTech doesn't have to worry about those things. They choose the most digital savvy customers, they don't have legacy processes or systems, and they have investors more concerned about their ability to scale than profitability. Look at Amazon, they didn't really start making big profits until they'd been in business for a good 10 years. Incumbent banks can't commit to 10 years of losses to rebuild. FinTechs just need to worry about raising the next round, and that comes down to scale and growth, not profitability.

In respects of innovation, however, this is where FinTechs have clear economic advantages. Their smaller teams, lack of legacy, the latest technology stack and their general willingness to break with conventions mean that they can deploy capital far more efficiently to create innovative customer experiences. Large incumbent banks will never be able to get the same bang for their buck as those small, agile, first principles teams.

Ultimately this will lead to parings of FinTech, technology players and incumbent banks. Banks who refuse to partner with these more efficient players will find it effecting their bottom line and speed to market increasingly, and this will be under the microscope of market analysts. It's the same reason why markets will, over time, start to discount banks who are reliant on branch networks for customer access—simply because challenger banks will consistently demonstrate much cheaper acquisition costs, and thus the ability to scale and take market share in a way that can't be defended by branch networks.

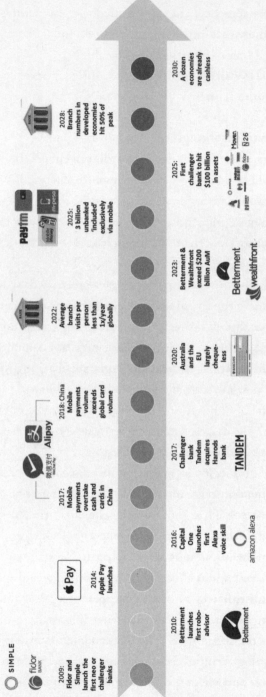

Figure 5: The Bank 4.0 roadmap.

Put all this together and the future is super-exciting—but super-disruptive for those that avoid rapid transformation.

The Bank 4.0 roadmap

The chart opposite represents the milestones we've seen in the Bank 4.0 transition thus far, and the likely milestones we'll see over the next decade as we move towards embedded, ubiquitous banking.

At the core of the Bank 4.0 world will be a simple, dramatic change. More people will be getting access to a basic banking service or value store through their mobile phone than through a branch. By 2025, most people will think of some device-based value store as their bank account, rather than a physical artifact—such as a chequebook or debit card—they had delivered by a bank.

More critically, the foundational elements of the Bank 1.0 world will rapidly start to decline in importance of delivery. Branches, agents and brokers based on information asymmetry will give way to contextual, behavioural offerings tailored to your personal world in a way that the traditional financial institution could never deliver via a face-to-face experience. Many will deny this shift up until the very moment they realise it's too late.

Conclusion

Blockbuster, Borders, Kodak, and their ilk have taught us one thing about the scale of disruption that we're seeing in financial services. Simply, that *no industry is immune, and no one admits they are being disrupted until they have to file for chapter 11.*

It will be the same in the Bank 4.0 space. For many CEOs and board members, they'll be hoping that they can retire before the organisation has to go through these radical changes. But putting these decisions off only guarantees that the disruption will be more impactful when it hits.

At the core of Bank 4.0 is a redefining of how financial services fits into the lives of the consumers, businesses and organisations that use those services. Technology is inevitably redefining that and in doing so is not just reducing friction and making delivery more seamless, it's finding ways to reframe financial services.

When we look at major technology leaps that changed entire industries, entire economies and the way society works, the biggest innovations occurred through first principles thinking and design. The printing press moving from handwritten copies to mass production; horses and steam-driven locomotives restricted to designated tracks, to automobiles that didn't require jobbers to come and collect the waste deposits left by those horses on city streets; factories that moved from handcrafted items with limited scale, to production lines that could daily churn out products by the thousands.

SpaceX, which in just 14 years reduced the cost to orbit Earth by 95 percent compared to other commercial rocket manufactures, and NASA's own efforts over 50 long years of gradual iteration and development of the same technology. An iPhone that bankrupted Nokia's and Motorola's phone division and set the benchmark for every smartphone made after it—and which materially changed the way we behaved and reset the industry so that Apple dominated for nearly a decade after this flagship device.

First principles thinking not only creates rapid innovation, but also rewrites the rules governing the industry's economics and market dynamics. It changes the baseline of how society operates around the core utility they've innovated on. Right now we see strong evidence that the likes of Alipay, Tencent WeChat, M-Pesa, the challenger banks of the world and others are all using elements of first principles thinking to start from scratch and deliver banking more efficiently at scale.

Let me ask you this simple question: consider everything we've discussed, technologies like AI, voice-smart assistants, digital onboarding, robo-processes and investment, behavioural experience design, and the like. If you were starting from scratch today building a bank from the ground up, would you really require customers to visit a building, sign a piece of paper, wait to get delivered their plastic debit card or chequebook to get a bank account? Or would you build it differently?

We already know the answer. No challenger bank in the world is building branches. No tech giant requires a wet signature on an application form to lend you money or help you save. The answer is clear—you'd definitely build it differently. So why are you still doing it the Bank 1.0 way for a basic account offering?

The focus now is on surfacing core banking utility in real time, not putting products on new channels. Bank platforms of the next 10 years will be differentiated through innovative use of technology, experience design, leveraging off network effect and creative ways to tap into customer behaviour.

Bank 4.0 is a fundamental paradigm shift in delivering banking services, embedded into the lives of customers when and where they need those same services. Bank 4.0 is about the emergence of banking that is everywhere through ubiquitous technology capabilities. Advice at scale through AI; revenue and relationship based on instant service capability; bank accounts that help you save and don't reward you for spending; millennials that reject credit, and seek simply an answer to their problem or question.

Money that isn't paper-based. Revenue that isn't paper-based. Relationships that are not people-based. Banking everywhere, but never at a bank.

The biggest "bank" in the world at the end of next decade will be phenomenal at technology delivery. The functions of the business will be built around delivery, and not products—those business units will be utility- or experience-based. The biggest banks and financial institutions will have phenomenal reach and scale, rapidly based on either being embedded in a technology you use everyday or in networks that enable network effect.

By the end of the next decade the largest "bank" in the world will have close to three billion customers in 100 countries, and be worth almost one trillion dollars. I'm making a bet that "bank" will be Ant Financial and in 2025 it will already have surpassed ICBC, the largest bank in the world today, in respect to customer numbers, assets, deposits and market capitalisation. By 2025 you won't be competing against other banks, you'll be competing against technology players like Ant Financial and Amazon. If you're still competing as a bank, it will be like taking on these guys blindfolded.

Things just got real—if you're not running fast and changing everything from the ground up, you're probably got a tough few years ahead.

For me, this makes banking exciting, cool, dynamic and interesting. If you're a risk adverse banker that sees this level of change as a fundamental threat, you should start looking for another job. Maybe go work for Kodak or Blockbuster…

Thanks for reading, and thanks for being a part of the dialogue. I hope you are ready for what comes next, because it's coming whether you're ready or not.

Welcome to the future—welcome to Bank 4.0.

Endnotes

1   Electronic Recording Machine for Accounting (BofA and MIT 1953).

Glossary

ACH: Automated Clearing House.

Adoption Rate: How quickly it takes new technologies to be adopted by the public at large.

AML: Anti-Money Laundering—the efforts through legislation, regulation and through systems to track, identify and stop the laundering of illicit funds into the mainstream banking system.

Android: An open mobile phone platform developed by Google and, later, the Open Handset Alliance. It consists of the operating system (on which everything runs), the middleware (allowing applications to talk to a network and to one another), and the applications (the actual programs that the phones will run).

AOs: Algorithmic Operations.

API: Application Program Interface.

App: Short for application—a program or piece of software, especially as downloaded by a user to a mobile device.

App Phone: A phone that provides open application support not limited to the phone handset, manufacturer's operating system and applications; most common instances are the iPhone, Droid and NexusOne.

Augmented Reality (AR): The overlaying of digital data on the real world.

Avatar: A computer user's representation of himself/herself, or alter ego, for use on computer systems.

B2B: Business-to-Business—as in intraorganisational communication, collaboration and commerce; normally electronic, and usually using websites and/or web services.

Basel II and III: The second and third of the Basel Accords, which are recommendations on banking laws and regulations issued by the Basel Committee on Banking Supervision.

Big Data: Data sets the sizes of which are beyond the ability of commonly used software tools to capture, manage, and process within a tolerable elapsed time. Big data sizes are a constantly moving target, and as of 2012, range from a few dozen terabytes to many petabytes of data in a single data set.

Bitcoin: A type of P2P digital currency.

Blog: A contraction of the term "web log"—a type of website usually maintained by an individual with regular entries of commentary, descriptions of events, or other material such as graphics or video.

BPO: Business Process Outsourcing—the practice of outsourcing some or all of the business's back-office processes to an external company or service provider; common with call centres and IT support.

BPR: Business Process Re-engineering—re-engineering business processes to either reduce costs or improve the flow of a process for customers.

CapEx: Capital Expense.

CES: Consumer Electronics Show.

Churn: This refers to customers moving from a service provider within one specific product category to another, based on price, value or some other factor.

CLID: Caller Line Identification—a system that identifies a customer based on the phone number they use to call a service provider.

Cloud Computing: An emerging computing technology that uses the internet and central remote servers to maintain data and applications; players include DropBox, YouSendIt and Flickr.

CPM: Cost per Impression—in online advertising, it relates to cost per (thousand) impressions.

CRM: Customer Relationship Management; sometimes Credit Risk Management.

Cross-Selling: A method of targeting and selling new products to an existing customer.

Crowdsourcing: Tapping into the collective intelligence of the public at large to complete business-related tasks that a company would normally either perform itself or outsource to a third party provider. It enables managers to expand the size of their talent pool while also gaining deeper insight into what customers really want.

CSR: Customer Service Representative—staff who work within the call centre to assist customers with enquiries.

CTI: Computer-Telephony Integration/Interface—a system that integrates telephone systems with computer networks.

CTR: Click-Through Rate.

Digital Natives: Y-Gen and younger users of technology.

DM: Direct Mail.

Durbin Amendment: The Dodd-Frank Wall Street Reform and Consumer Protection Act of 2010, which reduced fee income for banks of credit and debit card swipes at the point of sale in the US.

ECN: Electronic Communications Network—an electronic network that facilitates trading between stock or commodities exchanges.

EMV: An international standard for smart credit cards that have a built-in CPU chip. Used with brand names such as Chip and PIN and IC Credit, the smartcard provides greater safety than a magnetic stripe because it can support sophisticated security methods and make decisions on its own.

ETFs: Exchange-Traded Funds.

FAQs: Frequently Asked Questions—questions asked frequently by customers and put on the company's website to expedite answers.

FMCG: Fast-Moving Consumer Goods—products that are sold quickly at relatively low costs.

Geolocation: The technique of identifying the geographical location of a person or device by means of digital information processed via the internet.

Gilder's Law: Proposed by George Gilder, this law states that bandwidth grows at least three times faster than computer power.

GPR prepaid cards: General Purpose Reloadable prepaid cards.

GPRS: General Packet Radio Switching—a packet-oriented mobile data service available to users of 2G and 3G cellular communication systems in Global Systems for Mobile communications (GSM).

GSM: Global Systems for Mobile communications—the primary standard for digital mobile phones, in use by 80 percent of the global mobile market.

Haptic Touch: Technology that interfaces with the user through the sense of touch.

High-Counter: The typical teller station within a branch for conducting over-the-counter transactions.

HNWI: High-Net-Worth Individual—the most attractive client segment for retail banks; HNWIs typically invest US$150,000–US$1 million in investment type products.

IC: Integrated Circuit.

IDV: Identity Verification.

IM: Instant Messaging—a protocol for communicating between two parties using text-based chat through IP-based clients.

IN: Innovation Newspaper.

iOS: Apple's mobile operating system for its iPhone, iPod touch, iPad, Apple TV and similar devices.

IP: Internet Protocol—the primary protocol for transmitting data or information over the internet.

ISP: Internet Service Provider—a company that provides internet access to customers.

IVR: Interactive Voice Response (systems)—the automated telephone support systems you hear when you call a 1-800 helpline or customer support number, which uses menus and responses via touch-tone and/or voice response for navigation.

IxD: Interaction Design—a customer-led design methodology for improving the interaction between customers and systems.

KPI: Key Performance Indicators—metrics (or measures) used within corporations to measure the performance of one department against another in respect of things such as revenue, sales lead conversion, costs, customer support, etc.

KYC: Know Your Customer—an internal compliance regulation to ensure accurate identification and validation of a customer and understanding of his transactional behaviour.

LAN: Local Area Network—a computer network covering a small physical area, such as a home, office, or small group of buildings.

LOLA: A Siri-like technology (see Siri below) through the internet and via voice.

Low-Counter: Typically a desk station within a branch where the relationship manager can sit with customers and potential clients and advise them on available products and services.

Lo-Fi Prototype: A simple method of prototyping products, interfaces or applications and testing with target customers or users.

LIBOR: London Interbank Offered Rate.

LinkedIn: An online social network for business professionals.

Metcalfe's Law: Attributed to Robert Metcalfe, this law states that the value of a telecommunications network is proportional to the square of the number of connected users of the system (n^2).

MFI: Microfinance Institution—an alternate form of bank found in developing countries that provides microcredit lending.

MIRC: Magnetic Ink Character Recognition.

Mobile Money: Bank-like services delivered over a mobile device to enable payments between two parties; successful providers include M-Pesa, Edy, G-CASH, MTN Money, T-money, Suica.

Mobile Portal: A website designed specifically for mobile phone interfaces and mini-browsers.

Mobile Wallet: An electronic account, dominated in a currency, held on a mobile phone that can be used to store and transfer value.

Moore's Law: Named after Gordon Moore, this law basically states that the number of transistors on a chip doubles every 24 months.

NFC: Near Field Communication—a short-range high-frequency wireless communication technology which enables the exchange of data between devices over about a 10-centimetre distance.

OCR: Optical Character Recognition.

OpEx: Operating Expense.

OTC: Over the Counter—refers to physical transactions or trades done on behalf of a customer by a trader or customer representative who has access to a specific closed financial system or network.

P2P: Peer-to-Peer or Person-to-Person—a method of passing information or data via IP-based communication methods between two individuals connected to the internet via computer or mobile devices.

PayPal: A leading P2P payment provider; others include Square, i-Zettle, ClearXchange, Dwolla, PingIt, PopMoney, QuickPay, Venmo, ZashPay.

PCI Compliant: Complying with Payment Card Industry data security standards.

PFM: Personal Financial Management.

Pod: Modular customer engagement station.

POS: Point of Sale—the location where a retail transaction occurs; a POS terminal refers more generally to the hardware and software used at checkout stations.

PPC: Pay-per-Click—a method of paying for appearing in search engine results by bidding and paying for specific keywords; you then pay at the successful bid rate every time a user/visitor clicks on your link.

Prosumer: A portmanteau word formed by contracting either the word "professional" or "producer" with the word "consumer"; in respect of this publication, it identifies the role of the modern consumer of content who is also a producer of content on, for example, YouTube, Facebook and Twitter.

PSTN: Public Switched Telephone Network—the traditional copper-wire and exchange-based landline telephone system.

RFID: Radio Frequency Identification—a short-range radio communication methodology that uses "tags" or small integrated circuits connected to an antenna that when passed within the range of a magnetic reader is able to send a signal.

RM: Relationship Manager—a dedicated customer service manager assigned to look after specific customers, usually high-net-worth ones.

ROMI: Return on Marketing Investment.

SDK: Software Development Kit—a package provided by a mainstream software or operating system provider to the developer community to assist them with application construction.

SEO: Search Engine Optimisation—the science of optimising websites so that they appear in the top results for search engine enquiries.

SIM Card: Subscriber Identity Module (SIM) securely stores the service-subscriber key (IMSI) used to identify an individual subscriber on a mobile phone.

Siri: Siri on iPhone 4S lets you use your voice to send messages, make calls, set reminders, and more.

Skype: A technology allowing web chat.

SMS: Short Message Service—a system of communicating by short messages over the mobile telephone network.

Snail Mail: The term used by proponents of digital technologies to describe traditional mail and the postal system.

Spam: Unsolicited bulk email sent out simultaneously to thousands of thousands of email addresses to promote products or services.

Stored-Value Card: Monetary value stored on a card not in an externally recorded account; examples are the Octopus, Oyster and Suica systems used to replace public transport ticketing.

STP: Straight-Through Processing—the implementation of a system that requires no human intervention for the approval or processing of a customer application or transaction.

T-DMB: TV via Digital Multimedia Broadcasting.

TiVo: A brand and model of digital video recorder available in the US, UK, New Zealand, Canada, Mexico, Australia and Taiwan.

Touch Point: Any channel or mechanism by which a consumer has day-to-day interaction with a retail service company, such as a bank, in order to transact or conduct business.

TVC: The industry abbreviation for television commercials.

Twitter: A social media website that supports microblogging between participants in the network; similar to an SMS broadcast system for the web.

UCD: User-Centred Design.

Upselling: A system of selling an additional service of a higher margin or total revenue within the same product or asset class to a customer, typically upgrading from one class of product to another.

URL: Uniform Resource Locator—an "address" or identifier that is used to locate and retrieve documents hosted on the World Wide Web.

UT: Usability Testing—the science of testing how users interact with a system, product or interface through observation.

VBC: Video Banking Centre (Citibank, circa 1996)—an interactive, 24-hour personal banking centre providing access to personal banking experts through integrated voice, video and data connection.

Virtual Currency: Currencies such as Linden dollars, QQ coins, Project Entropia Dollars (PED), etc that exist in the virtual world and can be exchanged for real currency by users.

VoIP: Voice Over Internet Protocol—an internet-based protocol that allows users to use voice communication such as over a telephone system.

VSC: Virtual Support Centre—a call centre virtually supported by customer service representatives who typically operate from home (ie homesourcing).

WAP: Wireless Access Protocol—the original protocol for simple internet browsing or simple menu interactions via 2G (digital) mobile phones.

Web 2.0: Web applications that facilitate interactive information sharing, interoperability, user-centred design and collaboration on the World Wide Web.

Widget: A generic type of software application that is usually portable and works across different operating systems and devices.

WiMax: Worldwide Interoperability for Microwave Access—a telecommunications technology that enables wireless transmission of data from point-to-multipoint links to portable and fully mobile internet access.

XML: Extensible Markup Language—a set of rules for encoding documents electronically.

Yelp: A website that lets users review businesses ranging from plumbers to pet shops and that has a check-in service for mobile phones.

About Brett King

Brett King is an international bestselling author, a renowned commentator and globally respected speaker on the future of business. He has spoken in over 50 countries, to more than a million people, on how technology is disrupting business, changing behaviour and influencing society. He advised the Obama White House, the FED and the National Economic Council on the future of banking in the United States, and advises governments and regulators around the world. He appears regularly on US TV networks like CNBC, where he contributes on Future Tech and FinTech.

King hosts the world's leading dedicated radio show and podcast on technology impact in banking and financial services, called Breaking Banks (150-plus countries, 6.5 million listeners). He is also the founder of the neo-bank Moven, a globally recognised mobile startup, which has raised over US$42 million to date, with the world's first mobile, downloadable bank account.

Named "King of the Disruptors" by *Banking Exchange* magazine, King was voted American Banker's "Innovator of the Year", "the world's #1 Financial Services Influencer" by The Financial Brand and was nominated by Bank Innovation as one of the top 10 "coolest brands in banking". He was shortlisted for the 2015 Advance Global Australian of the Year Award for being one of the most influential Australians living offshore. His fifth book, *Augmented: Life in the Smart Lane*, was a top 10 non-fiction book in North America and was referenced by President Xi in his national address to the Chinese people in January 2018.

King lives in New York and enjoys flying, gaming and scuba diving in his spare time.

About Moven

In 2011, Brett King co-founded Moven as the first US direct to consumer neobank to offer account opening via a mobile app. The app's engaging design helps customers spend, save and live smarter. This innovative approach led to creating global demand from banks to offer Moven technology to their clients, resulting in the firm's transformational Moven Enterprise offering. To learn more visit moven.com or movenenterprise.com.